Praise for *The Extra Mile*

"*The Extra Mile* is one of those rare management books founded almost exclusively on reality. It delivers personal accounts of real leaders' experiences in energising their people and organisations to deliver. It's easy to read and to dip into and somewhat harder to put down!"

Kevin S. Beeston, Chairman, Serco Group plc

"With *The Extra Mile*, David MacLeod and Chris Brady have done something remarkably valuable. They've taken the vaguely defined concept of engagement and shown exactly what it does mean and, more importantly, exactly what it can mean for large-scale business success."

Robert B. Cialdini, Author, Influence: Science and Practice

"Eschewing the grand theory and strategy that often bedevils management writing, MacLeod and Brady provide an invaluable guide to the practical and messy business of engaging staff to achieve better performance. In a time of more fluid loyalties and drawing upon the 'real life' stories of leaders, they demonstrate conclusively how successful organisations in the future will need to go beyond the traditional focus on 'metrics' and touch the souls of those they employ."

David Bell, Permanent Secretary, Department for Children, Schools and Families

"*The Extra Mile* comprehensively addresses the issue of building competitive edge by harnessing the energies of an engaged workforce. The book is focused on the practical issues of how you need to act. Our economic well being depends upon our organisations being able to thrive in the more open global economy in order to meet the rising expectations of our citizens."

Sir David Varney, HM Treasury

"this is a great achievement."

Geoff Tudhope, Senior Independent Director, Cafedirect

"The basic argument is communicated in a thoughtful and practical way: in my opinion the book will help many people and organizations to perform better."

Philip Augar, co-author of The Rise of the Player Manager and ex-group Managing Director at Schroders

FT Prentice Hall

FINANCIAL TIMES

In an increasingly competitive world, we believe it's quality of thinking that will give you the edge – an idea that opens new doors, a technique that solves a problem, or an insight that simply makes sense of it all. The more you know, the smarter and faster you can go.

That's why we work with the best minds in business and finance to bring cutting-edge thinking and best learning practice to a global market.

Under a range of leading imprints, including *Financial Times Prentice Hall*, we create world-class print publications and electronic products bringing our readers knowledge, skills and understanding, which can be applied whether studying or at work.

To find out more about Pearson Education publications, or tell us about the books you'd like to find, you can visit us at **www.pearsoned.co.uk**

PEARSON
Education

THE EXTRA MILE

HOW TO ENGAGE YOUR PEOPLE TO WIN

David MacLeod and Chris Brady

FT Prentice Hall
FINANCIAL TIMES

An imprint of **Pearson Education**
Harlow, England • London • New York • Boston • San Francisco • Toronto
Sydney • Tokyo • Singapore • Hong Kong • Seoul • Taipei • New Delhi
Cape Town • Madrid • Mexico City • Amsterdam • Munich • Paris • Milan

PEARSON EDUCATION LIMITED

Edinburgh Gate
Harlow CM20 2JE
Tel: +44 (0)1279 623623
Fax: +44 (0)1279 431059
Website: www.pearsoned.co.uk

First published in Great Britain in 2008

ISBN: 978-0-273-70394-5

British Library Cataloguing-in-Publication Data
A catalogue record for this book is available from the British Library

Library of Congress Cataloging-in-Publication Data
MacLeod, David.
    The extra mile : how to engage your people to win / David MacLeod and
Chris Brady.
        p.   cm.
    Includes bibliographical references and index.
    ISBN 978–0–273–70394–5 (hardback)
    1. Employee motivation—Great Britain. 2. Personnel management—Great
Britain. 3. Corporate culture—Great Britain.   I. Brady, Christopher, 1947–
II. Title.
    HF5549.5.M63M323 2007
    658.3'14—dc22   2007036168

10 9 8 7 6 5 4 3 2 1
11 10 09 08 07

Typeset in10.5pt Iowan Old style by 3
Printed in Great Britain by Henry Ling Ltd., at the Dorset Press, Dorchester,
Dorset

The publisher's policy is to use paper manufactured from sustainable forests.

Contents

List of Figures

Preface and acknowledgements

FROM DAVID MACLEOD:

It was during my experience helping to reinvigorate the Dulux brand that I first became aware of the power of engagement. That wasn't what we called it at the time, but I nevertheless began to recognize how inspiring and enthusing everyone involved was central to the creation of a range of new products and new ideas, including the hugely successful Dulux Natural Whites. It was an observation that stayed with me as I went on to manage a series of business turnarounds in the industrial specialities sector, in the UK, throughout Europe, and then globally. More and more I appreciated the enormous potential that could be released by harnessing people's creativity and energy, and encouraging them to believe that goals were attainable. I realised increasingly that levels of 'engagement' in an organization are predictors of success.

This realization was echoed when I was then seconded to work in the Cabinet Office. Having chaired various forums for Permanent Secretaries and Chief Executives, I became even more convinced that there was a common language, a common approach, which could relate to almost any sector of the economy, and on which results could be built.

Such was my conviction that I decided to change career to focus on this issue; if I could help distil what I had used and observed, and, in the process, enable a more productive and satisfying working life, which would benefit employees and organizations alike, then this seemed to be a contribution worth making.

I then sought a partner for this journey: and in Chris Brady, at that time Associate Dean of the Cass Business School, I found someone who shared my belief.

FROM CHRIS BRADY:

I have been lucky enough to have had the opportunity to observe engagement in action in a wide variety of situations during a diverse working life. This has ranged from business academia: I am currently Dean of the Business School and Professor of Management Studies at Bournemouth University, to the world of sport; where I was a semi-professional footballer, a qualified UEFA 'A' license coach and managed at senior semi-pro level. During sixteen years in the Navy, where lives and livelihoods were always at stake. Also as a young man working at the front line of engagement I have experienced the power of engagement at the sharp end of many businesses, where my experience ranged from being a line worker at Chryslers in Detroit to a claims clerk in the City, to a land surveyor with the Ordnance Survey, to a manager of a bookmakers.

As a believer in much of what Henry Mintzberg has to say, I did it his way – I had all of that experience and *then* did the research using the mountains of evidence that we gathered through the course of writing this book. The good news is that the research confirmed and strengthened everything my experience told me was true.

FROM DAVID AND CHRIS:

Together we set out, over the course of four years, to explore the world of engagement. We particularly benefited from the input of Julian Powe, who over the last 20 years has built both a depth and breadth of experience in helping organizations to achieve change. We harnessed a team of researchers drawn from Cass and Towers Perrin. We trawled through all the published literature, a short summary of which is included in the book. We drew on the conclusions from various research studies, drawn from more than 33 million respondents. We wanted to explore the evidence that linked engagement to performance and we wanted to put that in a broader society wide context. From this analysis we discovered a compelling case that engagement predicts performance.

We set up seminars of experts, including those who were studying engagement in business schools, consultants who had helped to implement it in organizations, and engagement 'practitioners' –

people leading organizations. We harnessed the expertise of a range of specialists in different fields: Betsy Kendall, Director of Training & International Department at OPP with her deep insight into analysing thinking preferences; Ian Dodds whose built a very successful consultancy in the area of harnessing diversity; Gillian Stamp of BIOSS with her profound understanding of the importance of levels of activities in organizations; Bob Janes of R & J Ltd. who researched patterns of thinking for us, to name but a few. We worked closely with colleagues in the UK and internationally. We talked extensively with Roger Maitland and his team from ISR who have been researching in the area of engagement for more than 20 years. As our emerging themes developed we tested and shared them through a series of workshops.

We benefited hugely from over 50 in-depth interviews with leaders drawn from a variety of business sectors. The aim was to compare, constantly, what we were hearing and seeing from those for whom the effort to instil engagement in the real world was a daily affair, with what the research was saying. The aim throughout has been to write a book that would be practically helpful for those leading organisations (or wanting to lead organizations) rather than the more academic book that could have sprung from all this research.

And this is the result. The question we are trying to answer throughout is how your organisation can find, and how it can go, that extra mile. All of our research showed us that engagement is multifaceted and often complex. It relies on concepts such as trust, respect and pride that are easy to pay lip service to but more difficult to abide by in the hurly burly of the workplace. It relies heavily on management attitudes, and cannot be grafted on to an organisation where the basic structure or communications are shaky. It should inform, and can be affected by, the day to day behaviour of everyone in your organization. Given all of this, we realized that implanting engagement was never going to be a quick-fix solution: ground work must be laid, and effort must be expended, in order to reap the benefit.

Engagement, too often, is a buzzword that is bandied around as something desirable, but with little insight as to how to achieve it. If you are at the bottom of the hill looking up at this elusive beacon, it can be difficult to know how to start climbing. To us, the road to engagement is built first on strong foundations – of good strategy and leadership – and then on specific pillars which need to be present in your organization for engagement to flourish. We have, therefore, structured this book in a way that, while presenting a systematic investigation into the theories that lie behind engagement, also leads you along the path towards implementing it.

In the first section, we investigate the importance of engagement, and ask why it is that it is becoming increasingly vital. It is here that we lay out the statistical analysis, and analyse the drivers, definitions and taxonomy of engagement.

In the second, we analyse the key part that leadership has to play in putting in place the foundations that lead to engagement, and what the leader can do to ensure they are.

In the third, we dissect the seven pillars of engagement: the specific areas on which the engagement levels within your organization can be built.

We hope that this will be a book that will be of practical use: often, the most difficult thing to do is to get started. So throughout, we have included, where appropriate, tips on what you can do on Monday morning to start off on the road to engagement. Some will be more appropriate to you and your organization than others: they are intended not as a rigorous programme to work through but to stimulate your thinking.

Above all we want with this book to turn engagement from a buzzword into an attainable reality. Engagement is a path to success: we hope this book shows you both why, and how, to achieve it.

davidtmacleod@aol.com
cbrady@bournemouth.ac.uk

Dedication and acknowledgements

From Chris: To Eleanor, who means so much to me
From David: To Sue, Hannah & Henry

We would like to thank all our interviewees who so generously gave their time and so willingly offered their experience and ideas. We benefited hugely from the commitment of our extensive team of researchers who either made specific and valuable contributions or who contributed throughout our journey, especially Andrew Walker, Ibrahim Rasheed and Rocky Dellamano. We are also greatly indebted to our colleagues in Towers Perrin, Towers Perrin – ISR and Cass who have contributed so much data (33 million respondents!), so many insights and so much experience to helping shape our arguments through a series of meetings and workshops throughout the last 4 years. They, together with our subject experts and business leaders, have done so much to harness business academic insights to hard edged practical experience.

Sally Farrow so diligently transcribed all our interview recordings and Celia Hayley did much by turning some of our business English into something that reads so much better.

Gill Hanscombe has been with us throughout the ups and downs of the journey offering unstinting loyalty and support.

We would like to thank Helena Lawrence who designed the schematics and Tatiana Estevez who made an important contribution to the production of the manuscript. At all stages through the progress of the book from idea to finished product, Liz Gooster, Julie Knight and the Pearson team have been incredibly supportive and helpful.

We are indebted to so many people but in the end we as the authors bear the responsibility for what follows in this book.

Editor's note: Three of the interviews (with Grobbler, Sweetenham and Woodward) were personal interviews by Chris Brady and David Bolchover, which first appeared in the Sunday Times on July 10th, July 3rd and June 19th 2005 respectively.

INTRODUCTION

Why bother with engagement?

You are a leader and you have pulled out all the stops in order to shape your new strategy. You have researched the market, assessed your competitors, brought on board the best strategic thinkers. You have decided on a way forward that you know is going to provide a winning edge. You are absolutely clear about which way your organization should be headed, and excited about the possibilities that the future holds. All you need to do now is to make it happen.

Enthusiastically, you pitch it to your people; you share with them all the insights you have gleaned, outline the advantages of your new direction, carefully ensure that you have explained what it means for each different area. And your people have assented; they are on board. You are confident that this is a new dawn for your organization, and that you are heading up a united team that is marching into the future.

Three months later, while advancing confidently forward, you turn around to check how the rest of the organization's doing – only to find that there is nobody with you, or that they are so far behind as to make no difference.

Where are they?

The answer is, they are doing exactly what they have always done. They are not disagreeing with your plans; they are not trying to be obstructive. They probably think your ideas are good ones, and are excited that somebody is going to take the organization into these new waters. The problem is, they don't realize that this somebody is meant to be them, and they don't care enough to start making it happen. *They are not engaged.*

When your employees come in to work, are they thinking about the possibilities of what *can* be done, or only what needs to be done? Are they resolving on the best way to tackle their morning's work, or are they thinking about the end of the day when they can set all of this aside and start doing what really interests them? Do they think of the business simply as the organization that pays their monthly wages, or are they proud of belonging to it? Do they understand why the organization is moving in the direction that it is? Do they respect their bosses, their managers and their colleagues, or do they regard them as necessary evils? Are they *engaged*, or are they simply doing what they must to get by?

If you are a manager of any sort, you should be very interested indeed in the answers to these questions. You should be interested not because you want your office to be a cheerful place, or because you want to get your employees past the Monday-morning blues. You should be interested because *engagement levels predict profitability*. You should be interested because engaging your people is a vital factor in winning.

Paying attention to your people's engagement is not therefore a 'soft' issue – the facts, as we lay them out in **the focus is on engagement as a tool for success** this book, show conclusively that engagement is *the* hard issue. The subtitle of the book was not chosen by chance: the focus is on engagement as a tool for success, not as an end in itself. Its message is that you should be paying as much attention to the engagement of your people as you do to your products and strategy.

The role of strategy

Note that we are saying *as much* attention, not *more*. The quality of your people and even their treatment cannot deliver a defunct business model or an outdated product. A sound strategy is still vital. It is just that the developing of sound strategies is not surrounded by the mystique it used to be; we know what needs to be done – AND so do your competitors. The battleground is increasingly moving to who implements and that means who engages their people best.

Richard Baker, CEO of Alliance Boots, puts the emphasis on implementation:

> 'It is 10% strategy and 90% execution and the execution is all about everybody in the organization getting it and doing it. You can have a great strategy in the board room but if the people on the shop floor, in a factory or on the sales floor don't give a damn about what the company is trying to do, then execution of whatever you might dream up in the board room will fall over.'

The leader who wants to promote engagement within his organization must always start by engaging with the business environment outside it. From Marks & Spencer to the Sinclair C5 to the US presence in Vietnam the world is littered with endless instances of organizations which have not so much misread the environment or market but almost wilfully ignored it.

Failing to engage with the external environment before focusing on internal engagement will not bring success. Worse, paying attention to people issues at the expense of strategic ones will ultimately be disengaging in itself. As we will see throughout the book, in order to be engaged, the workforce needs to have confidence and trust in those responsible for policy; they need to feel that they are in safe hands. Staff knew that M&S had the wrong ranges in stock – everyone that is except the management. For years, American soldiers returning from Vietnam told of an 'unwinnable war'. Few commentators considered it likely that the C5 would succeed in the marketplace. The people cannot align with a policy so obviously at odds with reality. The quest for engagement is reliant on and should start with the external environment and with a sensible strategy.

The extra mile

So a good strategy is a pre-requisite, and we assume that you have at least the core strategic themes worked out. This book is about what comes next: how to bring your people with you on the journey and how to make sure that each of them is putting in that extra inch[1] of performance that will power your organization towards success.

It is not about employee happiness; it is about untapped potential. In the end organizations are not factories and buildings, they are the sum total of the efforts that their employees put in. We need to treat our employees as adults, engage their talents and watch them grow so that the organization grows. The theory and practice that we offer in this book are not complex but neither are they followed. Leaders and managers have claimed to have become 'sophisticated', they have become professional. They haven't. What they have done is to become lost in a plethora of systems and sophisticated, complex, strategic, analytically based, 'evidence'-based approaches that 'tell' employees what to do rather than encouraging them to care.

Our research tells us that this is not the way to build a successful, enduring, resilient business. In the eighties many companies focused on the shareholder above all else, but where are they now? Nor is the answer to parachute in lots of half-measures and faddish initiatives and away-days to make your company more 'employee friendly'. What employees want is to be engaged with their work. They *want* to understand, they *want* to take pride in the organization, they *want* to care. The job of the leader is to make sure that nothing stands in the way of that impulse.

what employees want is to be engaged with their work

Engagement is not a magic wand, it is a mindset that should run from the top of your organization to the bottom. Each employee is called to willingly give just that little extra, the sum of which makes up an extra mile.

NOTE

[1] Clive Woodward, former England rugby coach and head of performance for the British 2012 Olympics, used the fictional speech given by Al Pacino in the film *Any Given Sunday* as motivation for his world champion team. Watch and you will know why we used the term 'inch'.

WHY ENGAGEMENT?

To achieve engagement, it is first necessary that you understand it and believe in its importance in achieving high performance. In Part One, we seek to define engagement, to untangle the research that surrounds it and to see how businesses are doing at it. Most importantly, we investigate why it is vital in the business environment, and in particular why it matters so much in today's changing society

1 What is engagement?

What is engagement? The simplest definition is this: it is an employee's willingness to put discretionary effort into their work in the form of time, brainpower and energy, above and beyond what is considered adequate. Engaged employees have a desire and commitment for *always* doing the best job. They grip any task with energy and enthusiasm, often going above and beyond to increase or influence quality, costs and customer service. They bring fresh ideas, infuse their teams with their own engagement and are less likely to seek opportunities to work elsewhere. They believe in the purpose of their organization and demonstrate that belief through their actions and attitudes.

Harnessing engagement involves tapping into the discretionary energy of your workforce to increase their productivity without damaging quality. It can be observed in simple ways. Does the salesman try one more time to convince their client, or does the production manager try to think up ways to go from good to outstanding quality? Are they all personally interested enough in the success of the organization to care? Do company systems promote and reinforce constructive and creative work, or reward the mediocre as much as the outstanding?

A caveat: employee engagement does not simply equal employee happiness. The purpose of this book is not to provide ways of making your workforce more cheerful; it is to make them better performers. One of our interviewees, David Varney, recently appointed as special adviser to Gordon Brown and previously Chairman of MMO2, British Gas and a director of Shell, says this:

> 'We're brought up to believe, of course, in the mythology that it is a happy group that is going to be more productive. But we also know that some groups are so happy that they're contented to the point at which they ignore the customer . . . So I think it's too simple to say that if I make them happy then they will be productive.'

The purpose of promoting engagement is to increase performance, efficiency and company resilience, not just to build a happy workplace. Mere contentment, in fact, may be the enemy of engagement. Sir David Barnes, CEO of Zeneca (AstraZeneca) 1993–2000, says that we all work better with a little stretch in the system. We don't want a totally benign system. Engagement is a tool to be used to make your organization function better, not primarily to make your employees feel better.

In seeking to harness this elusive quality, organizations have an advantage: in general people actually *want* to be engaged. Lucian Hudson, Chairman of the Tavistock Institute and Head of Communication at the Foreign and Commonwealth Office, sees it almost as a unit of energy:

> 'The concept of a job well done. At its simplest, people derive enormous pleasure, satisfaction, motivation from the sense that they've done the job well. And that's the fundamental unit.'

Sir David Omand who was UK Security and Intelligence Coordinator (Cabinet Office) and previously Permanent Secretary of GCHQ, has a similar view:

> 'The essence of small group management is capitalizing on the innate wish that almost everybody has to do a good job and be respected for doing a good job. [They want] to be regarded as the best on the block: and you can foster that.'

Richard Baker of Alliance Boots puts it plainly:

> 'There are 100,000 intelligent people in Boots who want the company to be successful.'

Indeed, if recognition, satisfaction and respect are not coming from the workplace, it is likely that employees will find it elsewhere. Anyone reading this book knows people who turn up at work, do exactly what is required of them, do a perfectly adequate job and leave at 5.30. Then they go home, where they run an outstanding youth football team, get totally involved with various community projects, engage in some fantastic creative hobby. They are, therefore, able to be engaged, but not, apparently, with work. What if we were able to get them to bring this creativity, energy and inspiration into the workplace? Imagine the value we would add to our organizations.

One of our interviewees, confirming this point, described an adviser at one of his call centres. At work, the limit of her decision-making ability was capped at £25. Outside of the company, she was a magistrate whose decisions had the power to affect lives. It is unlikely that the £25 limit was encouraging her discretionary effort to be spent at the call centre.

Whatever their outside activities, people by and large do not come to work to do the wrong thing. Indeed, the opportunity to do challenging work has been identified as the fourth highest factor in attracting people to a job in the UK.[2] Employees would prefer to feel that they are making a definite contribution to a worthwhile and successful organization. Sir David Barnes of AstraZeneca describes it in terms of latent energy:

> 'I have this view that most employees are capable of a huge amount more than they are allowed to do by the system. It's a bit like stored energy . . . but how do you constructively release that energy?'

Such comments indicate that in great organizations, the workforce not only wants to work but is liberated by management to do so. When they do so, that effort must be recognized. And not only must they be recognized, but that recognition must be acted upon – rewarded or punished.

consequences – both good and bad – should be built into the organization

Consequences – both good and bad – should be built into the organization to encourage and reinforce discretionary effort.

What's in it for the organization?

All of this sounds fine for the individual, but why should employers make the effort? Employees may prefer to be engaged, but indulging them might seem to be a luxury rather than a necessity. The answer lies on the bottom line. We explore this thoroughly in the next chapter, but consider this: for any mid- to large-size company the workforce is likely to constitute one of its most expensive investments, and at present in most companies it is being vastly underexploited. Only 12% of the UK workforce can be considered as highly engaged[3] and the consequences, as detailed more fully in Chapter 2, are financial. Research shows a clear link between engagement and staff retention such that more than two thirds of highly engaged employees have no plans to leave their current jobs. Richard Baker of Alliance Boots sees it at store level like this:

> 'Sales tend to grow better in a store where the motivation and morale are high, the absenteeism tends to be lower and therefore the mechanistic jobs are being done more efficiently.'

At Royal Bank of Scotland (RBS) they take employee engagement very seriously indeed. Neil Roden, Group Director of Human Resources at RBS, confirms that they see engagement not as a 'soft' issue but as a vital function of management:

> 'I think when we talk about it in the UK we have tried to produce a stereotype that is kind of wishy-washy and . . . soft. And I think partly that's a kind of psychological device designed to cover up the fact that we are not very comfortable working in that space . . . the Americans are much more comfortable in saying, I'm going to be nice to David not because I want to be nice to David but because I know that if I'm nice to him he's going to give me 10% extra and that 10% extra is worth $5000 dollars to me; so if I've given him $500 to get that $5000 that's actually a good deal. I think sometimes people don't see that ultimately this is about the bottom line.'

Not that we are advocating what Roden describes as the more American approach, but this is about engagement for performance.

In the US, the SAS Institute, the world's largest privately held software company, is a leader in its market. It is now in its third decade of double-digit annual growth, with revenues in excess of US$1 billion. This success is fuelled in large measure by its ongoing commitment to research and development (R&D) but also by the decision of its founder, Jim Goodnight, to make the workplace an inviting environment. *Fortune* once referred to SAS Institute as the 'closest thing to a workers' utopia in America'. The on-site healthcare, for example, has saved upwards of US$5 million a year while the retention rate (less than 4% turnover against an industry norm of above 15%) saves more than US$50 million in recruitment and redundancy expenditure.

It is not only staff attraction and retention that are affected; it is the quality of the output. Adam Crozier joined the Royal Mail as CEO in February 2003 at a time when the organization was embattled; public perception was of a failing state-owned organization, and losses were running at £1.5 million per day. Within three years, profits had reached £2.2 million per day, on-time delivery of first-class mail had reached a decade-long high of 92.8% and the number of letters lost had been cut in half. Clearly the journey of modernisation at the Post Office is not over but a great deal has been achieved. For Crozier, productivity is linked inextricably to efficiency and in turn to dedication. Among other initiatives, he has instituted a policy of anonymous 'have your say' surveys for his entire workforce. These cover areas traditionally regarded as 'soft' – enjoyment of the workplace, employee view of line managers. These can, department by department, be measured against output. What Crozier has found overwhelmingly is that 'there is an absolute correlation between the best-performing units in the hard measures and the best-performing units in the soft areas'.

productivity is linked inextricably to efficiency and in turn to dedication

We have seen this at a practical level ourselves. In the mid-eighties, David was Marketing Manager at Dulux (ICI). One of the staple products of the company, Brilliant White paint, was losing market share, pressurized by cheaper 'own-brand' paints. The morale of the sales force was low, and falling.

Charged by his Marketing Director to come up with a way to turn around the Brilliant White sales, it would have been easy simply to do a redesign of the can or to produce a new advertising campaign along well-trodden lines. It would have been easy, and would almost certainly have failed. David was engaged enough with his company to want to do more: he trusted his Marketing Director's assessment of how important the issue was, and he wished to return that invested trust by delivering. His response therefore was to approach the project in a more creative, more lateral-thinking way. He in turn engaged a team around him, gleaning input from everyone he could think of: for the technological side he turned to R&D, for colour advice he went to a colour consultant, he brought the advertising agency and a creative into the process and canvassed the opinions of the key customer accounts and his international peers.

This process was a complicated one, with various false starts and of course a clamour of conflicting voices. The breakthroughs, in fact, came via a small piece of information from an international partner – that a range of off-whites had been successfully marketed by a company in the US – and from feeding that piece of information to the colour consultant who came up with the original three Natural White colours. This was then harnessed by the sales force (who suggested putting the distinctive emblems on the cans) and by the advertising agency which further developed the concept.

In retrospect, it might seem an obvious move. At the time, it was fraught: the costs of producing a multiple range at a time when sales were worryingly low were daunting; some of the sales force objected that there would be no room on shelves to stock the range; the manufacturers objected to the technical demands of the new paints, and the original Brilliant White remained a problem.

The results were extraordinary: when the first reports came back, the typical paint orders had jumped from three to four cans per store to several pallet-loads. The plant went from working five days a week to working 24 hours for five days a week, and eventually to working 24 hours seven days a week to keep up with demand. It was a dramatic turnaround in the fortunes of the company, and a byword for success in the industry.

It was engagement that led to this success: the extra energy and interest that everyone involved in the launch invested in it were repaid handsomely.

Similarly, an eye to engagement issues can be invaluable to the success of mergers and acquisitions (M&A) deals. In recent years these have become increasingly financially successful. In the most recent M&A cycle companies involved in M&A deals worth more than US$400 million outperformed the market by 7.0%. By contrast, share performance of companies involved in similar deals at the same point in the earlier M&A cycles of 1998 and 1988 underperformed the market by 2.5% (in 1998) and 6.4% (1988).[4]

One of the key reasons for this newly found success is much greater focus on the issues surrounding the integration of people. There is growing acknowledgement that retention and engagement of employees at all levels of the organization in post-deal integration have a direct impact on the operational success of M&As, which in turn is a key driver of M&A financial success.

By including human resources (HR) earlier in the M&A process, by focusing on the engagement agenda, M&A teams have also grown more successful at identifying key people and cultural issues during the due diligence stage. This, in turn, has enabled companies in the implementation phase to execute people strategies that support planned synergies swiftly and efficiently.

In fact, a survey on M&A activity in 2004[5] found that there was a high correlation between deal success and early HR involvement – especially when the key issues that were addressed early included executive issues (such as selection of the top **it is clear then that engagement is not a fad** team and the establishment of effective leadership) but also extended to include the integration of the broader workforce (such as the development of a corporate culture for the new organization).

It is clear then that engagement is not a fad. In fact, it is not even new. Intuitively we have always known that an engaged workforce will outperform a passive one. Now we are seeing the numbers to prove it. Engaging your workforce is not a luxury that you can afford to put on the back burner because it's a significant investment. It is absolutely vital to the success and, indeed, the survival of your organization. As Eric Peacock, Chairman of the Academy for Chief Executives and of Baydon Hill PLC, sees it:

> 'It's *the* issue. The market place is awash with opportunity for market penetration and with money for investment. One of the biggest obstacles to progress is around the talent management agenda. Getting awesomely good talent, keeping it and (within that) the engagement agenda is really the difference that makes the difference.'

Justin King, CEO of Sainsbury's, puts it even more strongly:

> 'In my business, with 140,000 people, engagement is my number one concern. In businesses of scale, you don't even get started without engagement.'

It is just as relevant to organizations that don't directly face the consumer, as David Spencer, Divisional MD, Smiths industries 1998–2002 and currently CEO, National School of Government (NSG), confirms:

> 'All factories are basically the same thing: there's production lines running and at one end goods come out. But some factories are buzzing with a real kind of entrepreneurial passion. They want to do it leaner, faster, more efficiently, with higher quality, with less failure. And in other factories you go into they don't seem to give a damn and consequently knock out rubbish.'

How do we recognize engagement?

To a certain extent people cite instinct: many of our interviewees, stressing the importance of getting out and about in the organization as often as possible, thought that an engaged atmosphere could be felt pretty quickly. 'Within ten minutes of arriving at a plant or factory or establishment you know whether this is a place that is well run', says Sir David Omand, previously UK Security and Intelligence Coordinator. Eye contact and body language are indicators of morale, both towards senior management and between members of teams. Honest and forthright conversations with all levels of the organization are useful, as is the good crude test of asking everyone from the front line to middle management the same questions about the organization, and seeing whether the same answers come back at every level. Experience can help you judge engagement based on what you are told and not told, the calibre of presentations, the speed with which communications are returned. Lord David Currie, Chair of Ofcom and previously Dean of the Cass Business School, sees it like this:

> 'You sort of smell it, don't you . . . that engagement of people as people. What goes on in meetings, how people talk to each other. You get the sense of energy, engagement, commitment, belief in what the organization stands for.'

However, as he goes on to warn: 'There may come a point in an organization where you want to test those intuitions and do a serious bit of analysis. One's intuition may be wrong and one has to guard against the danger that you are being told things by a group of people who you interact with but the reality is a bit different.' Added to which, in operations of any scale, it simply may be impossible to cover enough ground to visit every branch and department in person often enough. You should be wary of simply trusting your own judgement. You may think you're doing a good job at this, but our research tells a different story. If only 12% of employees could be described as fully engaged, then it is highly likely that yours fall into the other 88%. In lieu of, or allied to, intuitive judgement, there are a number of more specific, and measurable, engagement definitions that you should examine.

More than 1 million people surveyed worldwide on the subject of engagement identified nine factors that come together to define engagement.[6] An engaged employee:

❖ understands how their job **contributes to the organization's success**

❖ understands how their role in the organization **is related to the organization's goals, objectives and direction**

❖ is **personally motivated** to help in that success

❖ **cares** about the future of the organization

❖ is **willing to put in effort beyond what is normally expected**

❖ derives a sense of **personal accomplishment** from their job

❖ would **recommend their organization** to a friend as a good place to work

❖ believes that their **company inspires** them to do their best work

❖ is **proud** to tell others that they work for their organization.

For the purpose of this book we have chosen to group the nine factors under two sub-sets of alignment and engagement.

Alignment

'I think it is critical because unless you have got people aligned . . . you haven't got a hope in hell.'

Peter Erskine, Chairman and CEO, Telefonica O2 Europe plc

In the list above, the first two statements, we would say, form the underpinning of *alignment*. Alignment, put simply, is clarity from the workforce on exactly *what* their job is and *why* it is important. Alignment is crucial to true engagement – it is virtually impossible for an employee to sustain engagement if they are not aligned – but as we will see there is sometimes a tension between overall organizational alignment and individual engagement.

What does alignment consist of? An aligned (as opposed to engaged) employee *understands how their job contributes to the overall success of the organization*. What is vital is that that understanding should be accurately based in the organization's actual strategy. A basic understanding of how and why your task is important is a foundation stone of all engagement. Alignment needs to work at the job level and at the organizational level. People need to be clear what is expected of them day to day, and they benefit hugely by really understanding the strategy of the organization (asking and having answered the question, why?). People's decision making at the day-to-day level will be significantly benefited by their understanding of the organization's strategic intent. This works at a rational level, at the level of knowing what to do.

An aligned employee should *understand how their job relates to the group's overall goals, objectives and direction*. The employee must see their job in the context of the wider organization, not simply at a functional level but at a strategic one. Colin Green, President of Defence Aerospace, Rolls-Royce to 2006, says: 'In getting people to fight the battles you need to convince them of the righteousness of the cause.' There is of course a strategic imperative here. It is worse then a waste of energy for a group of managers to try to launch the company into Asia if the senior management have decided that the strategic necessity is South America. Sir Martin Sorrell, CEO of WPP, the world's largest advertising agency, put it very simply: 'If you asked me what is the biggest issue, it's about getting people aligned. Once you have everybody aligned you can take the world over. You can't have people pulling against the strategy.' Consequently, a deep understanding of the company's goals and direction underpins the rational side of engagement. The Japanese refer to this alignment as 'Wa', loosely translated as 'harmony'.

once you have everybody aligned you can take the world over

The most obvious requirement in an alignment process is effective communication. Kevin Beeston, Executive Chairman of SERCO, says:

'It's no good having a strategy if you keep it to yourself. It has to be articulated in a way that people can deliver it ... unless the people on the ground do actually understand their role in delivering your strategy and your organizational ethos and all the rest of it, then you won't succeed, it's as simple as that.'

Or, at an even more basic level, it simply means communicating to people the importance of what they do, as David Spencer of NSG points out:

> 'I think for me the shining light on getting people aligned, for instance in an aerospace factory, is to get them to understand which part of the aircraft they are making. Although they can sort out a tube with a fitting on the end, it's very hard to relate that to a Boeing or a fighter aircraft until you actually see it in situ on the plane. Then suddenly you realize that it's a critical safety component without which the thing will fail. And therefore the level of commitment and involvement is quite different to if you had allowed that individual on the production line to remain in the dark.'

For communication to be effective, the company's overarching aims must be clear, simply communicated and attainable. Ian Watmore, former Head of Accenture in the UK and now Head of the Delivery Unit at the Cabinet Office, sees it like this:

> 'You have got to have a clear vision, one that can be expressed simply but which has depth to it. If it is too complicated it won't resonate with people, if it's too simple it will sound trite, so it has got to be simple but with depth.'

However, simple does not mean simplistic. The concept must be simply communicated to make the message accessible. As Geoff Mulgan, who used to be head of the No 10 Strategy Unit and now is Head of the Young Foundation, puts it: 'The job of the leader is to get to the simplicity on the other side of complexity.' Richard Baker of Alliance Boots puts it this way: 'You need to get past the facts of the matter to the heart of the matter.' Adam Crozier of Royal Mail is adamant about the importance of communicating throughout the organization:

> 'It is very important for there to be absolute clarity from the top of the organization to the bottom of the organization ... what it is you want people to do and how you want them to do it. Because everybody wants to know what's expected of them and what part that plays in where the company is going, and in my experience the vast majority of people do want to have an idea of where the company they work for is going.'

A true understanding of where the company is going is a key factor for the engaged employee. Efforts are made meaningful, interest is sparked by an understanding of the bigger picture and by the sense of contribution to it. Employees actively seek leaders with decision-making abilities and the opportunity to influence those decisions. It is also important to recognize that it is a two-way process. From the employers' point of view, employees with an understanding of the overarching vision have the wherewithal to make independent decisions that won't cut across the strategy. It will make the organization stronger. Dianne Thompson, whose company Camelot has had to weather various media storms over the years, explains it like this:

> 'I need my people to be engaged in believing where we're going and how we're doing, so that they can withstand the attacks we get from outside. In my top priorities, growing sales is number one, and keeping my people engaged is number two.'

While alignment is hugely important by and large, it is an area in which British organizations have successfully focused their energy in recent years – 84% of respondents to our questionnaires felt able to agree with the first requirement of alignment, and 73% with the second. We shall examine it, therefore, as a pre-requisite of meaningful engagement, rather than as a separate topic. Alignment is something we must constantly strive for, but it represents only the first step towards a truly engaged workforce.

Engagement

If alignment is about ensuring employees know what to do then engagement is about them wanting to do it. While alignment and engagement are inextricably linked, the former is largely a rational activity and the latter is predominately emotional.

> 'Finding ways to get people to care about what they do is the way I put it, because the worst thing that anyone could ever say in this organization is, "I don't really care

▶

about that." If you can get them to care then you are 95% of the way there ... that's the key: getting people to care about what they do even if it's an incredibly mundane, habitual thing.'

Adam Crozier, CEO Royal Mail

In parallel with comprehension must come motivation. Here the boundaries between rational and emotional engagement begin to blur. Emotional engagement means that the employee is inspired, invested and interested enough in their job to equate company success with personal success. Engagement has many variables. Ensuring that an individual correlates success for the organization with personal achievement will depend on the terms that the individual chooses to define success. These will be partly financial, but they are also likely to include more intangible qualities, such as non-financial rewards, psychological satisfaction and recognition for achievement. Moreover, it is perfectly imaginable that an employee can be interested in their job function itself without feeling an emotional connection to the wider organization. Conversely, it is possible (though less likely) that an employee could feel a great loyalty to their company without being particularly inspired by the tasks they perform there.

Of the remaining seven definitions of engagement above, we can see that they range from statements which incline towards loyalty to the company (*I am proud to tell others I work here, I would recommend the company to a friend as a good place to work*), through motivation (*I am willing to put in effort beyond what is normally expected, I am personally motivated to help in my company's success*), to inspiration. Of the questions used in the research to define engagement, perhaps the one that best sums up the whole subject of emotional engagement is this: '*My company inspires me to do my best work.*' It is worth noting that this crucial statement, which in effect binds up many of the facets of engagement, scored only a 40% agreement rating – less than half of the score of the question that best sums up alignment. Such a disparity points out, forcibly, that although most of our employees are well aware of what is expected of them and why, significantly less than half of them, *by their own definitions,* feel that they are giving less than their best in the pursuit of those goals. It is for this reason that this book, while recognizing the necessity of rational alignment, focuses mainly on engagement.

Engagement and alignment

In fact, one of the things we wrestled with in the development of this book was the relationship of the terms 'engagement' and 'alignment'. Was engagement emotional and alignment rational? If one speaks of rational engagement, does that negate the need to talk of alignment? The truth is that irrespective of the terms, there is clearly both a rational and an emotional component to the relationships between the organization and the workforce, between the leader and the led, the manager and the managed. It is a relationship which occurs at all levels and is equally important to all of them. The preceding elements of this chapter have explained the basic ingredients of both the rational and the emotional. Here we seek to explain why, to truly harness employee

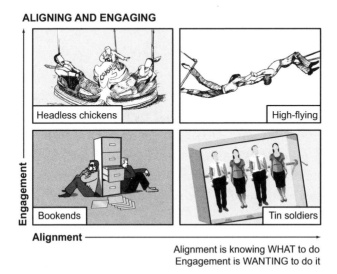

Figure 1.1 Engagement and alignment grid

engagement, both must be present. For the purposes of the ensuing discussion, assume that when we talk of alignment, we are tending towards the rational, and when we speak of engagement, we are leaning towards the emotional.

In response to this issue, we have developed the four-box model in Figure 1.1, which clarifies and brings to life the vital roles that both alignment and engagement play.

Bookends

Companies which demonstrate both low engagement and low alignment are disorganized and inefficient: either they occupy a market niche so safe that they are surviving despite their working practices (in which case the likelihood is that at some point they will find themselves vulnerable to competition), or they are on the way out but don't know it. The people inside them act like bookends: static and passive, merely propping up the existing organization. These are the workers who inhabit the offices described by David Bolchover in his book *The Living Dead*.[7]

Tin soldiers

Raising the levels of alignment of the 'bookends' will at least, by giving their processes more direction, raise their game. What it won't do is give them an innovative edge. An organization like this could be characterized as one made up of tin soldiers, all lined up correctly with everything in place, but without the dynamism to go anywhere. Think of the worst examples of public-sector workplaces where process dominates performance.

Headless chickens

Conversely, an organization with high levels of engagement but low levels of alignment will simply become chaotic. Vast amounts of discretionary energy applied by everyone with no overarching goal will result in mayhem as various impulses collide and conflict. The people within it will be like headless chickens. True engagement, without alignment, is unsustainable in a coherent organization since it will become dissipated, and ultimately unsuccessful. Think here of highly talented individuals *not* playing for the team but nevertheless highly engaged – think Geoff Boycott. Cristiano Ronaldo of Manchester United (in his early days). Great individuals but not great team players. Interestingly, Ronaldo demonstrates greater alignment and thus greater value to the organization.

true engagement, without alignment, is unsustainable

The research shows that organizations have done a much better job of aligning their people than they have of engaging them. Respondents' scores for agreeing they are aligned are more than twice as favourable as they are for engaging them.

High-flying

It is only when both rational and emotional commitment are present that a workforce can be said to be fully engaged and that such engagement can be leveraged for the most effect. Think of the ER team when a crisis occurs. They all work to the limit of their ability; each has a job to do, their own part of the operation to execute. But they are all working towards the same clear, overriding goal – to save lives.

However, it has to be recognized that there is a potential paradox here. The paradox is that achieving alignment can, on occasion, mean forcing people to do what they feel they would prefer not to. It is the manager's job to recognize and manage this tension so that individual engagement doesn't suffer (or only in the short term), but also so that organizational anarchy doesn't occur. According to Kahn (1990),[8] people are 'inherently ambivalent' about their levels of involvement in an organization. They are constantly engaging and disengaging in order to find the optimum balance point between having the room to express themselves and playing into their role within the organization. Therefore the first challenge for employers is to shift that tipping point to sit closer to the organization's needs by engineering jobs and the work environment.

The message here is simple – do not neglect either element of the engagement equation. Your people need to be clear about what to do and also about the fact that they want to do it. The ingredients of the dish are as we have described and the proportions must be carefully measured to provide the exact balance which your organization needs. Probably most of us are aware of the need for that balance. The next question is, are we providing it?

NOTES

[2] Towers Perrin Global Workforce Study, 2005 – UK data compendium.
[3] Towers Perrin European Talent Survey, 2004 – Reconnecting with employees.
[4] Towers Perrin, 2007 – M&As – the long and short of it.
[5] Towers Perrin Track M&A report, 2004 – Unlocking the value of M&A.
[6] Towers Perrin Global Workforce Study, 2005 – UK data compendium.
[7] Bolchover, David (2005) *The Living Dead. Switched off, zoned out – the shocking truth about office life*, Capstone.
[8] Kahn, W. A. (1990) 'Psychological conditions of personal engagement and disengagement at work.' *Academy of Management Journal*, 33, 692–724.

2 How are we doing and does it matter?

The brief answer is: a lot worse than we think we are. A research project carried out by the Chartered Management Institute and the DTI showed that while two-thirds of directors thought that their organizations were characterized by a good buzz and a feeling of energy, only one third of their middle management agreed. How would your organization score? Statistically, the chances are that it would not do very well. While 48% of directors thought that their leadership was in touch with how their workforce was feeling, only 21% of those in middle management agreed.

Towers Perrin has been measuring and analyzing employees' workforce attitudes – and the financial impact of these attitudes on their employers – since the early 1990s. As such, its ongoing research provides some valuable insights into levels of engagement.

The 2003 Talent Report[9] comprised over 35,000 one-to-one questionnaires across North America and the interest this report generated in a nascent but underserved area of HR study quickly led to the survey repeated in Europe in 2004 with over 15,000 unique employee interviews. In 2005 another more ambitious research study was undertaken into employee engagement[10] which was to date the world's largest single survey of employee engagement. It was conducted in parallel in 16 countries to satisfy two questions:

❖ What does the level of employee engagement look like across the globe?

❖ What factors drive employee engagement in these leading global markets?

What drives engagement in the UK

An engaged employee is one who is willing and able to contribute to company success. Engagement is the extent to which employees put extra discretionary effort into their work, in the form of time, brain-power or energy. Just 12% of the UK workforce describe themselves as highly engaged (see Figure 2.1). While low, the figure is just above average for the European countries surveyed.

The important message is that 65% of UK employees are moderately engaged while 23% are actively disengaged. Organizations, then, have a huge opportunity to sway the massive middle of ambivalently minded staff. Even a smallish percentage swing towards engagement has the capacity to change the attitudes of a large number of employees.

Figure 2.2 shows the numbers against the various issues. These issues can be used by any company and the answer benchmarked. Those interested in the theories which underpin the research method-ology used should look at Annex B. The top ten drivers of engagement in the UK are shown in Figure 2.2. It shows what employees rank as the most important and the least important drivers of engagement, with 'senior management interest in employee wellbeing' being the most important driver of engagement in the UK. Next to each driver

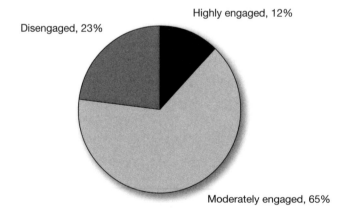

Figure 2.1 Percentage of UK workforce that describe themselves as engaged[11]

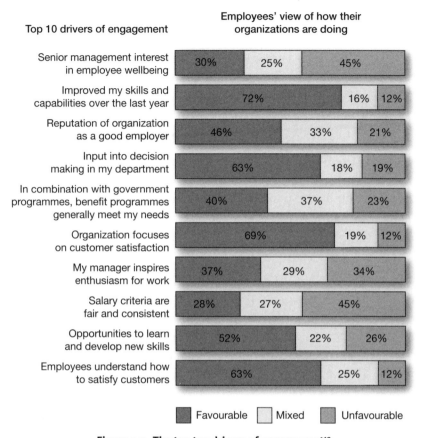

| Top 10 drivers of engagement | Employees' view of how their organizations are doing |

Figure 2.2 The top ten drivers of engagement[12]

are the survey results showing how well we are actually doing with respect to each one.

Irrespective of the theories, it is what the research shows that is of value. While it shows poor level of engagement in the UK, the overall picture for alignment is good. The most straightforward indicator of alignment – *I understand how my job contributes to the overall organization* – generates an 84% agreement rate. A further 73% could relate their role to their company's overall goals and objectives. Clearly for generic research across a range of organizations we can measure only how clear people are on what is expected of them. What we can't measure is whether their view coincides with the more senior management view or indeed whether they understand – and buy into the company strategy.

The factors relating to alignment – such as the opportunity to improve skills, or the organization's focus on customer satisfaction – also score relatively highly, while those that pertain to engagement – managerial attitudes, company reputation and the 'inspiration' factor – show large gaps between employee expectation and the reality. Levels of overall engagement are, interestingly, hardly affected by age. However, they are affected by seniority. Broadly speaking, and as might be expected, the ratio of highly engaged employees goes up as the surveys reach the higher echelons of the company. But not, perhaps, as much as you might assume. The percentage of highly engaged senior executives and directors stands at 20% against 9% for non-management.[13]

The same study also analyzed *retention* – rather than engagement – factors and concluded that the most important retention criterion is

this is evidence that talent gravitates to talent

the belief that the organization is managing to retain people with the required skills. This is evidence that talent gravitates to talent. Again, arguably, UK companies do not score very highly, with only 23% of employees believing that their company does well in retaining talent.

Other engagement views

Perhaps unsurprisingly, the key to inspiration for most people lies in their leadership. Backing up our own findings, a plethora of reports details what constitutes 'engagement'. An indicative selection is provided here to establish the consequence of observations about engagement.

A recent article by Bradon and Thomas defines employee engagement as 'the term which defines the quality and strength of the relationship between an employee and their organization'.[14] Top companies see their employees being proud of the organization and being happy to recommend it to a friend as a quality place of employment. Interestingly, the report upon which the article was based also deals with rewards and found no significant correlation between an employee's feelings about pay and benefits and how they viewed their company. This idea is supported throughout our studies and confirms that the employer/employee relationship is complex.

An ISR report[15] described the key drivers of employee engagement:

- ❖ Company has high ethical standards.
- ❖ Core values of the organization are clear.
- ❖ Employees respect management.
- ❖ Employees are treated with respect (this was statistically most important for the UK).
- ❖ Management seeks opinions of employees.
- ❖ Core values of the organization are readily applicable.

A Corporate Leadership Council (CLC) report identifies leadership (in terms of values, ethics and respectfulness) as the most important issue influencing employee engagement. Career development is second, followed by empowerment and employee decision making, then company/brand image. CLC research[16] involving over 50,000 employees yielded the following results and conclusions:

- ❖ Engaged employees perform 20% better and are 87% less likely to leave an organization.
- ❖ More than 10% of employees are fully disengaged.
- ❖ There are no high or low engagement groups based on gender, tenure, or position.
- ❖ Engagement levels are closely tied to company strategies and policies.
- ❖ Emotional engagement is closely linked to effort.
- ❖ Retention is related to both emotional and rational engagement.
- ❖ Compensation is linked to an employee's intent to stay.
- ❖ The role of the manager is critical in determining engagement levels.

This is why this book is structured as it is – before a dedicated engagement programme can flourish, it is necessary that there is a sound, engaging leadership. Leaders need to examine first themselves and then their top team, before talking an engagement agenda into the workforce. Common sense suggests that management, both immediate and senior, holds the levers that can engage or disengage a workforce; the statistical results of our research bear this out. Senior management's interest in employee wellbeing heads the list of engagement drivers. Interestingly, for the middle management level, it is also the most significant driver of employee retention; people join companies, they leave managers.

a good leader both challenges and trusts his team

Inspirational leadership is a slippery concept and arguably the key ingredient of inspirational leadership is mutual trust. A good leader both challenges and trusts his team. However, without the reciprocal trust of the team in that leader, the leader's trust in them is useless. As Martin Taylor of Syngenta puts it: 'This is absolutely crucial – why should we be working for somebody we don't trust?' His words are echoed by Neil Roden of RBS:

'If people don't trust the organization, they do behave in a way that absolutely reflects that lack of trust. Because if you work in an organization and you don't trust that company, does that have no effect on you? Of course it does. Are you going to take risks for those people ... no. Are you going to be more looking after yourself than anybody else ... absolutely.'

That inspirational leadership lies at the heart of engagement is backed up by the views of many of the CEOs and leaders we interviewed:

'People are most inspired when you hold out for them the promise of what they could be rather than what they are.'

Lucian Hudson, Chairman of Tavistock Institute and Communication Director, FCO

'To be a good manager, you have to love managing. This passion will ensure your dedication to the job. It will also be infectious, increasing the commitment of others and inspiring them to attain their own goals.'

Jurgen Grobler, England rowing coach

'My purpose is about growing people and letting them find their own greatness.'

Eric Peacock, Chairman of Baydon Hill PLC

Inspirational leadership consists of many facets, including involving the workforce, telling stories, being visible, being authentic and being successful. However, suffice to say that above all, engaging leadership must be underpinned by trust: a two-way contract between workforce and management.

The good news is that the workforce is hugely interested in leadership and is looking to leaders for direction and for inspiration (see Figure 2.3). The bad news, as we shall see later in the chapter, is that they don't believe this is what they are receiving.

Largely, the message is that although employees believe that their management is doing a reasonable job of representing the company externally, communicating with shareholders and customers, taking steps to ensure long-term success, they are less impressed by senior management's attitude to the company internally. The figures show that there is a vast disconnection between leadership and workforce. Shockingly, only 25% of respondents believe that their management is aware of the issues they face in their work on a day-to-day basis; only 30% of employees believe senior management's oft-repeated assurances that they care about employee wellbeing. Employees believe that their leadership is not communicating with them honestly (72% are neutral or agree with this), is not supportive of innovation (56% are neutral or could not agree with this) and does not make an effort to be visible and accessible (only 37% agreed it did).

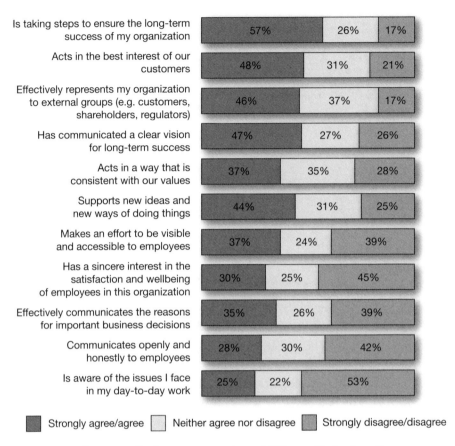

Figure 2.3 Senior management capabilities and behaviours[17]

Chartered Management Institute and DTI research confirms these numbers. Their surveys measured the gaps between what employees want and what they believe they are getting from their leadership. While 96% want their leaders to be good communicators and listen more than they talk, only 43% believed that they do; 79% wanted a genuine shared vision with their leadership, against the 38% who saw it in practice. Although the respondents to the Global Workforce Study are most positive, relatively, about senior management's competence, only 57% of those questioned agreed that their leadership was taking steps to ensure the company's long-term success; even about this basic building block they were ambivalent.[18]

Supports and promotes teamwork — 57% | 22% | 21%

Recognizes and appreciates good work — 55% | 21% | 24%

Treats employees with trust and respect — 53% | 22% | 25%

Holds people accountable for performance and goals — 53% | 29% | 18%

Encourages and empowers people to take initiative in their work — 51% | 24% | 25%

Acts quickly if I ask for help solving a problem — 49% | 22% | 29%

Encourages new ideas and new ways of doing things — 48% | 26% | 26%

Communicates clearly and openly — 47% | 23% | 30%

Provides performance goals that are challenging but achievable — 44% | 29% | 27%

Ensures that employees have access to a variety of learning opportunities — 45% | 26% | 29%

Shares valuable work experience or technical expertise that I can learn from — 44% | 25% | 31%

Manages performance reviews fairly and effectively — 43% | 29% | 28%

Gives me frequent feedback on my performance — 41% | 24% | 35%

Inspires enthusiasm for work — 37% | 29% | 34%

Helps employees understand how they influence the financial performance of their organization — 33% | 33% | 34%

Understands what motivates me — 35% | 27% | 38%

Effectively coaches and builds the strengths of employees — 34% | 30% | 36%

Consults employees before making decisions that affect them — 35% | 23% | 42%

■ Strongly agree/agree   □ Neither agree nor disagree   ■ Strongly disagree/disagree

Figure 2.4 Views about first-line managers

Views about first-line managers are marginally more positive, as shown in Figure 2.4.

A smallish majority believe that their first-line managers support teamwork, recognize good work and treat their employees with trust and respect. However, the facet of management which employees believe to be most important – inspiring enthusiasm – is perceived in practice by only 37% of respondents. Only 35% believe their management understands what motivates them and that only 51% encourage and empower the people beneath them to take initiative. As we will see later in the book, first-line management plays a key part in the development and harnessing of engagement.

There is also a vast disconnection between what the workforce wants from its leadership and what it believes it gets. Given these kinds of statistics, it is perhaps not surprising that overall engagement is so low.

The employment deal

Beyond the role of leadership in inspiring engagement, employees are also looking at their organizations to see whether the employment 'deal' is fair and attractive. Clearly, and crucially, people want to be fairly judged, rewarded and, if relevant, promoted. Salaries, especially crucial in attracting valuable staff (competitive base pay is the number one attraction driver), must remain fair and consistent. Only 28% of employees perceive that they are,[19] a worrying statistic given that this is the third most important factor in retaining staff.

Opportunities for learning and development are rated extremely important in attracting, retaining and engaging employees across the workforce, and especially in non-management roles where it is cited as the foremost engagement factor. Also key in engagement is the employee perception that they have some input into decision making within their department.

Of more concern is the fragility of the sense of co-ownership that is so important to engagement. In a European-wide survey in 2004,[20] 46% of respondents disagreed that 'if the company is successful, employees will share in that success'. Only 34% believed that their company provides challenging work. Even more striking is the disconnection employees perceive between their efforts and the consequences they reap. A mere 28% believe that they receive regular and meaningful performance feedback. Only 23% believe that their advancement is based on performance: further evidence of the alienation felt by high performers who perceive inequity. It also provides a huge opportunity for employers who want to exploit the latent asset in their businesses.

The overall picture we get is that employees feel hard done by. What they want is to feel as though they have input, control and will take home some kind of share in the organization's success. A kind of shared destiny. In return for this they are willing to invest their discretionary energy. And they want to make this bargain with senior leadership they can trust: this, in particular, is what they feel they are lacking. Employers seem ever more remote: leadership is not really communicating with the front line both in terms of the basic direction of the company and on the wider issues of company ethos, values and vision. The result, unsurprisingly, is disillusionment and a slackening of energy.

The lessons are clear. Organizations are currently talking a good engagement game, but their people are not feeling the effects. Talking the talk and not walking the walk destroys trust and lack of trust disengages and disengaged employees destroy value.

Does it matter?

Obviously, we think engagement matters. We have written this book because we believe that it is both relevant and important. Our interviewees agree. In fact, everybody concerned with the wellbeing and performance of organizations seems to agree. Engagement is the 'in' topic. But is everybody right? Does it really matter that much? Historically, there has been a good deal of research conducted on the relationship between the satisfaction/morale/contentment/development of employees and the return of any investment by an organization into increasing any or all of the above. See Annex A. The weight of evidence supports the view that there is a virtually inevitable correlation between the performance of a business and the engagement of its employees.

The stories

Why resource engagement? Because it pays. During our research we found two outstanding examples of best practice in the field of engagement and we examine them closely in this chapter. The first is the Nationwide Building Society.

Nationwide Building Society

In 1994 the board at Nationwide embarked on a market strategy to become the 'champion of the consumer'. It positioned itself as 'trustworthy, honest and fair'. This approach was epitomized in its marketing campaign. On behalf of the consumer, Nationwide highlighted and fought against the cash machine charges applied by leading high-street banks as well as the implicit charges which applied on currency exchange.

In 2000, Philip Williamson became Chief Executive and promoted his belief that 'People Capital' is an essential component of a successful organization. People Capital is defined within Nationwide as 'the value our people bring to our business through the impact they have on our members' advocacy and ultimately our business results'. The company's mission is to create a culture that increases employee engagement levels and aligns the entire workforce to a clear strategy.

A group of employees travelled to the United States to learn from organizations renowned for having highly engaged and committed staff, compelling products and high levels of sales and profitability. The experiences highlighted two important

▶

factors: the importance of creating a unique community and the effect senior leaders can achieve by showing a personal and authentic interest in their people. These lessons were taken home and Nationwide developed the PRIDE initiative which is now synonymous with the company culture and brand. PRIDE is a set of attitudes and behaviours which all employees are asked to adopt.

PRIDE stands for:

Putting members first

Rising to the challenge

Inspiring confidence

Delivering best value

Exceeding expectations

It encapsulates Nationwide's commercial outlook. It shows the company's belief that its people will make the difference. Nationwide says that 'if we identify, understand, optimize, communicate and exploit the value of our People Capital both internally and externally, our business will become increasingly successful'.

Have they done this? PRIDE has become firmly embedded in the organization through a comprehensive implementation programme. There are 200 designated 'Pride Partners' who champion the PRIDE values and encourage all employees to live and achieve them. Senior leaders are passionate about PRIDE and endorse it by living the values and leading by example. Philip Williamson says: 'You've got to let your people know that you're on their side. It's not us and them. I never use the word "staff" in Nationwide; I will not allow anybody to use the word "staff in" Nationwide. We talk about a team, people, togetherness, but it is not management and staff. We are a team. I do my bit.'

PRIDE is also built into the company's performance management systems so that each employee (regardless of level) understands what PRIDE means to them in practice. The Nationwide performance management system assesses employees' performance against PRIDE to ensure that they are living the values and displaying the appropriate behaviour. Nationwide even recruits and assesses potential employees based on the system. PRIDE is always centre stage.

The annual PRIDE event is a celebration, which in recent years has taken on a more commercial outlook but retains the positive employee and customer focus. Awards are given to employees who excel in the PRIDE values and even suppliers can qualify. To take an example, one year a refurbishing supplier gave some very valuable input into how to improve customer satisfaction in a local branch. When the ideas were incorporated successfully the supplier was given a PRIDE award.

▶

The core PRIDE values are complemented by corporate social responsibility. Major Nationwide sites are powered by renewable energy, the company distributes bicycle reflectors for child safety and contributes to Macmillan nurses.

PRIDE helped Nationwide to finish top in *The Times* Best Organization poll in 2005.

While this is, of course, both gratifying and interesting, more important is the PRIDE effect on the bottom line. Nationwide has established a system to measure employee engagement levels and the effect this has on business results. With around 16,000 employees and a wage bill of about £450 million (representing about 50% of management costs), the company sees the need for data and analysis on the added value to realize and evaluate this significant investment. Project Genome is the Nationwide term for the internal process of identifying, characterizing and mapping the key drivers of engagement or 'corporate DNA'. Importantly, this research is intended to establish their effect on and importance to member commitment and business performance (i.e. the service-profit chain). The data is obtained through an all-employee survey, which is issued each year and has now been running for 13 years. There is a strong internal commitment to the survey, with an 89% response rate.

The information gleaned from the survey is used to improve the characterizations of the employee brand and to increase employee engagement, with the aim of improving the value members derive from doing business with the company. It covers a number of issues, from employee satisfaction and commitment levels, to hire and promotion costs, sickness and absence rates and workforce demographics. The survey shows the success of the PRIDE values:

❖ Employee satisfaction is measured at 79% (substantially above the other organizations).

❖ Employee commitment is measured at 85%.

❖ 89% of employees feel Nationwide is an employer of integrity.

❖ 79% of employees are satisfied with their work–life balance.

❖ Group absence levels are low at 3.3%.

❖ Group turnover is 8% compared with the benchmark of 14%. On this measure, the organization has saved an estimated £18 million in training and recruitment alone.

Nationwide has developed a predictive business tool (or simulator) based on three different products which quantify the impact of the five key drivers. The three products are mortgage sales, personal loans and household insurance sales. The simulator shows what effect an increase or decrease in, say, the average length of

▶

service would have on the number of mortgage sales. The predictive examples show that if Nationwide can increase the average length of service from 10.2 years to 11.2 years, this will result in an increase in customer commitment by almost 1%, which will improve mortgage completions against target by almost 2%, yielding an additional net present value of around £5.6 million. Similarly, an increase in employee perceptions of coaching leads to almost a 1% increase in personal loan sales against target.

The second example of best practice is the Royal Bank of Scotland.

Royal Bank of Scotland

RBS has 135,000 employees and 30 million customers in 30 countries. It has £871,432 million of assets and staff costs of £6,647 million (2006). It is the tenth largest bank in the world. The group's activities range from retail to commercial and investment banking. It places a premium in collating – and using – engagement data. Data on employee attitudes is gathered via an annual anonymous survey which is directed at all staff and has an 86% response rate. The survey is conducted online or on paper and is run by ISR, an independent firm. Surveys are also carried out with joiners and leavers, and there are surveys to take the 'pulse' on particular topics and surveys with newly acquired businesses.

The raw survey responses are stored so that managers can compare data directly as well as at the aggregate level for business units and cost centres at different levels. Qualifier data collected includes demographics, length of employment, position, geography, gender and benefits preferences – this allows segmentation and analysis on these lines. This survey data has been combined with pooled data from RBS's 30 systems across the world as part of a virtual data warehouse. An important part of this process was standardization of the data and standardization of employee research across the RBS group.

Its annual employee survey provides an impressive volume of useful information – the high response rate (86%) and quality of data (i.e. honesty of responses) is related to the way it is conducted independently and the fact that it is run by a third party (ISR). Using an external survey organization also allows standardization of metrics and direct comparison of performance with that of competitors. Internal benchmarking is being accomplished with the assistance of another third party (the Saratoga Institute). It has a policy of publishing much more human capital information than most organizations do. Specific human capital measures for RBS

▶

and its competitors are, for example, included as part of the group's annual accounts.

RBS has developed a detailed model of how its human capital is related to business performance. It uses analysis of extensive datasets to correlate specific HR metrics to specific business outcomes. All the internal research on human capital issues, from call centre performance, through management effectiveness, to employment case law, has been collated. RBS's HR staff have worked with divisional executives from the businesses to jointly agree their own human capital measures and the competitors they want to benchmark their business performance against. Later chapters will show exactly how they have gone about measuring and using this key information. For now, what concerns us is the results they have perceived.

What have been the consequences of using this information?

Once data from the warehouse has been processed and statistically refined, the resultant information is used to give managers a detailed breakdown of performance in attraction, engagement and retention of the best people. It also informs the business's leaders as to how the people management is affecting the business's performance. A human capital board has been set up with both business and HR executives, and the group uses the data to objectively prioritize human capital initiatives according to their business impact. A range of human capital measures is published as part of the annual accounts and benchmarked to competitors' performance. The key internal outputs of RBS's human capital model are 'impact diagrams' which illustrate the impact of different human capital factors on engagement and which highlight the opportunities for concentrating on particular issues which could boost or threaten engagement.

As they are now part of the same database, operational measures such as headcount, absence rates, costs, productivity and turnover can be compared relatively easily with engagement drivers directly and the relationship monitored automatically and continuously. HR staff have access not only to internal comparisons across call centres (for example) but also to the correlations and implications for engagement of management and leadership effectiveness at the individual level.

At an aggregate level, RBS's analysis of its data shows that increased productivity and increased engagement are positively correlated (0.51), with a 5% variation in productivity possible. Staff turnover at RBS is also negatively correlated with engagement (−0.43). A 1% reduction in staff turnover is estimated to be worth £20 million per year and a 0.1% reduction in absence is worth an annual £1 million for RBS. Engagement was also shown to be positively correlated with participation in the RBSelect flexible benefits plan: engagement was 20% higher for employees selecting

▶

three or more flexible benefit options. This has allowed detailed planning and changes in resourcing, reward, organizational development and employment relations.

For Neil Roden, the reasons for committing such energy to engagement analysis are obvious. First of all, 'not caring about people and not caring whether they come or go doesn't seem a very sensible strategy when getting good people is very difficult. So to me it is the same as customers – it's much easier to hold onto a customer you've got than get a new one. It's exactly the same for employees – (they are) much easier to keep than to acquire.'

The evidence

Our research bears Roden out on this. The need to create an engaged, motivated workforce has long been a basic pillar of the HR function. Until recently the link between employee engagement and the company balance sheet was largely intuitive, so a leap of faith has been required to believe that improved employee engagement could lead to a rise in profitability. The research referred to previously developed employee engagement 'linkage' methodology to provide managers with powerful metrics to show the financial impact of improving the level of employee engagement.

The 2004 employee engagement survey[21] determined the levels of employee engagement in France, Germany, Italy, the Netherlands, Spain and the UK and statistically evaluated the relationship between employees' engagement levels and the performance of their companies.

The analysis found that those companies with higher average employee engagement have significantly higher operating margin relative to their industry – and vice versa. While this is not a proven causal relationship, it is another important piece of evidence that links engagement and financial results, the weight of which in aggregation is becoming overwhelming.

it is another important piece of evidence that links engagement and financial results

It is estimated that a 15% increase in engagement correlates with a 2.2% point increase in operating margin. This conclusion was reached by researching levels of engagement in 250 companies in the US and correlating this with operating margin, grouping companies by industry segment.

This kind of analysis is critical in helping companies create a business case for improving employee engagement. A growing number of companies have conducted this kind of financial modelling.

ISR research found that companies with highly engaged employees have lower staff turnover rates, lower absenteeism, higher customer satisfaction and loyalty, fewer safety incidents, higher quality and more efficient production, as well as enhanced sales performance. ISR's latest research reveals the difference an engaged workforce can make to the financial performance of an organization. ISR compared the financial performance of organizations with a highly engaged workforce with their peers with a less engaged workforce, over a 12-month period. This was based on a 12-month study involving 664,000 employees from 50 global companies across a range of industry sectors. (A three-year study reflected the same conclusions but analyzing operating margin and net profit margin.)

Some of the research findings are striking (see Figure 2.5):

❖ The most dramatic result is seen when evaluating changes in operating income. In the group of **companies with high levels of employee engagement, operating income improved by 19.2%** over 12 months, while in companies with low levels of engagement it declined by 32.7%.

❖ Over the same period, the group of **companies with highly engaged employees saw a 13.7% improvement** in net income growth rate and those with less engaged employees saw a 3.8% decline.

❖ The group of companies with **highly engaged employees saw earnings per share (EPS) rise by 27.8%** and companies with low levels of employee engagement saw EPS decline by 11.2%.

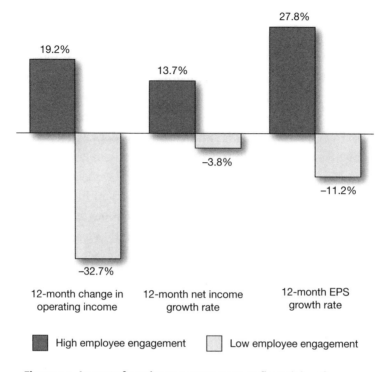

Figure 2.5 Impact of employee engagement on financial performance

B&Q, the DIY retailer, has been able to definitively link employee engagement scores to greater productivity, less retail shrinkage (inventory losses attributed to shoplifting and employee theft), less employee turnover, greater customer loyalty, higher sales and higher profits.[22]

Engagement and the customer

An increasing number of individual companies have looked at the direct link between levels of engagement within an organization and the level of its customer satisfaction. Often, this is an easier way into convincing senior management of the importance of increasing their employees' engagement. The link between employee engagement and customer satisfaction is irrefutably positive and common sense.

Customers interacting with engaged employees have a more positive experience when compared with dealing with a disengaged employee. The better experience leads to higher satisfaction. Higher satisfaction leads to more repeat business and word of mouth leads to new business. The statistical nature of this positive effect can differ greatly depending on the nature of the organization's business, whether it is business-to-business, business-to-consumer or public sector. However, that better employee engagement leads to higher customer satisfaction which leads to better performance (efficiency, revenues and profit) is common to all.

Engaged employees also believe that they can have a direct impact on the financial performance of the company As Figure 2.6 shows, engagement affects whether employees believe they can impact quality, costs or customer service. Broadly, highly engaged employees

Figure 2.6 Highly engaged people are empowered to deliver business results

believe they are 50% more likely to impact quality/costs/customer service as moderately engaged employees, who in turn feel they are 50% more likely to impact these measures than disengaged ones. It is another positive reason to engage employees.

The final financial benefit to raising an organization's employee engagement comes from lowering the turnover of staff. The Global Workforce Survey[23] shows that disengaged staff are more likely to leave: 11% had plans to leave and 41% were open to offers compared with 1% of engaged staff planning to leave and 26% open to offers. In the short term this is not necessarily a bad thing. Disengaged staff are largely unproductive and can have a negative effect on the rest of their team's engagement. But if the problem persists – with new joiners becoming disengaged and leaving – then the organization has huge inbuilt labour costs. The hard costs (advertisement/recruitment agency fees) and soft costs (HR, time of other interviewers and the process of 'onboardment' with low productivity in the first few months of tenure) vary from position to position, but some surveys suggest that the combined hard and soft costs can be as high as one year's salary.

The emotional connection

The reason why an employee's emotional connection to their work is so important is, it would seem, hard-wired into our brains. Our instinctive, emotional responses operate at a different level from our rational thought, as the following summary shows.

How the brain works and why the intuitive/instinctive (emotional) brain is so important:

> Our brains are astonishingly complex organs, containing an almost unimaginably large number – around 10,000,000,000 – of richly interconnected neurons. Surprisingly little of our brain is devoted to rational thought. Paul MacLean[24] offered his Triune Brain theory as a useful way of looking at how our brains work. He suggested that our brains have three functional parts: the *R-Complex* or 'reptilian'

▶

brain, including the brain stem and the cerebellum, runs basic processes necessary for survival and gathering the most basic information from the outside world; the *Limbic system* or 'mammalian' brain, including the amygdala, hypothalamus and hippocampus, where we experience emotions, some aspects of personal identity and memory functions; and the *cortex* and *neo-cortex*, the 'human' brain, which enable higher-order skills that we think of as 'human', including reason and speech.

Although these three divisions interlink and interact, they perform largely separate functions for us. Very little of this complexity is related to 'thinking'; most of it is entirely out of our conscious awareness and is dedicated to the minutiae of living – dealing with what we see, hear, feel, taste and smell; with the mechanics of movement; monitoring our nervous system; etc. Consciousness is related only to the frontal cortex, around a quarter of our brain.

In fact, we live much of our lives without conscious thought. Think of an experienced driver following a well-known route. Even such a complex, potentially life-threatening activity can be done effectively without conscious intervention; the driver's 'mind' wanders off on some pressing line of thought about a meeting later in the day whilst some other part of his brain processes the controls of the car, the traffic flows, the radio in the background and filters out everything that is 'normal'. We might call this expertise. Yet as soon (one hopes) as something is out of the 'normal', internal conversation is interrupted, the mind is alerted and he can take conscious control of driving until the potential hazard is passed. Similarly, in what is known as the Cocktail Party Effect[25] – our ability to pick out our name being mentioned in a conversation on the other side of a chatter-filled room – it seems that our mind filters out most sensory information, until, that is, it suddenly becomes relevant. We can't do this with our conscious mind; it simply isn't possible to pay attention to a specific conversation and to deliberately scan through the background noise for some particular message. And yet, if the message is clear enough and strong enough, we can do it effortlessly and without thought.

All of this is extremely beneficial – it's vital for our ability to cope. The mammalian and reptilian parts of our brain are constantly assessing information and relating it to established patterns in order to judge whether we need to deal with it in the cortex (an oncoming lorry, the sound of your name across the room) or ignore it. If there were no filter we would be in complete information overload.

Much of our unconscious, out of awareness, thinking works by analogy – this situation seems to be like 'this other situation', so let's do the same as we did then. It is this kind of analogous thinking that lets us visit an unfamiliar situation – going to a new restaurant, to take a trivial example – and to do so with confidence. We know the kinds of things to expect in a restaurant (tables, bar, menus, etc.) and we look for the clues as to where they are in this 'particular' restaurant; again, most of the time this

▶

happens without conscious thought. We frequently apply the same unconscious thinking when we are in business meetings, when we recruit people, or when we make business decisions.

However, the danger is that if we get information that doesn't fit our established patterns we often ignore it or skew it to fit a preconceived notion. This can be a real problem as we force fit misconceived preconditioned solutions to issues. If we want to change these conditioned patterns of thought and action we need to work extremely hard to do so.[26]

Relying solely on either the conscious or the 'emotional' unconscious path to decision making is fraught with difficulty. Overemphasis on the 'rational' framework can be counterproductive. Because it is never possible to know the information, the logical, cognitive pathways can be brought to a state of paralysis. However, gut-led 'unconscious' thinking can let one down at precisely the moment when it is most needed – when something unexpected happens. The answer, then, is that effective thinking is best done by bringing into play both rational analysis and 'intuitive wisdom'.

overemphasis on the 'rational' framework can be counterproductive

It is very important to listen to people's feelings as well as the words they are saying. By doing so you are tapping more deeply into their patterns of conditioning and so their 'true feelings'. Only by addressing these can you create real change and in this case really engage people in whatever your chosen way forward is. Hearing the message or possibly feeling it can be difficult if we have been tutored to pay attention only to the logic. And yet most of us have the experience of knowing that something doesn't smell right, that we have a gut feeling that we're missing something important, that the facts don't quite add up – all of these are external expressions of an internal mismatch. When this happens we are well counselled to pay attention and not to dismiss the message until we are sure that it is groundless.

When the logical decision is aligned with our internal experience we can feel the difference: there is a sense of alignment, a sense of purposefulness and a confidence in delivery that can be lacking if the alignment is not present. And if we are not aligned, then we can be certain that – unless we are unusually good actors – the people around us, our colleagues, staff and employees will get both messages. They will hear the words and feel the incongruity and they will sense that all is not well. They will hesitate and be uncertain in their communications, the uncertainty will amplify and the organization will be left ambivalent, awaiting clear direction and guidance.

It makes sense!

Inspirational leadership knows that the reward for focusing on employee engagement can be extraordinary results. Ian Smith, Senior Vice President of Oracle in the UK, pointed us in the direction of the following, his favourite example and a fitting conclusion to this argument:

> 'The successful companies, the really successful ones, know that you grow through building good customer relationships, that you nurture and protect, and the most successful companies are the ones that continue to focus [on that]. The company in the US that has grown shareholder value the most in the last 30 years is not a high-tech company, it's South West Airlines. And through all of the problems in the American airline industry they continued to deliver outstanding financial results. Why? Because they were committed to 20% growth? No. They have a simple phrase: 'The customer comes second.' Meaning you employ the right people and if you look after the people and make sure those people know what they're doing to service the customer, that's where the focus of attention is . . . They focus on their employees and they focus on those employees who deliver excellence and that pulls through their revenue performance. Pushing revenue performance eventually fails; pulling revenue performance through quality customer satisfaction [works].'

NOTES

9 Towers Perrin US Talent Report, 2003 – Working today: understanding what drives employee engagement.
10 Towers Perrin Global Workforce Study, 2005 – Winning strategies for a global workforce.

[11] Ibid.

[12] Towers Perrin Global Workforce Study, 2005 – UK data compendium.

[13] Ibid.

[14] Bradon, P. and Thomas, Z. (2006) 'Falling in love with your job.' *The Sunday Times*, 5 March, pp. 8–9.

[15] ISR White Paper: 'Creating competitive advantage from your employees: a global study of employee engagement.' www.isrsurveys.com

[16] Corporate Leadership Council (2006) *Employee Engagement – top things you must know and do.* http://www.corporateleadershipcouncil.com

[17] Towers Perrin Global Workforce Study, 2005 – UK data compendium.

[18] Ibid.

[19] Ibid.

[20] Towers Perrin European Talent Survey, 2004 – Reconnecting with employees.

[21] Ibid.

[22] Tritch, T. (2003) 'B&Q boosts employee engagement – and profits.' *Gallup Management Journal*, 8 May.

[23] Towers Perrin Global Workforce Study, 2005 – Ten steps to creating an engaged workforce, key European findings.

[24] Senior Research Scientist, Emeritus in the Department of Neurophysiology at the US National Institute of Mental Health.

[25] Cherry, Colin, 1953 and Arons, Barry, 1992 source: http://en.wikipedia.org/wiki/Cocktail_party_effect – accessed 20 April 2006.

[26] The analysis adapted from a study by Bob Janes, who works with people and organizations in transition – bob@bobjanes.com

3 Why is engagement so important now?

The 'why?' factor

Is engagement a new topic? Has the need for it always been there? Of course, organizations have always valued loyal, hardworking, motivated employees. But we would argue that the need for engagement has become increasingly vital in the modern business environment. The reasons for this are complex and interwoven, but they start perhaps with the newfound importance of the question 'why?'.

People learn by observing their environment and asking questions. So too do organizations.[27] Consequently those organizations must encourage their employees to continually question systems, processes, direction and management. However, to do so requires mutual trust. The management must trust the employees to be the best they can and the employees must trust the management to deliver on its promises.

Although not a role model in most facets, Enron was a role model in one aspect: the most significant reason that Enron became so successful, so quickly, was that at its core were executives who understood the centrality of the 'why'. Beneath the Enron logo were two words that encapsulated the corporate philosophy: those words were 'Ask Why'. As Kenneth Lay, the disgraced and deceased Chairman of Enron, put it: 'Always ask why things are done the way they are and then why they couldn't be done another, more productive way.' Lest we forget, Enron was named in *Fortune* as 'America's Most Innovative Company' for six consecutive years. The culture was pioneering, inventive, inquisitive. Unfortunately for all who relied on it, however, it also became greedy and dishonest. The greed blinded people to the need for questioning. The eventual whistle-blower was simply asking why the accounts were as they were and, more importantly, not receiving a plausible answer. That's when trust dies. Employees need to question why we do things the way we do them and they need to understand why we are headed in the direction we are going. People don't readily

people don't readily and wholeheartedly commit if they don't understand why

and wholeheartedly commit if they don't understand why. If you haven't taken the trouble and time to explain why we are taking a particular course of action, don't be surprised if they don't take much trouble in implementing it.

The death of deference

In the evolution of the new 'change is good' society there has been a simultaneous death of deference. Not only has the question 'why' become acceptable, it has almost become obligatory. Make no mistake, the death of deference is not only a good thing – it was essential to releasing the potential of all those inhibited by a rigid, ossified hierarchical system. Too often this death of deference can be mistaken for a lack of respect and sometimes it is. It need not be that way. It is right that we are unafraid to ask why people are in a position to dictate to us.

Politicians should face trial by media and by the public. It is fantastic that we live in an age where even the Women's Institute will slow-handclap a prime minister. From the way we talk to our doctor to the familiarity with which schoolchildren interact with their teachers, the social norms have changed. Familiarity, real or perceived, prevails. At universities, for instance:

'Students once would only dare to approach a lecturer with a meek knock and a humble "excuse me Professor", but now they bombard lecturers with e-mail messages at all hours of the day to make banal or impertinent queries in a manner that ranges from the overly familiar to the downright rude.'[28]

Somewhat surprisingly, this is true even in organizations where we would expect deference to be a built-in part of the structure. According to Admiral Sir Mark Stanhope, who is Deputy Supreme Allied Commander Transformation, NATO:

'The difference in leadership qualities of our people in the services now to those 50 years ago is that the "why" culture now exists ... 50 years ago if you said jump and you had one stripe on your arm people did so, you were respected as an officer; people are now respected for [what are] probably the things they ought to be respected for, which is who they are: what their qualities are, what their characters are, what their ability to lead is [or not].'

We are all programmed now to ask 'why?'. The perceived differences between bosses and employees have become minimal; the 'them and us' culture is under constant challenge. Reinforcing this trend is an increasing focus on individualization. Margaret Thatcher's famous quote of 1987, 'there's no such thing as society', seems to be increasingly true insofar as it applies to people's perceptions of themselves. In any position of authority, then, leadership must stem from something other than position: leaders will have to think harder about how to get people to do what they want.

If the death of deference can be observed throughout society, in the business world its effects are far-reaching. In a deferential culture, the reason employees did things was because they were told to and because doing the things you were told to do would, eventually, lead you up the career ladder. A typical employee went up his organization level by level and aspired, perhaps, to title rather than achievement.

That title would, in turn, earn the right to make the decisions, to give orders. Advancement along the recognizable chain of command earned you power, and knowledge. You held more information than your subordinates, and your boss, in turn, held more than you. Company structures underpinned this; each department was a vertical silo. The assumption was that your manager had his reasons for giving you a task. 'Why' was a question both irrelevant and potentially dangerous. There was little mileage in rocking the boat. It was paternalistic; the era of the company man – and it normally was a man – who played it the company way. The contract between employees and employers was clear: you worked hard for them, and in return they would look after you. There was an absolute distinction between management and workers which inevitably led to the creation of powerful trades unions. The conflictual nature of the workplace came to a head in the UK during the Thatcherite restructuring of labour relations. Since that time, the unions have lost much of their power; their influence is now more likely to be exerted through persuasion rather than threat. In the modern workplace, almost all employees have their individual relationships with the organization.

While the paternalistic culture of the past could lead to clarity and to efficiency, it could also result in a clumsy overemphasis on the internal rather than the external. Company culture, the insistence on doing things 'our way', allowed for organizations that were efficient within themselves but not alert to change – the near demise of such giants as IBM and Marks & Spencer is testimony to this effect. Ian Smith, Senior Vice President (SVP) Oracle UK, for instance, was trying to implement some cost-saving initiatives at one of his previous employers. His potentially cost-saving question 'why', in that environment, fell foul of the old hierarchical structure:

> 'So I said, "what if we didn't all own our own cars and we didn't own all our garages and our own employees servicing them?" Well, that's an innovative idea ... and they were really excited about this until suddenly somebody said, "wait a minute, does this mean there's a possibility of someone having a better car than the boss?" and I said, "Well, of course," and they just suddenly said "right, next item please!" And that was it, and for years afterwards they didn't introduce a single reason why they didn't go for this significant cost saving. Just because culturally they couldn't accept the fact that the boss would have a worse car than his subordinates.'

More importantly than any of its potential shortcomings, however, this culture is simply not one that employees are prepared to accept any more. There are clear indications that people's perceptions of their work have altered due to tangible changes such as the tenure of work (e.g. the end of the job for life) or technology (e.g. the rise of virtual teams and teleworking). There has also been a shift in trust from the overarching corporate 'brand' to individuals. Research carried out in the mid-nineties[29] confirms this. There has been a shift to more flexible, less hierarchical ways of organizing work which means that people place less trust in the structure of the institution and more in personal relationships and networks of people.[30] Unfortunately for the employers, these networks tend not to be associated with them.

Why this shift in attitudes?

Spin

The modern employee can see the spin and is not impressed by smoke and mirrors any more. During the last 20 years, 'The media, industry, politics, the establishment and the arts conspired to bring us not their constituent parts, but a presentation of what they would like us to think they were. During the 1990s a widespread sense developed that presentation had become all'.[31]

the modern employee can see the spin

Previous generations of workers were, perhaps, less sophisticated in their appreciation of the effects of spin. The modern workforce, however, is less gullible and 'shareholders are becoming more demanding and environmental groups more hostile. The rise of online media and the increasing attention that broadcasters pay to financial news mean that companies are having to respond, ideally with carefully crafted messages, more or less in real time'.[32] When it becomes clear that even shareholders and corporate activists are no longer tolerating spun justifications of blatant greed, then from the employee's perspective, the dissonance becomes unacceptable. Employees inhabit the organization as well as being part of the outside world; therefore they are finely attuned to any mismatch between the external story, internal communications and the reality of what is going on in the organization.

Even governments are beginning to realize the potential damage their own spin can cause. Peter Hain, the UK's Minister for Europe, stated: 'We have undoubtedly suffered from a lack of trust from the average voter and all the kind of spin and stuff that there's been going on.'[33] Employees witnessing that kind of spin from their own organizations experience precisely the same loss of trust as voters. The issue is exacerbated when internal communications are 'spun' and employees are confronted with messages that they know to be untrue. Checking stories and blogging the results is now commonplace. As a consequence, those leaders who are seen to be spinning are viewed as disingenuous and undermine their own credibility and their own future communications. For chief executives, who spend 30–40% of their time on communications,[34] this is potentially disastrous.

Pensions failures

Perhaps the most important thing to remember about 'spin' is that over time it fails. If anyone doubts it they should visit Jeff Shilling, former CEO of Enron, in jail. In Britain, the scandal of the pension fund shortfalls has seriously dented public confidence in the Establishment. In fact, employees often opt for the safety of public-sector pensions over higher salaries as a career choice. Total company pension fund shortfalls in the UK were up to £160 billion in 2005 compared with the defined benefits they promised.[35] This has led to extreme nervousness among pensioners and current employees alike, and has provided yet another reason to distrust those previously thought to be trustworthy.

Perception of 'fat cat' pay

Yet another reason to distrust those who claim to lead you is the perception of their propensity to reward themselves disproportionately. As stakeholders with both financial and psychological investment in their companies, employees are just as aggrieved as shareholders are when the custodians of the company walk away with excessive amounts of its cash. Never is trust more damaged than when payouts for the bosses occur simultaneously with the arrival of P45s for the employees. The perception is that executive pay is being funded by taking away from the employees. This contradicts the implicit and even explicit contract that members of an organization sign up to when they join it – that in some sense social justice should prevail. It is clearly hypocritical when companies preach the performance-related pay sermon but reward managers who have presided over disastrous performance. For example, early 2006, the Economist reported that Cable & Wireless announced the loss of 3,000 jobs – more than half the UK workforce. But just two months later the company unveiled a £220 million payout for top managers.[36]

Even where companies have recognized the destructive effect of inequitable executive reward and taken steps to reform it by linking pay to performance, trust can be damaged when the policy is flouted. Research carried out by Bies and Tripp[37] identified changing the rules retrospectively as an act that frequently violates trust. Employees need to feel their rewards are aligned with those for senior management. Most people accept that levels of reward will vary significantly but their direction and consistency must be the same for all levels of management.

High-profile scandals

Recent scandals at Enron, Ahold, Tyco, WorldCom, Barings Bank and others have been high-profile examples of the leadership of corporations actively betraying others' trust. It is important to accept accountability in these situations. Nevertheless, despite the fact that the dishonesty probably originated with a small number of people in all of these cases, the effect was to cast doubt on the motivations of all members of the organization and to disproportionately damage the interests of the innocent bulk of employees. Just as trust involves a measured judgement of risk, the corporate scandals of the last decade betrayed trust by transferring much more risk than agreed to customers, suppliers and workers – quite literally in the case of Enron's LTCM's (Long-Term Capital Management's) entire business model. In fact, it was the *point* of the LTCM model.

Equally damaging to public confidence and employees' trust in their companies was the apparent complicity (or at best neglect) of the auditors in many of the cases mentioned above. With the failure of these guardians of accounting trustworthiness, the penumbra of suspicion enveloped other clients' affairs and contributed to a reduction in firms' abilities to credibly claim to share the goals and positive motives of their employees.

The complete demise of Andersen is evidence of the power of trust (or lack of it) in the market place. The Andersen brand was one of integrity; its corporate behaviour in the Enron scandal was so contrary to that brand that it killed the company. A collapse in trust collapsed the company. The search for trust is not, therefore, a touchy-feely nice thing to have but an integral component for corporate survival.

In the aftermath of scandal, the introduction of controls such as those of the Sarbanes-Oxley Act of 2002 reflected the erosion of public trust in corporations and piled huge costs onto those organizations. However, intense risk management is having its own detrimental effects on the business at employee level. Individuals are being dissuaded from taking calculated risks on behalf of their organization by the all-embracing compliance culture.

individuals are being dissuaded from taking calculated risks on behalf of their organization

Rousseau, Sitkin, Burt and Camerer[38] point out that this type of culture reduces the 'relational' and 'calculative' elements of trust, and increases dependence on 'institutional' trust (i.e. there is a move towards relying on the solid structure and ubiquitous presence of the organization within people's lives to evoke their trust). But as we have seen, the modern trend is towards weakening trust in institutions. The potential effect of this combination of factors is the collapse of all types of meaningful trust between employers and employees.

Overscrutiny of performance

Despite the advent of new technology, working patterns and flattened organizational structures, the old 'command and control' attitudes to management (among both management and employees) have not dispersed.[39] The combination leaves workers feeling under constant scrutiny – simultaneously accountable to everyone and no one. A clear example of this occurred in 2003 when British Airways' check-in staff went on unofficial strike. They believed that the introduction of swipe card access systems would be used to track their movements. The perception was heightened by the apparently arbitrary manner of the introduction of this new working practice which not only managed to further erode trust and goodwill between management and employees but also cost British Airways an estimated £40 million.[40]

More generally, employees are left responding to excessive performance communications from all directions rather than the true drivers of performance – customer needs and the market. The breach of trust cuts both ways between employers and employees – employees who do not trust performance evaluation to be fair feel pressured to 'game' the system in ever more imaginative ways; this in turn can precipitate even more intense monitoring as trust in the relationship is eroded.

Continual change and loss of trust

Continual faddish change runs the risk of alienating people from both the decision makers and the drivers behind the decisions. Lee and Teo found a negative correlation between employees' satisfaction and trust, and the extent of change being asked of them.[41] Asked to shoulder changes, employees can be left feeling that they are taking the brunt of the firm's risk from changing environments.

In Britain in particular we are guilty of a short-termist attitude: worryingly low levels of investment in research and development, and in capital equipment, have left certain industries and organizations looking vulnerable both from the outside and, crucially, from the inside. The modern employee is far more aware of how well the business is doing and where the money is going. Business is a spectator sport now. It is no longer the black box it used to be. Not only can workers now see inside the black box but apparently they are not happy with what they see. Workers no longer trust their employers – 66% of people believe that there has been a decline in trust and 77% believe 'trust' is an important issue.[42]

A Chartered Institute of Personnel and Development (CIPD) study (Guest and Conway, 2004) indicates that trust within UK organizations is declining, with 41% of workers having little or no trust in senior management compared with 25% having a lot of trust. The survey also indicates a significant fall in trust at the team level, with a 10% decline in trust in employees' immediate line managers over just two years.

In a 2005 survey, Mercer Consulting found that the numbers of UK employees trusting their managers to communicate honestly had fallen from 39% to 36% since 2002. Employees' trust fell even more dramatically with the length of time they were in the post – 57% of employees who had worked for their present organization for less than a year trusted their managers' communications; only 25% of employees with 15 or more years' service were as trusting. The pattern is repeated in the US where only 40% of workers trust senior management to be truthful.

High levels of global competition combined with a lack of trust have made the workplace an uncomfortable environment.

Individualization

Allied to this atmosphere of scepticism and insecurity, and mirroring the societal impulse to individualization, employees have a stronger sense of self. In simple terms, that means that employees want more and demand more. They want more input, more responsibility. Research has shown that in the UK, they want a better work–life balance, the opportunity for career advancement and the opportunity for challenging work. After competitive pay, these are the top factors that employees have directly identified as being important to them when they choose a job[43] and these factors are relatively consistent across different age groups and job levels.

Having attracted talent, organizations need to keep it. Of the factors that drive employee retention, the opportunity to learn and develop new skills is key (the second highest driver).[44] Employees want to feel a measure of control. 'People no longer do as they're told; they will do things better if they are included in decisions,' says Martin Taylor of Syngenta. People are more assertive. They are surer of their rights. The young are willing to change careers and jobs more frequently in the early stages of employment in order to find something that suits them. Aside from the 15% of the European workforce who are actively looking for new jobs, 41% are passive job seekers – not necessarily looking but open to the opportunity.[45] Working hours tend to be more flexible, the boundaries between work and life less rigid. As Gill McLaren, Director of Strategic Planning and Insights at Coca-Cola, asserts:

> 'The key thing about today's working young adults is the balance between life and work and the blurring of the two. They generally desire more flexible hours and more of an ability to mix the two up. They expect at work to be able to use the internet to sort out holidays, download music or e-mail friends but then are happy to take their laptop home in the evening or weekends to get the remaining work done. If companies insist on a more classic and rigid working style and don't offer this degree of flexibility, they are likely to struggle to attract and retain young people.'

The uncomfortable truth is that in a knowledge economy talent chooses organizations, not the other way around.

This new-age worker has arrived, or possibly was created by new organizational imperatives. There is now more than ever a need for the

this new-age worker has arrived

workforce to be more cooperative, open and trusting. Where once competition was essentially regional, globalization and the revolution in communications have now exerted huge pressure on organizations to share information, almost instantly, with a wide group of employees, shareholders and a variety of other stakeholders. This entails cutting across traditional lines of authority. The old model, characterized by a single line of command to all parts of the front line (customer interface, supply of goods, service, etc.) and a straightforward chain of information up and down the organization, might have been cumbersome, but it did mean that management had a firm handle on their own areas of responsibility. It was a system which could survive when markets were more homogenous, less intensely competitive and organizations did not need to be quite so responsive to the market as they are today – there were likely to be fewer than ten market segments compared with, say, Tesco's current count of 70,000 customer groups.

Trust, under the traditional system, was arguably a less important issue than it is now because the culture was more rigid. In today's more complex organizational environment, single lines of authority can no longer work. You can no longer design an organization with clear lines of accountability. Increasingly, you need people to take their own decisions within the framework of the organization's strategy. Market intelligence comes from a variety of media sources, and the internet and company intranets generate information that is instantly available to a wide spectrum of people.

Large organizations in particular have to cope with both local and global customers and suppliers. Decisions have to be made locally and quickly in response to more rapidly changing circumstances but also take account of a wider circle of influence. Global companies need their suppliers to be equally global. Those suppliers, in turn, will need to be able to respond not only to the wishes of head office but also to their regional customers and their market. Typically in a global company any one person will have three separate lines of influence bearing down on them: function, region and global business unit. To be adequately responsive and therefore competitive, it is necessary to work across these lines of influence quickly and coherently. For this to work without leading to chaos, everyone who forms a part of this web must have a well-developed understanding of the principles and strategy involved. In short, they must be engaged and aligned.

An interesting analogy for the development of company structures over the last 40 years is that of the development of IT systems. During the seventies, all computing architecture was necessarily centralized around huge mainframe computers which held data in hierarchical silos of information, much as a traditional company structure had sharply delineated departments converging only at the head office. As technological know-how and customer service needs grew, local area networks were developed. These held lots of data on a range of subjects in local pockets, reflecting the prevailing ethos of empowerment and the blurring of boundaries. As the need for instant information and global businesses grew and communication speeded up, IT systems responded with 'open networks'. In behavioural terms the changes have led to the need for a greater level of trust to underpin a sense of interdependency, and an approach that has replaced the top-down style of management with one where the customer is the driving force. And, of course, because society has changed, the customer has changed too. Ian Smith of Oracle UK points out:

> 'Fifteen years ago the British consumer was typically British. They would queue up, both physically and metaphorically. They would put up with less than perfect service ... 15 years on that has changed; whether it's because of the privatization that has gone on, whether it's because of every newspaper be it tabloid or broadsheet having a consumer champion, because of *Watchdog* and Ann Robinson, it's totally different.'

In Britain, the change in the economy vis-à-vis the service and manufacturing industries has also had an effect. It may be an oversimplification to say that the country is now a service-based economy rather than a manufacturing one. Rather, what has happened is that the lower levels of both service and manufacturing are increasingly outsourceable and outsourced. It is the higher-end levels of employment in both sectors that, more and more, employees in this country will be concerned with – the levels at which it is more and more important to attract, retain and develop a high-quality workforce.

Even the term 'matrix management', first coined to reflect the above-mentioned tripartite management structures of region, function and business unit, is now in itself an outdated concept. It reflects the last attempt of those with a hierarchical mindset to design organizations which could reflect the growing complexity of the market place. It doesn't work. Recognition of the individualism of the talent worker requires recognition of the complexity of managing those workers. The aim must be to simultaneously engage and align those workers to deliver success for themselves, their colleagues and the organization. To do that, they must understand the strategic and tactical objectives of the organization.

In other words, in a business environment that is becoming ever more complex, changes are taking place in the way organizations relate to their employees. What was once arguably a simple equation is now a multi-faceted conversation.

Harnessing the 'why?'

Do all of these changes constitute a problem? Possibly, but they also constitute a massive opportunity. The new realities of the employee/employer relationship mean that the way to attract, retain and develop people is to forge an emotional bond between them and the company. In this emotional bond lies the capacity not simply to replace the old levers of authority but to improve on them. Making people really care about the organizations they work for may take a certain amount of work on the part of the employer. But if successful, this effort will be more than repaid. And the currency it will be paid in is engagement. The value of this is perhaps best summed up in the words of Keki Dadiseth, Director, Home and Personal Care, Unilever, who drove the hugely successful growth of Unilever in India. To him, the engaged worker performing a task:

'... would get a wonderful sparkle in the eye and get really excited about it. All of a sudden you can do three times more than you think you are capable of doing.'

No longer able to base their authority on the stripe on their arm or the title on their office door, employers must instead generate and maintain a system of mutual respect. The question 'why?' lies at the core of this. If you can harness it, not only can you build a structure responsive and adapted to the modern business environment, but you will have access to a largely untapped resource: the discretionary effort of your workforce. The aim is to create an environment where the question 'why?' does not need to be asked; the reasons for instructions or requests are inherently understood because of the transparency of the corporate and personal communications. The process is twofold: establishing communication so that the whole organization understands the basic reasoning behind company strategy, and, critically, delivering and sharing performance results so that employees can invest their faith in their leadership. Richard Baker of Alliance Boots offered the following:

> 'There is a little expression I learned at Walmart, when they owned Asda for the two and a half years I was there. Sam Walton's expression was "the more you share, the more they care". This is all about imparting information and taking chances with your employees by telling them how it is good, bad or indifferent. But tell them straight and tell them much more about the business than most businesses think employees need to know.'

there is (or should be) a virtuous circle at work

There is (or should be) a virtuous circle at work: employee trust is earned by making clear what lies behind company strategy and is rewarded with success in which they can share; they respond by providing the support and energy to move forward.

When David Currie took over as Chairman of Ofcom, he made internal transparency a vital tenet of the organization. As a regulator, Ofcom is highly visible to the outside world. He ensured that this was mirrored by constant internal explanation so that people were clear where decisions were made and why. Sir David Omand, UK Security and Intelligence Coordinator, similarly sees the value of this kind of internal business narrative in implementing strategy:

'It has to be a compelling story and if people don't understand why, and particularly why them, then it is unlikely that they are going to be able to interpret the strategic direction in the right sort of way.'

This **strategic** 'why' can then be reinforced with a more deep-seated answer to why should they invest their discretionary energy in the cause of your organization? Why should they become **engaged**?

Sir Digby Jones, former Director General of the CBI, is very clear and passionate about the significance of engaging the workforce. He puts it like this:

'At the end of the day if you harness the why, turn it to advantage, you rule the world because the rest will fall into place.'

The ideal situation is an organization where the question 'why?' is never necessary because everyone knows where the organization is going, why it has chosen that route and how it intends to get there. In such an organization, *all* employees (senior and junior) are both engaged and aligned. To see how that can be achieved – read on.

Notes

[27] Senge, P. (2006) *The Fifth Discipline: The art and practice of the learning organization*, Random House Business Books; Nonaka, I. and Takeuchi, H. (1995) *The Knowledge-creating Company: How Japanese companies create the dynamics of innovation*, Oxford University Press.

[28] *The Times Higher Education Supplement*, 24 March 2006.

[29] Miles, R. E. and Creed, W. E. D. (1995) 'Organizational forms and managerial philosophies: A descriptive and analytical review', in Staw, B. M. and Cummings, L. L. (eds.) *Research in Organizational Behavior*, Vol. 17, Greenwich CT: JAI Press, pp. 333–372.

[30] Saxenian, A. (1996) 'Beyond boundaries: Open labor markets and learning in Silicon Valley', in Arthur, M. B. and Rousseau, D. M. (eds.) *The Boundaryless Career: A new organizational principle for a new organizational era*, New York: Oxford University Press, pp. 23–39.

[31] Pitcher, G. (2002) *The Death of Spin? Communication in the 21st century*, London: Demos.

32 *The Economist*, 12 July 2001, 'The spin doctors get serious'. http://www.economist.com/displaystory.cfm?story_id=693570 – accessed 1 June 2006.

33 BBC News, broadcast 23/06/02, Transcript of 'Breakfast with Frost', http://news.bbc.co.uk/1/low/uk_politics/2062555.stm – accessed 31 May 2006.

34 *The Economist*, 12 July 2001, 'The spin doctors get serious', http://www.economist.com/displaystory.cfm?story_id=693570 – accessed 1 June 2006.

35 Capital Economics, cited in *The Guardian*, 25 February 2006, 'Sainsbury's puts £350m into its pension fund', http://www.guardian.co.uk/supermarkets/story/0,,1717646,00.html – accessed 31 May 2006.

36 *The Economist*, 20 May 2006, 'Lowering the bar', pp. 31–32.

37 Bies, R. J. and Tripp, T. M. (1996) 'Beyond distrust: "getting even" and the need for revenge', in Kramer, R. and Tyler, T. (eds.) *Trust in Organizations: Frontiers of theory and research*, Thousand Oaks, CA: Sage, pp. 246–260.

38 Rousseau, D. M., Sitkin, S. B., Burt, R. S. and Camerer, C. (1998) 'Not so different after all: a cross-discipline view of trust.' *Academy of Management Review*, Vol. 23, No. 3, pp. 393–404.

39 Sørensen, C. (2004) *The Future Role of Trust in Work – The key success factor for mobile productivity*, Reading: Microsoft Corporation.

40 Arrowsmith, J. (2003) 'Strike grounds British Airways at Heathrow', http://www.eiro.eurofound.eu.int/2003/08/feature/uk0308103f.html – accessed 31 May 2006; BBC News, 22/07/03, 'Heathrow chaos continues', http://news.bbc.co.uk/2/hi/business/3085813.stm – accessed 31 May 2006; *Edinburgh Evening News*, 31/07/03, 'BA faces £40m bill for swipe-card row', http://news.scotsman.com/topics.cfm?tid=438&id=825432003 – accessed 31 May 2006.

41 Lee, G. and Teo, A. (2005) 'Organizational restructuring: impact on trust and work satisfaction.' *Asia Pacific Journal of Management*, Vol. 22, Issue 1, pp. 23–39.

42 Johnson, Mike (2004) *New Rules of Engagement*, Chartered Institute of Personnel & Development.

43 Towers Perrin Global Workforce Study, 2005 – UK data compendium.

44 Ibid.

45 Towers Perrin Global Workforce Study, 2005 – Ten steps to creating an engaged workforce, key European findings.

FOUNDATIONS FOR ENGAGEMENT

Engagement, if it is to be more than a management fad, has to be built on strong foundations. There are three of these: a robust business plan that employees can engage with, a committed leader whom employees can believe in, and a strong, top team that can lead the agenda. This is not a book about strategy, therefore we are assuming that your business model is sensible, strong and ready to withstand the market place. What we concentrate on in Part Two is senior leadership: how it should behave and what it should believe in in order to achieve engagement

4 The leader; walking the walk

> 'Leadership is not about making clever decisions and doing bigger deals, least of all for personal gain. It is about energizing other people to make good decisions and do better things. In other words, it is about helping release the positive energy that exists naturally within people. Effective leadership inspires more than empowers; it connects more than controls; it demonstrates more than decides. It does all this by engaging – itself above all, and consequently others.'
>
> Henry Mintzberg[46]

Every leader believes themselves to be one who works hard to inspire and engage the workforce. Motivation, loyalty, commitment – everybody feels these are important qualities in an organization and therefore ones to which they are convinced they pay attention. If you are one of those leaders who believe they engage their staff, the statistics say you are probably wrong. Remember the research – the UK workforce (and the worldwide workforce) is *not* highly engaged. And since the quality of leadership – at every level – plays such a large role in engagement, the chances are that your workforce is *not* highly engaged and it is *your* fault.

For openers, you need genuinely to care more about your staff. Not just say it, show it. The statistics tell us that a belief that the senior management has a sincere interest in the wellbeing of the workforce is the foremost factor in engagement.[47] If that is true then it is a test that UK senior management is failing miserably: 45% of respondents simply do not believe that their leaders are interested in their wellbeing. A further 25% felt they did not know for sure either way. So, while leaders may believe they are doing a good job at one of the basic facets of driving engagement, 70% of their workforce disagree.

Genuine interest in the wellbeing of employees is just one of the characteristics which employees wishing to be engaged might reasonably expect their management to demonstrate.

According to the research undertaken by the Chartered Management Institute and the DTI, employees are looking to their leaders to lead the development of a vision and to create trust and respect in the organization, yet fewer than four out of ten see this in their leaders.

Another study[48] showed that around only one third of employees believe their senior management acts in a way consistent with their values, i.e. approximately two thirds of employees are either neutral or disagree that this is the case. This same study shows that 72% of employees are either neutral or disagree with the statement that senior management communicates openly and honestly with employees. Employees are hardly more convinced that senior management has communicated a clear vision for long-term success. So although you may want to believe you are an effective leader, research shows us that if this is the case you are in a minority.

So how do you ensure you are in the 'effective' group?

David Bell, Permanent Secretary at the Department for Children, Schools and Families (DCSF) and previously Her Majesty's Chief Inspector of Schools (HMCI), thinks there are two sides to the leadership role:

> 'Leadership, I think we can safely conclude, is a complex mixture of doing and being. It is about good management and about getting things done, getting your 'doing' right, but it is also, I believe, about a way of 'being'. The two are not exclusive.'

A good leader is good at providing success – the 'doing' of leadership. But in order to keep delivering that success, a leader will have to rely on his people, and for this reason he had better behave as a good leader too or risk losing the foundations on which success is built. It is to the behavioural ('being') side of the coin that we turn first.

The 'being' side of leadership

Who is the authentic you?

As usual, Shakespeare has said it already: 'To thine own self be true.' It may sound simplistic, but you must be yourself. Why? Because employees are, by and large, smart. They can smell management that merely pays lip-service to the latest management fad. Obvious as it may sound, employees will not believe in your vision, your strategy, your engagement

'people aren't daft – they can sense sincerity or insincerity'

agenda, if they don't think that you believe in it yourself. When Philip Williamson, CEO of Nationwide to 2007, says, 'People aren't daft – they can sense sincerity or insincerity', we know intuitively that he is right.

Interestingly, the list of engagement drivers pertaining to leadership contains some telling nouns – sincerity, consistency, clarity. Gill McLaren at Coca-Cola reinforced that these characteristics are the most important and enduring. Rather than being confronted by such management fads, 98% of employees surveyed listed 'an open and honest' face as something they would like their leadership to demonstrate. As we showed above, they don't believe this is what they are getting. (Only 28% of UK respondents believed that their senior management communicated with them openly and honestly.) Henry Mintzberg, the management guru, agrees and argues that to engage people you need to be able to connect with them on various levels, you need to understand and relate to them and to their experiences, and you need to be seen as someone who is authentic and not just another 'management-speak suit' who can rattle off the latest theory without knowing what is really happening in practice. This is where trust is so important – do workers trust that their managers connect with their experience, or do they believe that they are so far removed and caught up in their own ideas that they cannot genuinely connect with what is happening in the employees' world?

Richard Baker sees it like this: 'It is leadership by example – you can't get others to do it if you're not doing it yourself, so it has to be authentic.'

However, even before the leader connects with the workforce there is a prior task. It is to identify what you want your employees to engage with (your strategy) and the way in which you want them to go about it (your values and behaviours). Both strategy and values need to be deeply held, thought through and carefully identified. A smart idea without a genuine belief in that idea will not deliver. Consider the story of Jeff Tetlow, for example, in the box below.

In 1994, Jeff Tetlow was the Conoco Project Director on the development of a huge gas field called Britannia in the Central North Sea. The scale was enormous. The gas field was 3.5 trillion cubic feet and would be responsible for an output equating to 8% of the average UK daily consumption. The investment was of the order of £1¼ billion. Concerned that, at that time, the industry norm was becoming increasingly inefficient and expensive, Jeff had been looking for ways to execute projects better, and knew that they would have to take a new and different approach. What he and his colleagues came up with was an alliance system: a new idea in that industry. The standard practice would have meant putting out the different parts of the job for competitive tendering and dealing separately with each appointed contractor to get their part of the job done. Instead of this, Conoco came up with a system of profit sharing. Once a reasonable cost for the project had been agreed, Conoco would pay all the direct costs to the contractors (i.e. there was no risk for those companies), but would also share with them 50/50 any savings that were made by coming in under that target, thus encouraging them to work with Conoco, and with the other contractors, towards a common goal of keeping costs down and schedules on time.

The process started at the point of appointing the contractors. They were chosen not merely on the merits of their budgeting and schedule forecasts but on what ideas they could bring to the concept of working together. The first thing they were asked was not whether they could work together but how exactly they would do so. The result of this alliance structure for the Britannia gas field project was strikingly successful. With minimal in-fighting and close communications between all parties, the project came in 20% under budget and two months early.

▶

Jeff Tetlow had the smart idea which worked and one would think would have become the industry norm. Wrong! Nearly ten years on such alliances are still a rarity. Why is this? Jeff Tetlow believes it is that those who have tried to emulate the Britannia success *didn't really believe in the idea of alliance*. Where Jeff and his team had been passionate about the idea, choosing contractors for their ability to buy into the big idea and to add their own ideas, those who tried to copy it took on only certain aspects of the idea. They implemented the contractual side of the arrangement, but without a genuine belief. They consequently failed to convince all the partners and failed to ensure that everyone involved stayed on track.

This is a story about the authenticity that is demanded by employees. Jeff had the courage of his convictions. He had worked out in advance a strong, decisive, even radical plan of action. He made obvious, observable changes to the working methods. The approach worked because those who implemented it were prepared to take a risk and also worked hard in the planning stages. Once the project was under way, constant communication ensured that it didn't slide out of control. Throughout, Jeff sent signals that this was a concept that he believed in and was prepared to fight hard to make work. As much as the clever and radical system, it was this visible determination and obvious commitment that delivered success for his formula. His aim at the start of the project was not specifically to promote engagement, but its success finally rested on the engagement of all involved, from the top downwards.

Sir David Omand believes that any process of change – including the drive towards engagement – within an organization starts with the kind of honest dialogue that can come only from an honesty that can cascade down throughout the company:

'It is about authenticity, authenticity of explaining why change is needed, producing the convincing story but not trying to bullshit and just parrot some line that has been provided centrally . . . you can replicate that one level down, two levels down, three levels down so that even in a small workgroup people will look to their boss and [ask] are they just doing this because they have been told to do it? Do they actually believe in this story? And it's when they all start to believe it or the critical mass starts to believe it that the thing starts to move and then it starts really quite quickly.'

What then do we mean by 'authenticity' in this context? We mean that words must be consistent with deeds. Authentic leaders live their values every moment of the day. For Jack Welch 'leaders can't have an iota of fakeness'.

Rob Goffee and Gareth Jones, in their book *Why Should Anyone Be Led By You?*,[49] argue that authenticity is a critical element of leadership:

'Our growing dissatisfaction with sleek ersatz, airbrushed leadership is what makes authenticity such a desirable quality in today's corporations – a quality that unfortunately is in short supply. Leaders and followers both associate authenticity with sincerity, honesty and integrity. It's the real thing – the attribute that uniquely defines great leaders.'[50]

However, it is not sufficient to be authentic – you must be seen as authentic. The workforce needs to be able to relate to you. This requires you to present different faces to different people. Establishing your authenticity is neither a question of laying yourself entirely bare to those around you nor of giving yourself free rein. Goffee and Jones refer to it as 'managing your authenticity', a concept that may sound paradoxical but which is a neat way of describing the process whereby you choose which facet of your essential self is most appropriate and most useful in any given situation. This works only if behind these facets lies a strong, and unchanging, set of core characteristics and beliefs.

Once words have been uttered by leaders, they are committed to them. The result is that they either act consistently with the words or they are hoist by them. They cannot escape them.

A leader cannot, therefore, adopt a persona depending on the needs of the situation. Jack Welch, who identifies the importance of authenticity when discussing why certain executives who on paper seem ready for promotion never seem to get it, points out the dangers of such an approach. 'What was wrong? Finally we figured out that these executives always had a certain phoniness to them. They pretended to be something they were not – more in control, more upbeat, more savvy than they really were. They didn't sweat. They didn't cry. They squirmed in their own skin, playing a role of their own inventing.'

Authentic leaders manage their behaviours holistically, with particular emphasis on using their personal differences (e.g. quirks) to reflect their leadership objectives:

'Those aspiring to leadership need to discover what it is about themselves that they can mobilize in a leadership context.'[51]

There is, therefore, no single 'leadership' style that you must emulate. Instead, you must develop your own character traits so that your followers can believe that they are entering into an open and honest 'contract' with you. This may involve exposing flaws or weaknesses, but this cannot be helped and may actually endear leaders to their followers rather than compromise their legitimacy.

Above all, authenticity means that leaders deliver honestly upon their promises – fulfilling their side of the contract without compromising their personality. Sir Digby Jones, the Director General of the CBI until 2006, echoed this thought:

'People have got to see the leader deliver. They've not just got to listen to the leader saying how to do it, they have got to see him deliver, it's got to be transparent and open ... I don't think they need to see an infallible leader. I actually think they quite like to see a leader who's a human being, enjoys a drink, says "sorry, got it wrong, help me."'

This is not to deny, therefore, that we all have different moods and different roles. You can present yourself in different ways at different times and still be authentic. In fact, it is important that you do use different styles in different situations.

From a host of interviewees with views on the issue of leadership style, here are some notable comments:

'An ability to read people is a crucial attribute for any manager. You need to adapt your style according to the person you are dealing with. If you have only one style you limit yourself to getting the best only out of the one person who responds to it.'

Bill Sweetenham, England Swimming Coach

'In recent years there has been a substantive change in terms of what is required of leaders and the old days of command and control are gone. Today leaders at all levels need to inspire people to be fully involved in generating new and better ways of working. To stay ahead of the competition, a collective approach that unleashes innovation and creativity is essential.'

Nigel Crouch, of the Inspirational Leadership Programme[52]

'Leaders must wear different coats – the different coats you wear are simply a function of presentation, a way to get your message across. None of them should contradict or act against the basic message.'

Colin Green, President, Defence, Aerospace, Rolls-Royce

'You are you and in the end however good an actor you are you will revert to being you. One of the key requirements of a leader is a level of consistency. People expect you to get tired, people expect you to get cross. People expect human emotions but they do not want inconsistency.'

Admiral Sir Mark Stanhope, Deputy Supreme Allied Commander Transformation, NATO

So, for the purposes of engagement, the facets of your authentic self that you should aim to display are those that demonstrate your commitment to your organization and to your employees: care for their wellbeing, awareness of the challenges they face, an honest communication with the organization. To go back to David Bell of the DCSF, his definition of the ideal leadership behaviour is as follows:

'The being of leadership ... has a number of overlapping features – inner calm, resilience, judgement, realism about self, moral courage and compassion.'

Being seen to be authentic

Sir Digby Jones, when he took over the CBI, came into an organization which had had a succession of Directors General who were highly intelligent but possibly over-academic. It had become a rather elitist, establishment place. He had a vision for where he wanted to take it: he wanted its focus to go back to the membership. The purpose of the organization, he felt, was not to please the government but to be connected to its members, from the smallest business in Birmingham to the largest corporations in the country. He wanted to take a campaigning stance but at the same time he knew there was a balance to be maintained. He also needed to retain access to the government, to know that they wouldn't slam the door in his face. His first step was to let it be known that from now on the membership was to be the top priority. It was not an easy message to get across in a culture that had become quite comfortable under the old regime. So he had to proceed by demonstration:

> 'The delivery mechanism was the DG being seen to do it himself, the DG visiting the extra member, returning the extra phone call and constantly talking about the members. Everything was about the members, then choosing my fight with governments. I realized I was at times pissing off the government and it was uncomfortable when they had a go at me. Me standing there and taking it and being seen to take it and not changing, not rolling over, and suddenly the members thought, "He's not just telling me about this, he personally has taken the criticism, he personally is visiting the members all the time. What are we doing to support this guy?"'

People hear what they see – it is no good repeating your agenda if you don't demonstrate it in your own behaviour. The first place to implement the changes is around yourself. If you believe that the company should hold down costs this year, then you need to watch how *you* spend money. If you believe in harnessing diversity, you had better think deeply about the level of diversity in the team you have directly around you. If you want to have an

the first place to implement the changes is around yourself

egalitarian culture in your company, make sure that you haven't got separate facilities for management and employees.

Sir Digby Jones explains the same point in a simple fashion:

'You lead from the front and you ensure total honesty of action and they know that you are going to share with them the experience of change and they know that they're never going to be asked to do one single thing that you won't do yourself . . . rule one is that we are in this together.'

You should ensure your personal behaviours are modelling those you want to become the norm in your organization. As Gandhi said: 'You need to be the change you want to see in the world.' You should spend considerable time telling everyone exactly how you want them to behave and what you don't want to see in your organization by way of people's behaviours. Research[53] indicates that the best way to bring this communication alive is by telling stories which illustrate desired behaviours and which bring alive those behaviours you want to see permeating the organization. On their own, however, these stories will amount to little if they are not constantly reinforced by your actions and by rewarding the 'right' kind of behaviour with promotions, bonuses and public recognition, and by taking appropriate action, however tough, to punish the 'wrong' kind of behaviours.

You also need to be aware that, at an even more personal level, you are constantly sending out messages by your demeanour, by your conversations and by your habits. You are on show at every moment that you are in your organization. As Eric Peacock, Chairman of Baydon Hill PLC, explains:

'The leadership thing is what you do when nobody is watching and . . . I'm very conscious that when they are watching the impression which I give when I walk into any of the businesses can set a tone for the day. You know – am I coming in grumpy, am I coming in with a smile on my face, am I coming in radiating energy and enthusiasm? . . . I'm very, very conscious of the signals which I may give out.'

Who you choose to talk to, how you walk into the building each day, how you react to news, good or bad – everything sends a signal because you are the boss. It is for this reason that you need to be fully committed to the engagement agenda, or, as Mintzberg puts it in the quotation that opens this chapter: '[Leadership] does all this by engaging – itself above all, and consequently others.' Although engagement is driven from the top, it is not something that can be imposed from above. It requires you to lead by example, to believe wholeheartedly in the value of your organization, your strategy, your latest drive. And it therefore requires you to use yourself as the primary tool by which to engage others.

Concentrate on your strengths

Daley Thompson, determined to win his second gold medal in the decathlon at the 1984 Los Angeles Olympic Games, and chased hard by Jurgen Hingsen, knew that there was only one event, the 1500 metres, in which he was vulnerable. So he went to see a world-renowned coach and asked him to help him with improving this weak event. The coach thought about this offer and told Daley that he was not prepared to help him improve his performance in the 1500 metres. What he would do instead would be to help Thompson become so strong in the other nine sports that the result of the 1500 metres would become irrelevant. The strategy paid off. In Los Angeles Thompson entered the final event of the decathlon, the 1500 metres, knowing that as long as he finished he had already won gold. What he and his coach had understood was that you will do better by building on your strengths than by addressing your weaknesses.

Drucker has said we should waste as little effort as possible on improving areas of low competence. 'It takes far more energy and work to improve from incompetence to mediocrity than it takes to improve from first-rate performance to excellence – and yet most people in most organizations concentrate on making incompetent performers into mediocre ones. Energy, resources and time should go instead to making a competent person into a star performer.'[54]

While, naturally, you should learn any readily learnable skills, there is no point in trying to force on to your personality traits which sit uneasily with you. Instead, you should be looking to polish and hone the areas in which you feel your strengths lie. Someone who feels themselves to be an innovator should be looking for structured ways (lectures, conversations with inspiring people, etc.) to bring out that creativity. Someone who feels their talents lie with bringing out the best in others should examine this more closely. Are there, for example, opportunities to harness people's skills more effectively in different parts of the organization? Is there a formalized structure whereby they can distil and share their knowledge with others?

Before looking out into the wider organization to identify flaws and assets, you should apply this process to yourself: 'Question yourself before you question your team,' as Jurgen Grobler, England's most successful rowing coach, says. The pre-requisite is honesty: to understand your failings is in itself a strength.

For every characteristic in yourself that enhances your leadership, there will be ways of improving. It is up to you to identify them and **the first step is to find your 'authentic self'** seek out best practice and ways of developing them. You need to recognize that these will be personal and will vary from case to case. The first step is to find your 'authentic self'.

So, what should you do on Monday?

How do you turn this theory into practice? These are some ideas that can help you get started – practical steps that you can do on Monday morning.

1. **Demonstrate a genuine interest**

   Cut out Figure 2.3 and look at it every morning and evening to see whether you can 'tick every box'. If you can't, change things or leave.

Do what Sir Terry Leahy did at Tesco. He asked each member of his team to be sure that they really understood the personal preoccupations and aspirations of their colleagues on the next two levels down.

2. Communicate a winning persona

Get some quick wins, no matter how insignificant they seem. (But make sure they are consistent with your vision.) Bill Parcells,[55] the great turnaround coach of American football, explains that simply insisting that the players turn up looking smart can be the first step. They arrive and look at each other and think, 'we can do what the coach wants'. Each mini victory builds a new attitude – a 'can-do' rather than a 'cannot' approach.

3. Make sure you know who you are (i.e. how you come across)

Self-diagnosis. The first steps are relatively simple and, crucially, are taken alone. They require nothing but thought and honest self-searching. Book some time out and find a safe space. Begin with some questions to yourself (the answers should be written):

❖ What do you want your legacy to be? How would you like your obituary to describe you? The purpose of this is to discover what you are driven by: do you want to be the Dyson of your market, or simply to make a lot of money? Do you want to be an entrepreneur, a showman, a safe pair of hands? And in getting to that goal, how do you want to be perceived: do you want to be liked, or just respected? Do you want to be thought of as charismatic, as reliable, as thoughtful? Do you want to be an excellent manager or an inspiring leader, or do you think you can be both? Do you like to think in the long or the short term? If you find this process too woolly, formalize it: write a list of characteristics that you think are important and then trade them off for which is most important to you.

❖   Test the conclusions you have come to against the imagined responses of someone who was influential in your early life (probably a parent). Do you think they would respect the values you have outlined? Similarly, imagine the reaction of your closest friends.

Psychometric testing. Take a psychometric test. The Myers Briggs – MBTI – is a commonly known system of psychometric testing that has stood the test of time and is as good as any. Betsy Kendall, one of the foremost practitioners in this country, describes how it focuses on the way in which people take in information and prioritize that information to make decisions. It can be applied to understand oneself, to understand others and to understand how a leader of one type might be perceived by people with other types and preferences.

The guiding principles of Myers Briggs assume that type is inborn and individuals will be most effective when they recognize their type and work with it, rather than attempting to fix what is 'wrong' with them. The point of applying MBTI to oneself is not to discover whether you have the characteristics of a 'leader' but to uncover what your innate characteristics are so that you can hone them in the leadership context.

4. **Make sure you know who people think you are**

   External feedback. Having established to your own satisfaction what you think your authentic characteristics are, this is the point at which you test your conclusions against the perceptions of others.

   ❖   Draw up a list of those people who know you best: a mixture of family, friends, ex-colleagues, close business associates. Ask them to provide three things:

   • A short list of what they consider you to be good at/bad at, with examples.

   • A quality that they consider you value, with examples of how this is manifested.

   • An anecdote that best sums up how they see you.

❖ For a more formal approach, harness preferably an external group to conduct 360° feedback from those around you, ensuring that participants know that confidentiality is strictly maintained.

5. Be authentic and be seen as such

Using both oral and written communication channels, make sure that everyone in the organization knows what you believe in, in terms of both strategy and values. Be prepared to share some personal information. Then, even more importantly, make sure your behaviour is always consistent with your beliefs. Reiterate your beliefs regularly because the workforce changes and forgets. Present yourself and your values with confidence: alarm signals should be ringing if in presentations you are using lots of notes and presentation materials, if you are feeling uncomfortable and doubting inside, if your audience is looking bored.

6. Build on your strengths

❖ Divide up your life into reasonable stages, four or five blocks of time delineating reasonably homogenous roles: one for your further education, one for the first year or two of your working life, and then every three or four years of your working life since then, for instance.

❖ For each period list what you achieved, how you achieved it, what got in the way, what made it difficult and what really enabled your successes.

What do you want to replicate and what do you want to leave behind?

Identify the time you felt at the top of your game – when your capability best matched your role and you were neither in burn out or rust out. You are almost certainly looking for a period in your career when you were least conscious about yourself, your 'difficult relationships', the blocking issues.

❖ Using this list, identify your strengths. Having identified them, define beside each one what excellence consists of. List three actions that will help you exploit and improve them.

❖ Similarly (and similarly honestly), identify your weaknesses. Are they merely learnable skills that you have neglected, or are they characteristics which you know lie against the grain of your personality?

❖ Repeat the process every three months.

The 'doing' of leadership

'Being' an authentic, perfectly presented leader will count for little, of course, if the 'doing' of your leadership is lacking: you must ensure that your leadership is enabling the smooth running of the company, and providing success. One of the common failings of leaders is to operate at too low a level; to miss the big issues, be they internal or external, that will critically shape the fortunes of the organization. So what do you 'do', how do you operate in such a way that you don't miss these 'big' issues? How do you operate in such a way that levels of activity below you can be carried out efficiently and effectively?

Five levels of activity

A useful way to look at organizational levels is through the work originally developed by Elliot Jaques in the fifties and significantly built on by Gillian Stamp in more recent times. Jaques observed that in successful organizations of any type there are distinct but well-connected levels of activity. We have simplified these levels down to five.

With apologies to Jaques and Stamp, we have defined the levels in the simplest terms, for simplicity starting with Level 1 before outlining Level 5, the work of the leader.

❖ *Level 1* is the work undertaken at the front line of the organization, often interacting directly with customers.

❖ *Level 2* ensures the cost-efficient delivery of goods and services, and makes sure that any alterations in working processes, conditions or culture are put in place without damaging the ongoing drive of work. They will largely be managing those at Level 1. It is still a fairly linear equation at this point.

❖ *Level 3* is responsible for quality: ensuring that resources are allocated to the right place and that conflicts are dealt with. They have responsibility for internal best practice, acting as a control on Levels 1 and 2 and checking any tendency to extravagance. They are primarily concerned with internal matters: efficiency, streamlining, ensuring that all the parts of the engine are running smoothly.

❖ At *Level 4*, people start looking outside the company, ensuring that any external developments in processes or technology are matched by the company. They translate trends in the market place or advances in technology and make the information available to those at Level 3. Level 4 ensures that the organization is up to date and constantly improving. Leadership at this level should be providing a sense of direction and a consistent message.

❖ At the top is *Level 5*. Here strategic decisions are made, connecting the organization to the external environment to ensure that it remains relevant. Level 5 leadership should provide the values and mission for the organization. As Gillian Stamp says: 'Unlike the other levels of work, Level 5 has to engage with an open context, where anything might happen but decisions have to be made about what will and will not be assumed. Taking into account what is known, suspected or unknowable about the next ten years, decisions have to be made about what contingencies will be expected, prepared for or guarded against and the organization is structured, resourced and managed accordingly.' Level 5 is responsible for the sustainability of strategic intent. It is therefore necessary to discern potential for opportunity, instability or threat in the global complex.

For the organization to be coherent and cohesive, each of these levels needs to be present and healthy and above all properly interconnected. Level 1 needs to be efficient, responsive to customer needs and with the capacity to perform in-process problem solving if necessary. A prerequisite of this is the framework of planning, scheduling and information dissemination that Level 2 provides. Without effective Level 2 leadership, those at Level 1 will feel their contribution is not valued and their needs not attended to. Waste will not be controlled, costs and absenteeism will rise – they will not be engaged.

Similarly, unless leadership at Level 3 provides for systems, processes, standards and resources necessary to create and share current

costs are likely to increase while quality declines

best practice, people working at Level 2 cannot provide the framework needed by people at Level 1. If leadership at Level 3 is not clear, there will be resistance, loss of confidence and a mushrooming of grievances. Costs are likely to increase while quality declines.

Good, clear leadership at Level 4 should be setting a sense of direction so that changes are made in a way that aligns all those at a lower level. (Deciding what you are doing and providing the discipline to do it.) If this is to work, the channels of communication between Levels 3 and 4 must work in both directions. If the bright ideas of the Level 4 management are not grounded in the reality of the day-to-day experience of Level 3, confusion and disengagement will ensue. If management at an airline decides summarily that best practice is for air stewards to serve the sweets, meal and coffee separately, ignoring the fact that this is impracticable on a 45-minute flight, this is because of a disconnection between the levels. The upshot is disillusionment at the lower levels: they have in effect been presented with evidence to show that their leadership neither understands nor appreciates their jobs. Government can be particularly prone to problems like these: focusing too much on what the politicians say they want and not paying enough attention to what is practically possible.

As Gillian Stamp says:

'Clear leadership at level 5 will sustain reputation so it's the touchstone for all change. Everyone in the organization will be clear about his or her role in protecting it and will be proud and confident to represent the organization through the initial change and beyond. Where leadership at this level is not clear, costs of change are likely to run out of control, reputations will be at risk, changes resisted and likely to be inconsistent and eventually to stall.'

Examples of failure of management to provide Level 5 leadership litter business history. British Leyland through the latter half of the 20th century failed to position itself within what was by then a global and highly competitive automobile market. It didn't concentrate on making the right connections overseas and with other manufacturers to give it the critical mass that it was clearly going to need in the new world. In the public sector the Ministry of Agriculture, Fisheries and Food (MAFF) allowed itself to believe that its primary role was to work ever more effectively with farmers at a time when in the real world the agenda was moving away from farmers and into rural land management. Both suffered as a consequence.

Marks & Spencer in the late nineties/early 2000s concentrated on Level 4 work, doing what it did ever more effectively. But it failed to spot the macro changes in the consumer and competitor landscape.

Simply put, by ignoring or failing to see the changes around them, these organizations were creating an environment where Levels 1–4 were unable to add value to the organization.

It is important to realize that at Level 5 the numbers start to run out. You have to make judgements because a lot of your decisions are about the future. Beware of getting caught in what Jocelyn Burgoyne, the very impressive former head of the Canadian Civil Service and now with the Organization for Economic Cooperation and Development (OECD), describes as the Tyranny of Perfect Knowledge. You have to make judgements at Level 5.

David Bell of the DCSF puts it:

'Because to solely to rely on your gut, well your gut might just be equally wrong as it might be right. There is something here about experience again. There's something about the reservoir in topping that up ... [take] teachers at the end of their first years. One of the great things of going into a second year of teaching is you've got something to draw on. You've got what happened last year and every year you go on you've got what happened two years, three years and four years ago ... I can look back now and say, well, I've got 20 years of this stuff and I can still make an absolutely dreadful call tomorrow but I think there is something about saying generally speaking my instincts, if that is what they are, are usually not bad.'

Gary Klein, in fascinating research on practical decision making,[56] describes this phenomenon as 'recognition primed decisions' (RPD), the recognition that you have been here before, you have seen this situation and can, therefore, make rational, practically based decisions. It also helps you to *not* make a decision when you do not recognize a scenario, but instead to recognize that this is a new situation which requires new solutions. Klein's approach is a neat bridge between the analytical, information-heavy, traditional approach to decision making and Malcolm Gladwell's gut reaction approach as articulated in *Blink*.[57] Running parallel with RPD, analysis and experiential decision making is an ability to read people – Goleman's emotional intelligence[58] or more recently his 'social intelligence'.[59] As Gillian Stamp says:

'Because asking for, offering and receiving practical wisdom – or advice – goes deeper than asking for or providing analysis or technical support, it makes us feel open to the other person, so both vulnerable and generous. When the exchange works both parties feel enhanced and trust builds. But if there is a sense that practical wisdom is being withheld or it has been offered and rejected then trust is at risk.'

A trusting and responsive relationship with those around you is necessary, therefore, in order to use your practical wisdom effectively. But for those who are seeking a higher level of engagement, it comes with the added bonus of binding people closer to their jobs and to your organization.

What do I do on Monday at Level 5?

How do you represent the organization and its strategy externally?

1. Be properly briefed

As a leader, it is your role to represent your organization to the prime stakeholders. The chief requirement for this is that you are fully briefed and in total command of its aims and objectives. Gone are the days when stakeholders were in the dark about an organization's affairs. Now any diligent stakeholder can know a great deal about your organization from a brief visit to the internet. However large your organization, it is vital that no city analyst or business journalist knows more about any corner of your strategy than you do.

❖ Regular, probably weekly, meetings with divisional heads are essential. They must take priority over all activities and absence cannot be acceptable. They must be short, information-delivery sessions, not discussion groups.

❖ Employ a Chief Intelligence/Information Officer (CIO) who will be responsible for information management. This cannot be simply systems-generated data but also human intelligence from within the organization. The CIO should attend the Excom meeting.

2. The story

You must have a compelling story to tell about what you are trying to achieve and how you'll achieve it. It should be devoid of jargon and straightforward; it must be your elevator pitch. If you must use PowerPoint and charts, use them only to illustrate your points and to show figures. Complicated graphs and charts that show seven strategic objectives, ten supporting strategies, six enabling resources only elaborate what is currently being done rather than providing a beacon towards which the organization is headed.

❖ Take time to consult and refine the story, then stick to it.

❖   Make the story the central component of any induction
    programme.

❖   Regularly review the story to make sure that it is still true.

3. Setting targets and objectives

For an organization to become engaged, it needs to know it is
winning; this success must be measurable. So you need to set
targets and milestones. Unless the pain of not achieving a target
overwhelms the risk of taking action, nothing will happen.

4. Creating or maintaining an appropriate organizational culture

It is valuable to remember that it is the responsibility of Level 5
leadership to *decide* upon the organizational culture and not to
simply let it happen. One of the crucial decisions of the board,
for example, when appointing a new CEO is whether that
person fits the current culture (if the board wishes to retain it)
or fits the intended culture the board wishes the organization to
cultivate.

Find the few contributions that show you modelling – in the full
gaze of the organization – the desired culture and climate. For
instance, one CEO of a global international airline was
determined (in the interests of shaping a different culture and
climate) to introduce more performance differentiation into the
organization. He was ever-present in this task, challenging the
performance management data coming in from the business,
chairing all staff conference calls about the conduct of the
company's change programme, banging the drum about the
importance of performance management and making sure the
top team collectively and individually did an outstanding job on
performance management and differentiation.

5. Look to the future

The role of Level 5 leadership is also to peer into the future and
determine whether your organization has the products and
capabilities to survive. You need to evaluate markets adjoining

your business such that you can **you need to evaluate** determine who to acquire or what to **markets adjoining** divest. Your intelligence function will **your business** provide the information, it is the role of the leader to transform that into knowledge.

It is also the job at Level 5 to create the right partnerships – future partnerships. You need to determine how your market place might evolve so you can position yourself for sustainable growth. New technologies might require you to partner with new suppliers, new ways to market may become available, new consumer requirements may require you to develop new products in specific market sectors. All need to be carefully considered so you are not incrementally becoming less relevant to your market place.

While your marketing department, if competent, should be developing line extensions, product improvements and understanding market segmentation, rarely can they be relied upon to see the 'big' picture requiring the major shifts – that is Level 5 work. Only that level has the authority and the power to take the strategic leaps that result in new alliances being formed and old alliances being severed.

6. **Be ruthless about playing at the right level**

Jot down the outcomes and activities that you should be delivering at Level 5. They should be about strategic decision making, key partnerships, other relationships with key stakeholders, looking to the future, providing the lead on organizational culture. Take a look at your diary for the last three months. To what extent have you been spending your time on the right things? How much have you been stepping into the legitimate space of those around you? List the things that you have been doing which do not fit with the desired picture and quantify the time and energy involved. Think about the better use that could be made of that. Construct your diary for the next three months around the right activities. Take the discussions with your team about their space. Find a partner ruthlessly to review with you, week by week, the way you are spending your time, helping you to stick to the discipline of the right level. Say no when the old activities start creeping back in, keep stepping into the new. Weather the weeks of discomfort, for you and others, as you adjust to the new habits. Celebrate the successes that come your way.

One leadership team recently looked at their diaries and the way they had spent their time over the previous six months. On average, 60% of it had been wasted on work below their level, which actually obstructed the accountability of the next level down.

7. **Simplify your organization, apply the five-level test**

As a rule of thumb, challenge to the nth degree the appearance of levels in your organization beyond five.

8. **What you do when you do not and cannot know what to do**

Pick on an upcoming decision. Cut short the process that is pushing you to get 'just that extra piece of data, then we'll be sure'. Don't ask for it, make the decision now. Do not procrastinate. Look back at the effectiveness of the decision, learn to trust your instincts better and understand, so that you can harness them better, the resources that you are drawing on to hone your practical wisdom.

9. **Get a coach**

Consider hiring a coach/mentor. Not a 'tea and biscuits' type but someone who will really challenge and inspire you, within a supportive environment. If you want some idea of what a good coach does, look at Peter Shaw and Robin Linnecar's book *Business Coaching: Achieving practical results through effective engagement*, published by Capstone, 2007.

What about me?

This is about giving yourself permission to look after yourself.

As we have already established, as a leader you are on display and your demeanour and behaviour send involuntary messages to those around you. It is therefore important that you ensure that this message is not counterproductive; that you are not presenting yourself as worn out, frazzled and tetchy. Unless you are a highly skilled actor, the only way of ensuring this is not to be worn out, frazzled and tetchy. You must look after yourself.

Once, in a previous role, one of the authors arrived back from a business trip to the US and almost immediately had a session with someone who was facilitating a team-building activity. She took one look at him and said 'go home'. 'I don't go home at three o'clock in the afternoon.' 'You look knackered and drained and every time you walk down the corridor you are sending a strong signal out that however bad people thought things were, actually they're worse. Go home, reconnect with your family and come back when you are restored.'

It was good advice. What you think of as pushing yourself to the limits in the name of efficiency may actually be undermining engagement in those around you. That is why looking after yourself matters. Because you can engage others more effectively. If you feel you need to keep pushing yourself to the very limits, consider this: even if you managed somehow to double your output (almost certainly impossible), you would get only one extra person 'for free'. **create the conditions whereby your whole organization becomes truly engaged** Instead, create the conditions whereby your whole organization becomes truly engaged and you might well add 20% to their effectiveness; the equivalent of 100 people in a 500-strong organization.

Looking after yourself is not about work–life balance, it is about being at the top of your game. Of all the leaders we interviewed, the most effective and productive had very definite answers when asked how they kept up their energy levels. While the answers themselves were disparate, these extremely busy people had actually thought about their own wellbeing rather than handing over their lives to their companies. In doing so they had added huge value to their organizations. Here are some examples of how they answered this question. You will note that they range from those who, like Keki Dadiseth, the extraordinarily impressive leader who did much to build Unilever in India, like to absent themselves entirely from work during their downtime, to those who find that their topping-up comes within the framework of the job itself:

'My way – I usually leave the office at 5.30 pm. I do work on Friday evenings and after dinner so that my weekend is free. Saturday and Sunday is my wife's time. I don't have the tension of preparing for the next week. I work during evenings in the week only if there is something important. I have a walk, watch television and chat to my wife. I am not one of those high-powered chief execs who work 17 hours a day.'

Keki Dadiseth, Unilever

'At RBS we don't have a kind of "where were you at half past seven in the morning and why weren't you in the office at eight o'clock last night" type culture and I take all of the holidays I'm entitled to every year.'

Neil Roden HR Director, RBS

'Winning. Taking on and changing the UK government's policies – I really enjoyed that.'

Mike Turner, CEO, BAE Systems

'What keeps me fresh is the diversity of other things in my life.'

Dianne Thompson, CEO, Camelot

'I love my job, I love doing what I do. I think that I am moderately good at it. I am on a constant learning curve ... Just when I think that I am moving up a bit there is something else to learn. So it is a constant challenge for me. It is the constant new challenges that drive me.'

Anji Hunter, BP and No 10 Downing Street

'I have this love of international business so I like buzzing around the place doing deals, talking to people, getting to understand the details of what is going on, feeling how people are feeling, communicating. It's an enjoyable thing for me so I don't feel, oh, it's terribly stressful.'

Andy Green, CEO, Global Solutions, BT

'I am a very big believer in shutting it off. I play tennis, I go to the theatre, I play golf, I work like a lunatic when I'm travelling and all that sort of stuff, but I try and I just about get away with it. It's almost like when I step through that door – it's off. So I create the space to have the variety in my life rather than an obsession, I suppose.'

Mike Clasper, CEO, BAA to 2006

'I'm on the board of Ipswich Football Club, that's a bit of a passion. I've got three young kids who are all very active in sports ... but I do need that because if I didn't have let us say an obligation to Ipswich being a supporter and a director, if I didn't have kids who had demands in terms of being ferried around to rugby matches and all the rest of it, which I actually find incredibly enjoyable, then I wouldn't switch off. But I don't really need to be physically there all the time because I've got my PDA with me all the time, got my e-mail with me all the time, got my mobile with me all the time as we all do. I find it quite easy to kind of switch between one and the other, it doesn't phase me if I get phone calls on Saturdays or whatever, but equally it doesn't phase me if I go off on Wednesday afternoon and watch a rugby match. Because as long as you are in contact then you're there.'

Kevin Beeston, Exec Chairman, SERCO

'I do find reading and experiences of what other people do . . . I think that is a really powerful way of topping up. What have other people done in similar circumstances? And I have an endless fascination for hearing other people talk about their organizations and what they've done.'

David Bell, DCSF

Clearly, there are no hard-and-fast rules for how you look after yourself. For every top executive who likes to switch off entirely at the weekend there is one who cannot relax unless they know they are at the business end of a Blackberry. It would be both presumptuous and counterproductive of us to lay down any diktats on the subject. However, we *can* assert that looking after yourself will almost certainly include developing the ability to say no. It will include doing things that you find to be the sources of inspiration, whether that comes from the challenge of the work itself or from meeting people you find inspiring. The time spent on this is not self-indulgent. It is a part of the drive towards engagement. Just as you cannot feign authenticity, so you cannot feign your own energy. In maintaining your drive and purpose, you are topping up the drive and purpose of the whole organization. The energy coming from you will be magnified as it spreads throughout the company.

The people who will help you magnify and spread this energy are those closest to you: your top team. Having engaged with engagement yourself, it is they to whom you must turn.

NOTES

[46] Mintzberg, Henry (2004) *Managers not MBAs, A hard look at the soft practice of managing and management development*, Financial Times Prentice Hall, p. 143.

[47] Towers Perrin European Talent Survey, 2004 – Reconnecting with employees.

[48] Towers Perrin Global Workforce Study, 2005 – UK data compendium.

[49] Goffee, R. and Jones, G. (2006) *Why Should Anyone Be Led By You? What it takes to be an authentic leader*, Harvard Business School Press.

[50] Ibid.

[51] Ibid, p. 11.

[52] Nigel Crouch of the Inspirational Leadership Programme, driven by more than ten organizations. Nigelcrouch@f2s.com

[53] Sims, D. (2004) 'The velveteen rabbit and passionate feelings for organizations', in Gabriel, Y. (ed.) *Myths, Stories and Organizations*, Oxford University Press, pp. 209–222.

[54] Drucker, Peter F. (1999) 'Managing Oneself.' *Harvard Business Review*, March–April.

[55] At the time of writing, Bill Parcells is the Head Coach of the Dallas Cowboys NFL team.

[56] Klein, G. (1998) *Sources of Power*, MIT Press.

[57] Gladwell, M. (2006) *Blink: The power of thinking without thinking*, Penguin Paperbacks.

[58] Goleman, D. P. (2005) *Emotional Intelligence*, Bantam Books.

[59] Goleman, D. P. (2006) *Social Intelligence: The new science of human relationships*, Hutchinson.

5 The top team

In approaching this chapter, we found ourselves in a quandary. Our strong belief is that engagement is something that in a perfect world should obtain at every level of the organization. Why then should we approach the top team separately? Theoretically, there should be no difference between engaging the top team and engaging any other section of the company. What you do with your senior leadership should simply be repeated down through the levels. Yet experience – and common sense – told us that this was not true in practice. Yes, everybody else should be as engaged as your top team is, but that top team – your direct reports plus a few other critical leaders – also carry an extra level of responsibility. This is because, in the real world, it is they who will work with you to implement engagement, they who help mould the organization, and they who set the tone in their own areas of responsibility.

If the top team is not on board, not engaged, not aligned, then the impact of any programme will be diluted and conflicting messages will undo the process before it has begun. It is impossible in an organization of any scale that the leader will be able to reach every employee, or even every department, directly or on an ongoing basis. The members of the top team, for good or ill, represent the strategy. If they are lukewarm about a strategy, the organization will not commit. If the organization smells the possibility that the programme will fail, its instinct will be to do little to contribute. Equivocation in the top team is fatal: any fissure there will be widened to a chasm by the time it reaches the whole organization. The extra layer of engagement that the top team must learn to demonstrate, then, is *collective responsibility*. We might call this a kind of family value system, a united front, a pact or psychological contract. Whatever we call it, the key aspect is that the leadership represents *one* body that speaks with *one* voice; one strategy with which they are engaged, to which they are aligned.

If you cast your mind back to the dying months of John Major's Conservative government, you will remember that his Cabinet was characterized by a remarkable lack of collective responsibility. Major, at one point, referred to several of his ministers – his top team – as 'bastards'. This disharmony cost them dear at the ballot box. So it wasn't surprising that New Labour, on gaining the keys to Number 10, understood well the dangers of visible disagreement and took pains to make sure that they spoke with one voice. The members of that first Cabinet were in fact very different characters, often with hugely varying backgrounds and views – as we have since discovered, there was little love lost between some of them. Yet outside Number 10, they were careful not to let this show. Importance was attached to being 'on message', and whatever gibes were thrown at them for this, they succeeded in presenting a remarkably united front.

Such an approach is vital for strong leadership, and especially when a change programme is afoot. This is not to say, however, that it does not carry its own dangers. As the Blair government grew older and more fixed in its habits, it fell into a trap. According to the late Robin Cook, by the time of the decision to embark on the war in Iraq, the Cabinet had 'lost the habit of dissent'.[60] In other words the custom of *internal* disagreement and discussion had faded. Overly used to falling into line, the Cabinet neglected a hugely important step in collective responsibility: vigorous, healthy debate and discussion in order to reach the collective conclusion. They had become so used to agreement that when they did find themselves in severe opposition to the proposed strategy there were no mechanisms in place to allow them to challenge it. The result was a dubious war, a Cabinet where cracks began to appear in the previously rigid façade, and a country that felt betrayed by its leadership. The Cabinet was *not* acting as the perfect team: while appearing to speak with one voice, they were forgetting first of all to have the internal dialogues that would have forged a true common vision.

This applies outside the political sphere also, of course. As Peter Erskine, Chairman and CEO, Telefonica O2 Europe, comments:

'Constructive tension is magic. I don't want everyone agreeing – if they are all sitting around and smiling, you've got a real problem. Though clearly sometimes constructive tension descends into destructive tension.'

the challenge is to make sure that collective responsibility remains healthy

The challenge, then, is to make sure that collective responsibility remains healthy. It should be characterized by vigorous, impassioned debate *within* the four walls of the boardroom, and a unity and clarity of purpose *outside* those walls.

As Sir Brian Bender, Permanent Secretary at the DTI and DEFRA until 2005, puts it:

'The role of the leader is to inspire self-confidence, inspire therefore an openness to constructive challenge because from constructive challenge and arguments good things will come.'

But as Lord Currie of Ofcom stresses, those challenges must not be allowed to leak out into the public arena:

'One of the things we did very early on in Ofcom was to agree a very strict code of collective responsibility . . . so you've never had a comment in the press which says board member X disagreed with the policy . . . we've avoided all of that.'

This chapter is about walking that delicate line between *engaging* your top team so that they bring the full force of their intelligence to bear on the challenges you face, but also *aligning* them around decisions made so that they can in turn swing the rest of the organization.

There are three components to this process. Your first preoccupation should be with making sure you have the right *balance* of people in your team, turning your top team into a body which together forms the perfect leader. Having achieved this balance, you must next *collectivize* your team, working to distil a perfect vision. This balanced collective will be the exemplar which will be radiated around the organization, and so the final stage is that the team carry the vision into the organization, each acting as a conduit for the leadership.

Balance: the perfect leader

Imagine what the perfect leader of your organization would look like. A person who can see the big picture and also pay attention to the fine detail; someone who is courageous in all decisions but prudent at the right moments, somebody who combines creative and charismatic leadership with an analytical business brain, as well as embodying whatever particular professional characteristics are necessary in your field. Now remember the honest assessment of yourself that you performed in Chapter 4. Do these two images match up? Of course not. No one person could ever combine every single necessary virtue. But a team can.

We have also seen that it is better to concentrate on polishing your strengths to brilliance than struggle to bring your areas of weakness up to scratch. And yet it is a key criterion for an engaged workforce that they should be able to have absolute faith in the high quality of their leadership – and this quality cannot be patchily confined to those areas in which you feel most comfortable. It might seem, therefore, that there is an inherent contradiction: if you are going to concentrate on your areas of strength, how can your employees have faith that the leadership has all bases covered? By bringing your top team into play. The top team is the virtual perfect leader.

This 'team' often has at its core a successful leader who works in tandem with someone else. During the turnaround at Asda, Archie Norman provided the cold-headed business brain while Allan Leighton provided the charismatic leadership; at Granada, Gerry Robinson and Charles Allen brought different skills to the equation: Robinson provided the policy, drive and innovation, while Allen provided the operational detail and perseverance. Sir Digby Jones, who considers himself a leader rather than a manager, relied on his second in command John Cridland at the CBI to provide the day-to-day management of the organization.

These partnerships allow these leaders the freedom to concentrate on the areas where they excel, knowing that the other areas are taken care of brilliantly well. The effect can be achieved either by finding one individual who fits well with you, or by carefully choosing a small squad who will perform the same function. Note, however, that we are not talking about a joint leadership. It must always remain clear who the overall leader is.

Hiring people of great ability, but with skills that are different and complementary to your own, is the first step in creating a top team characterized by stimulating, creative and successful thinking, especially if you also take care to build an open, discursive culture. Resist the temptation to feel threatened by the calibre of those who form the layer beneath you. Good people will make you look good, not suffer by comparison. As Bill Gates famously said: 'A' people hire 'A' people, 'B' people hire 'C' people. You need to intervene to stop the first recruitment of a 'B' person.' Adam Crozier of the Royal Mail advocates hiring only those who you think could comfortably succeed you.

Recruit for values

However brilliant, varied and complementary the skill sets and personalities of your immediate circle are, what they must have in common are their values. Whatever it is that you prize highly and which will support the organization's success – enthusiasm, diligence, a sense of adventure – make sure it is reflected in those closest to you. A large part of the engagement programme lies in embedding a set of values into the organization. Like words through a stick of rock, they must run through the company, and this will happen only if they are wholeheartedly shared by the top team. As Howell James, Permanent Secretary Communication at the Cabinet Office, says:

'I always try to hire people with skills that I don't have but people who share the same attitude. Not that they are the same kind of people because I think it is awful when you get clones; [but those] that have similar attitudes and desire for success and have a similar view of how people should be treated.'

Simply by hiring a certain type of person, you send a message down the organization about what you find important. You can talk as much as you like about loyalty, for instance, but it will be worth nothing if one of your right-hand men has a reputation for playing politics. And before you assume that this is something you already take note of, remember that only 34% of the European workforce consider that their organization's senior management 'lead by example in demonstrating the values of the company'.

The values you want embedded in your own organization are, to a certain extent, particular to you, to the industry you work in, or to a particular direction you are trying to take. As Bill Shankley, the great Liverpool FC manager, said: 'We recruit for attitude – Liverpool attitude.' At the top level it is a given that skill sets will be there, but without the appropriate attitude they cannot provide a winning formula.

Only you can decide what values will be important to you. There are, however, some key attributes that employees are particularly keen to see in their leadership. These are necessary for the engagement agenda. The Chartered Institute of Management and DTI research pinpoints the three most frequently identified attributes desired by employees in their leaders (vision (79%), trust (77%) and respect (73%)). At present, only four in ten respondents see these demonstrated in their organization. As we have seen in Chapter 2, similar research also cites communication of a winning vision as a top-ten attribute desired by employees. It identifies that, as well as delivering success, they want their leadership to:

❖ act in a way that is consistent with the company values

❖ support innovation

❖ demonstrate a sincere interest in the wellbeing of employees

❖ communicate effectively, openly and honestly.

(Not coincidentally, these are all areas which are identified as lacking: considerably fewer than half of respondents could agree that their senior management demonstrated these qualities.) All this research throws up a wealth of significant words: respect, trust, vision, communication, inspiration. These rather abstract nouns are, perhaps, difficult to translate into useful and identifiable characteristics. We distil them into the following, observable personality traits:

Optimism: Because it contributes to the 'vision' that is so important to employees. James Crosby, CEO HBOS 1999–2006:

'I would choose the optimist every single day because the pessimist doesn't achieve anything. And if anybody sits in a room and says "I'm going to be the Devil's advocate", fine, say "off you go". I've never seen that as a process of any value whatsoever. Optimists can challenge the future but they can actually create the future. Pessimists only challenge the future, they are a negativity, so you need that sense of optimism, the belief that somehow, however difficult it looks, you can achieve it, God you need that ... I want words like pace, optimism and courage.'

Energy: to help you achieve it. You want to surround yourself with what Clive Woodward calls energizers, not energy-sappers. Don't forget that members of your leadership group perform dual roles: a supporting role to you and simultaneously a leader to a section of your organization. You cannot inject energy-sappers into leadership roles.

Respect: employees need to believe that those who lead them have a sincere interest in their wellbeing. This involves acknowledging work done, being open to new ideas and innovations, communicating the reasons behind business decisions. It is demonstrated by listening, by communicating, by being aware of the issues faced by employees. These are all characteristics that employees have identified as desirable – and often lacking – in their leadership.[61]

Openness/Honesty: Employees want to see their senior leadership acting in a way that is consistent with the professed values of the company, and they want to be able to believe in what their bosses tell them. You need your top people to deliver honesty in feedback.

Getting the right people on the bus

'First who ... then what.' This is the argument of Jim Collins in his seminal book *Good to Great*.[62] In his view, the best idea is to assemble a great team before setting the strategy. 'It is better to first get the right people on the bus, the wrong people off the bus and the right people in the right seats, and then figure out where to drive,' he writes. The central point is to hire the right people. Collins got that right; we disagree with his order of priorities. In our opinion, in order to know who it is you want on the bus you need first to have a broad notion of where you are trying to get to and what kind of terrain you will have to cover. There is little point in hiring agile, flexible, strong, skilful yet tiny athletes for your basketball team. Equally it makes little sense to hire a risk-averse retiring personality to the trading floor of an investment bank, or to put an entrepreneur in charge of a high-hazard chemical site. It is not until you have identified the external factors and your own leadership goals that you start to look for your co-drivers. They will help you refine, improve and if necessary shape your strategy, but they do not set the basic aims.

Changing the team, firing the blockers

During a conversation we had with a group of top CEOs we asked what they most regretted in their professional lives. By consensus the biggest regret concerned not making the changes in personnel that needed to be made. Having worked hard on your strategy and concentrated on getting those around you to swing behind it, it is still perfectly possible that one or two people will remain unconvinced. It is your responsibility to try to bring them on side, but if it becomes clear that they are a fundamental mismatch, you will have to move them out. If you tolerate people who are actively blocking your policy, or indeed those who are 'passive resistors', outwardly compliant but actually dragging at the strategy by their behaviour, it sends a message that you are not serious about the commitments made. Nothing sends a more powerful signal to the organization that you are very serious about the strategy and the kinds of ways of working required to achieve it than being prepared to move people who stand in the way. Do it fairly and do it quickly.

do not confuse blockers with challengers   A note of caution here. Do not confuse blockers with challengers. It is extremely healthy to have people around you who are prepared to challenge you.

In Thomas Ricks's *Fiasco*,[63] a significant book on the Iraq war, the author identified an instance of this mistake, perpetrated by Tommy Franks, Commanding Officer of American and Coalition troops in Operation Iraqi Freedom: 'Everything has to be good news stuff . . . you would find out you can't tell the truth.' Or, elsewhere in the same book: 'Franks' abusive style tended to distort the information that flowed towards him.' Ricks argues that this had disastrous consequences for the US position in post-war Iraq.

It is an aspect of robust debate and crucial to sharpening up your game. Such frankness is precious and rare. The difference between challengers and blockers is that the challengers, having taken you on, will come on board once the policy is set and will engage with it. Blockers will not. Eric Peacock, Chairman of Baydon Hill PLC, describes the differentiation neatly:

> 'We can live with the sceptics because generally speaking if you are prepared to invest enough time in discussing with the sceptic the points of difference hopefully you can get alignment and these individuals turn into your best advocates. Cynics we take a very different view on because they are cancerous and we move them out of the organization quickly.'

Clive Woodward, former England rugby coach, was one of the many leaders who stressed this point:

> 'You need to get the right people, all of them committed to achieve. If there are those who don't share that commitment, move swiftly to turn them around. If their attitude doesn't improve, get them out before the entire working atmosphere is tainted irreparably.'

What do you do on Monday to achieve balance?

1. Don't limit your recruitment opportunities

Don't automatically assume that recruitment for top team jobs should be done externally (see Pillar 6, Harnessing Talent). While this can seem the easy option, it is a leap into the unknown. As Peter Erskine, Chairman and CEO, Telefonica O2 Europe, says:

> 'All external recruits have outstanding CVs. They come with excellent references. They are also completely unknown to you. You essentially have no idea whether they will fit in. You are always to some extent taking a leap in the dark.'

2. Identify values

We have listed what we consider to be the key traits to look for when appointing your top team, if engagement is your goal. However, depending on the demands of your particular organization, or indeed your own preferences, you will want to add to this list. It is worth doing this in quite a systematic way so that you can come up with a checklist of five top values that you consciously look out for.

3. Do not second-guess yourself

Having made your choice of the people in your top team, trust them. People need to feel secure enough to offer honest, constructive, challenging feedback.

This does not mean that, having once allowed people into a magic circle, you give them an easy ride. There is a balance to be struck. Honest criticism contributes to engagement so long as it is sensitively handled. Here as elsewhere, a sense of even-handedness and consistency is all. Doubts will be sown if you blow hot and cold, or if you continuously single out one person for praise or censure. Every aspect of your behaviour should indicate that performance is the only criterion for advancement and that favouritism has no place. According to Jurgen Grobler, England rowing coach, what applies in the world of sport should apply equally in a high-performing business unit:

'There is no room for cronyism in any team or organization that strives for excellence. Who is best able to carry out a specific task or fulfil a particular role? That is the only relevant question in selection and recruitment.'

4. Competition is healthy

It may be that in a team full of energetic and ambitious people, more than one will be thinking of themselves as your potential successor. This is fine: you are not trying to erase their ambitions, and healthy competition can be a spur to achievement. It is up to you to make sure that it doesn't descend into politics, or that energy isn't being wasted by people jockeying with each other for position. You do this by making sure you are open and undevious yourself.

5. Be smart when moving people on

If you have to move people out, do it with everyone's dignity intact. People's jobs cease to suit them for all sorts of reasons – their training becomes obsolete, the structure of the company changes, their skills do not match with the new order. To act decisively but as supportively as possible is just common human decency, and it also minimizes the seismic repercussions among the rest of the team.

The best leaders do not shirk from this difficult task, but they strive and are able to maintain positive relationships with those who go. There doesn't need to be blood on the carpet.

Collectivize: the perfect vision

When employees look up to the top level of the organization, what do they want to see? They want certainty, success and a shared vision. They want to see a winning team – with the emphasis on both words: teamship and success. To put these things in place, you must exploit your team fully, harnessing the power of their various whys and building together a vision that they can fully champion.

In today's world, tackling today's problems, leadership requires immense imagination. It is a recipe for failure simply to rely on one's current frame to provide direction, shape and purpose. Innovation, hand in hand with inspiration, is the key.

Everybody has had the experience of wrestling alone and unsuccessfully with a complex problem, only to resolve it in discussion with others. In Einstein's phrase, 'you cannot solve a problem at the same level of thinking as created it'. Think of your management group as a fertile ground for ideas and solutions. You want them to question even the most valued tenets of the status quo; you want them to look both outside and inside the organization for potential dangers, challenges and opportunities. Mike Clasper describes the process he went through with his top team as follows:

> 'What I did is after about three months I identified ten or eleven senior managers who I had confidence in and I basically said, let's draw out what our purpose is, what our strategy is, what our vision is, on the basis that I think you know what our strategies are implicitly and all I'm going to do is try and take you through a process where we draw out explicitly what they are.'

The very basics of engagement should, in your most senior people, be already covered. They should already care about the future of the organization, be personally motivated to ensure its success, and be willing to go the extra mile for it. The next stage, that of building the collective responsibility, requires that you start to listen to them. They will be saying things that are worth paying attention to. As Lord Currie of Ofcom puts it:

'I'm very strongly of the view that collective wisdom is much more powerful than individual wisdom, so in none of the jobs I've done did I think that I knew the answers and usually I didn't. The key thing is to get the right people engaged collectively on the issues and to energize them.'

Such an approach, as well as supplying extra 'wisdom' to your decisions, carries with it the benefit of starting the process of buy-in. It breaks down the defences of those who might otherwise 'consent and evade'.

Consent and evade

David Bell (DCSF) identified a technique that is probably all too familiar to anyone who has been in a leadership position. He calls it 'consent and evade':

'I have recently realized just how resilient organizations are. They can soak up a huge amount of punishment in the form of initiatives and good ideas without budging at all. This often seems to be the result of a clever strategy called consent and evade, adopted by people at all levels, and especially at the top. It is in situations like these that leaders have to do things differently and that can mean being tough with top teams since they set the tone for the whole organization. This does not mean that you must peddle dogma; discussion and engagement are vital, but if you want to change, then you must change behaviours and that means not permitting people to consent and evade.'

This sums up a danger you run if you attempt to make pronouncements and expect your senior people to fall in behind them unquestioningly. They may not disagree openly, but they may not be as acquiescent as you think they are. The first step in avoiding this tactic is to engage your team in conversation, and not just in the kind of conversation where they parrot back what you feel you need to hear. Consider the following statement from another of our interviewees, John Hirst, previously a divisional CEO at ICI:

> 'To get alignment, to get commitment, what do you need? You need a big yes. What is a pre-condition for a big yes? The possibility of a big no.'

That 'possibility of a big no' is what Robin Cook was missing when he lamented that the Cabinet had lost the habit of dissent. It can be implemented only through proper impassioned debate. Real, honest, constructive feedback is something you probably think you already get. You almost certainly don't.

real, honest, constructive feedback is something you probably think you already get

This is not a stage you can neglect or skim over. Ian Watmore, former Head of Accenture in the UK and now Head of the Delivery Unit at the Cabinet Office, stresses the investment of energy that is needed:

> 'You shouldn't underestimate the difficulty and the time-consuming nature of getting the immediate and extended team brought into that vision. The old phrase that it's 10% inspiration and 90% perspiration applies here. You've got to get that vision right but then you have got to put a lot of time and leg work into getting people with you and actually it is best sometimes to slow down to get the team to come with you rather than to press ahead and snap the elastic that joins people together.'

The effective leader energizes his team in this dialogue and debate. He asks questions, encourages opinions, stretches perspectives and promotes a feedback culture. Here are two simple examples:

One organization was completely changing the way it regulated some key public services. The leadership team had to deliver the current approach *and* do all the complex thinking and consult with stakeholders to develop it for later implementation: the classic dilemma of managing business as usual and at the same time implementing significant change. This put the team under huge strain, tensions crept in and they noticed that debate was becoming stultified.

They broke through this by stopping and giving themselves direct, supportive feedback. At a couple of sessions, they spent time with each member of the team, including the CEO, in rotating pairs, telling each other, 'this is what I most value about the contribution you are making', 'this is the one thing I would like you to change in your current contribution', 'this is the one thing that we should change in our collective behaviour'. The confidence and data that this gave them enabled them to get back on track.

The leader of a global Fast Moving Consumer Goods (FMCG) company decided that the top team needed to stretch its perspectives. Completely unexpectedly, he took them on a one-week journey through the Costa Rican jungle, throwing them all on to each other's resources for survival. The profound conversations that they had in the process enriched their sense of mission and drive.

But all of this does not mean that the leader institutes a democracy. In the words of David Barnes of AstraZeneca:

'As I see it, the Chief Executive has the final shout . . . I make that decision. I don't guarantee that I will come down with the majority. Indeed I specifically reserve the right not to come down with the majority. I think the buck stops with me and I will make my decision on the basis of what I have heard.'

You might assume that taking such a resolute stance is likely to discourage honest contributions from your team. But if handled correctly, this basic rule should in fact free those around you to make their contribution in an environment where they know that all possibilities can be discussed, but that there is one central guiding intelligence.

Vision – purpose and strategy

All of this debate, discussion and energy are used in the service of distilling two things: your purpose and your strategy. Taken together, they add up to become your *vision*.

Purpose

Imagine a football team that concentrates only on scoring goals and doesn't worry about how many it concedes or where it finishes in the league. While scoring goals is obviously necessary in achieving that team's ultimate purpose, it does not constitute an end in itself and will not deliver absolute success.

For companies, profit is like the football team's goals. You cannot survive without achieving profit, and in the immediate term it is critical. But it does not constitute the final aim. The concept of 'purpose beyond profit' is an interesting one and much has been written about it in a highly sophisticated way, especially by Jim Collins and Jerry Porras in their book *Built to Last*[64] in which they identify that a common characteristic of the resilient organizations they study is that they all espouse a purpose above and beyond simply making money. They cite examples such as Merck (pharmaceuticals) – 'We are in the business of preserving and improving human life. All our actions must be measured by our success in achieving this goal'; Walt Disney (entertainment) – 'To bring happiness to millions'; Johnson and Johnson (healthcare products) – 'To alleviate pain and disease'.

Our point, however, is not a terribly sophisticated one. It is simply that since nothing moves forward unless there is real conviction behind its 'purpose', it is also critical for engagement. It is part of the 'story' that your organization tells its employees. Distilling this purpose is up to you and your top team, engaging as far as possible with what you and your colleagues personally care about.

Terry Smith, General Manager, Public Sector, Microsoft, talking about the early days of the company, underlines the need for this conviction:

'The original goal [was] to put a PC on every desk and in every home, and if you start off with that as your vision and you're in an industry that is really, really early days, the only people who are coming to work for you and with you are people who've got that emotional connection. They are directly connected to some massive (actually ludicrous in 1975) vision . . . At the start it was Bill and a bunch of bright people saying, we're going to set out to do something different. You can chart right the way through our history that that is actually what keeps people in the company and what drives and fulfils people.'

Richard Baker of Alliance Boots reminds us that sometimes organizations need to re-establish their core purpose:

'A journalist asked me, "so, what is Boots, what is Boots all about, who needs Boots?" I said, "it's Boots the chemist, I've never had any doubts, it's a pharmacy, it's a healthcare company. Yes, it does lots of other things, but the beating heart of this company is Boots the chemist."'

What you are trying to avoid, however, is the following type of scenario, outlined for us by Ian Smith, SVP Oracle UK:

'I was listening to something on Radio 4 about the time it takes for an ambulance to arrive in an emergency. There's a target for that called the eight-minute target. The target is you have to get to the end of it all within eight minutes 75% of the time. Some trusts have decided that that's an unfair target so they won't start the clock anything up to 4½ minutes after they've received the call. The point is, however, the eight minutes is not an arbitrary target, eight minutes is a well-researched piece of information that says if a person had a heart attack or something, if you don't get to them within eight minutes the likelihood of death or serious brain damage is much higher. Now one health authority achieves this target consistently. They interviewed the Chief Executive . . . and he said, "I'm not about targets; I'm here to save lives. My whole organization is here to save lives. If I make the targets so be it."

▶

[But at another health authority] they said, "Oh well, this is different, we're not like them, we have busier roads and you can't get the staff round here, etc." So I went on to the website of both trusts and went into the minutes of the board meetings and you go into the minutes of the more successful one and it's this: "How can we save lives? These are the lives we've saved . . ." Then I went on to the minutes of the other trust: no mention of achievement but they were deciding on what type of uniform the staff would wear. They were having a board meeting to decide on what uniform they wanted.'

Strategy

The advantage of starting the 'vision' process by identifying your purpose, rather than by leaping straight into strategy, is that it encourages co-ownership and buy-in. The process of refining your strategy should be one of energetic, passionate debate, as Lord Currie describes:

'What you have got to do is have a process where you allow people enough time to discuss the issues so you get the diverse set of views and you get them on the table and you debate them and you argue about them and obviously you have to reach a conclusion. Often if you have a genuine debate, the conclusion you reach is more sophisticated, more nuanced than it would have been if you'd made a quick decision because you are recognising those differences of view and you are embodying them in what you decide. But then you have to be absolutely clear that having decided it, we move on. People have to feel they have made their contribution; they have to feel they've been listened to, but ultimately if the decision goes against them they have to be willing to go with that.'

Or, as Peter Kilgour, previously of Exxon and now Towers Perrin, puts it:

'There's something about compliance without stifling, so on the one hand you want to encourage discussion, dialogue, engagement and involvement, but on the other hand when a team has agreed something it wants that to happen as opposed to individual members going off and doing their own things.'

once you have established your vision you need a strategy to achieve it Once you have established your vision you need a strategy to achieve it – for which you want people to be aligned and engaged. This plan should be based on Activity-Based Costing to ensure you know where you make your money. You should have an outstanding marketing department to ensure you understand and satisfy today's customers and (this is the clever part, why you need outstanding marketing people) both latent and likely future customer needs. Now read Porter to understand the basic dynamics in your market and your place within it. If you can then manage to employ an outstanding Finance Director and Marketing Director you can save yourself a huge strategic consultancy bill.

Winning

Perhaps the most important requirement of the perfect leader and the vision that they craft is that they are successful. Consider the following statements:

> 'My organization's senior management is taking steps to ensure the long-term success of my organization.'

> 'Senior management acts in the best interest of our customers.'

> 'Senior management effectively represents my organization to external groups.'

These are, in order, the top three drivers of engagement in the context of senior leadership. They are about winning. The first thing your employees want to see from their top team is winners. The reason is simple – they consider, rightly, that their future lies in your hands. The UK workforce is not overwhelmingly convinced that their leadership is doing a good job of this. Only 57%, 48% and 46%, respectively, could agree that their leadership was fulfilling these three functions.[65]

The trick is to tie up the 'winning' with the new vision so that colleagues, customers and other stakeholders see the vision in action, understand that this is the way the organization is going (and hopefully adopt similar behaviours themselves) and take increasing confidence from the new direction. For example, before its launch, Ofcom, the new telecoms super-regulator, gave a great deal of attention to a new approach to regulation. As they considered the first six months of their new life, the CEO and his leadership team decided on a few issues that they were going to major on and focus on exclusively, making absolutely sure that they were successful in tackling them and drawing external confidence and understanding as a result. They did so, and in looking back recently the media congratulated them on their excellent fast start which symbolized the new direction they were taking.

A newly appointed CEO of another organization was determined to freshen it up, starting with the leadership team. She put a lot of work into the sense of purpose and strategy but quickly decided that she had to model performance in the areas where the team had previously been weak. For instance, relationships with external stakeholders were critical to the future vision, so she went out of her way to spend 40% of her time with them. This brought success, the organization began to notice and a number of colleagues followed her 'winning' lead.

Successful CEOs exemplify the vision, its purpose and strategy in the 'winning' they do day to day. As a result, they are bringing it alive for their people and all external stakeholders. As we shall explore in Part three, this is the best way for the CEO and their leadership team to be the exemplars which drive the vision into the organization, each acting as a 'carrier'.

Do on Monday (for the perfect vision)

1. Where are you at? Where are you going?

There are various techniques for imagining the future for your organization. Simply demanding feedback, if the culture of your company doesn't already favour it, is unlikely to work. Use one of the techniques available. Take a step back and consciously encourage deeper conversations by building a shared picture of where the organization is at and where it is going. The manager of a large but beleaguered company asked a team to draw a picture of the organization as it was. The results were startling, and worrying: the pictures drawn were brutal – one person drew the headquarters of the building in flames to show the pain they were feeling within the institution. Once the pictures went up on the wall, the effect was striking. The overriding reaction was, 'what the hell are we doing to each other?' It was clear from this simple exercise that before any strategic intent was discussed, a massive cultural shift had to take place.

At DEFRA, a similar technique was used as a projecting tool. Each of the top team was asked to draw independently a picture of what the newly created department should be like. In Sir Brian Bender's words:

'It was very powerful because what was really interesting was that every single one of the pictures, one way or another, was about the coherence of the department, about having uniformity, joining up and so on.'

Other techniques for assessing the current state of the organization can involve imagining the organization as a person and the business environment as a swimming pool. Where does everyone in the meeting consider the organization to be? In the shallow end, in the deep end, or by the edge of the pool deciding whether to jump in or not?

A small company, Directing Creativity spun out of the Royal Shakespeare Company, enables clients to imagine the future by using theatrical skills. There are as many techniques as organizations – find the one which suits your company.

2. Feedback

Constantly practise both giving and receiving constructive

feedback. Consider carefully how you invite it and learn to take criticism in your stride. Never punish people for honesty, and open up your attention so that you take notice of any feedback offered, even if it is done in an oblique way. When giving feedback, start with positive, constructive feedback and move on from there to any negative comments. Ensure that any feedback sessions take place in a 'safe space'. Take advantage of any unusual scenarios to invite feedback. We call this the 'nightshift factor' – when out at the front line, one of the authors found that employees tended to be most expansive and open when he took part in factory night shifts with them. You need to ensure that feedback is 360° not 180° by bringing in external views from surveys, customers, stakeholders, etc. For more feedback ideas, see Pillar Three, Loudhailers to Conversations.

3. Envision success

It is extraordinary how often people take it for granted that they are working towards the same ends, without necessarily working out what those ends are. We asked each member of one team we worked with to write down the six main aims of the group. We wrote the answers on the whiteboard. The team found themselves looking not at six broadly aligned answers but at 25 separate goals. The first job, clearly, was to establish the team's priorities.

Divide your team into groups of 4–5 people. Give them no more than half an hour to come up with the three big environmental changes that are going to drive change within your organization. Then ask your groups to share their lists of changes, discuss and evaluate them.

With a consolidated list of the major environmental changes having been agreed, address what success might look like in the future. Ask each person to project themselves forward two years: the team is sitting with a large congratulatory bottle of champagne in front of them. The champagne signifies success: what does that success consist of? What achievements would be worth celebrating? Consider what the successful company might look like from several perspectives: that of the shareholder, the employee, the customer, the media. Spend time in syndicates discussing this and then through effective facilitation draw together the key themes that best describe what success would look like for your group.

4. **Identify the path**

   Having achieved a high-end definition of success, the group now needs to work out how to get there. Again the team should be divided into small groups to produce the top three or four enablers and the top three or four blockers to achieving the defined goals. For instance, the leadership team of a newly merged organization identified the quality of talent, the competitive landscape and the potential synergies between the two predecessor organizations as strong *enablers,* and differences in culture, uncertainty about the future and differences in systems as the main *blockers.* Therein lay their agenda for the implementation pathways.

5. **Try different ways to stretch the perspective of your team**

   a) *Bring in the personal voice*

      Connect with what you as a group really care about. Invite your people (during an out-of-office away-day, preferably over dinner) to reflect on what they personally really want to achieve; what they really care about.

   b) *Step out of the day-to-day routines*

      David Varney, on becoming Chairman of O2, spent little time in his office – rather than being shut away in an ivory tower his priority was to get 'out there' and learn the business through and through. Go to other organizations to bring a fresh perspective on your own environment. All the senior members of a government department went on a week's secondment to shadow senior people in a private-sector organization and brought back different perspectives on change and transformation. Get out of the office, spend more time with customers and other stakeholders, and spend time on the front line.

c) *Push the thinking beyond the usual boundaries*

Force a leap of imagination by using different scenarios. For instance, we recently invited the leadership teams of two organizations facing a merger to put together a pitch for the running of the newly merged business as though it were a tender bid. This produced a wealth of radical performance expectations, structural options, cost-saving ideas and other improvements. This encouraged them to see the organization as others might see it.

d) *Bring in the voice of the organization*

Use the perspectives of colleagues outside the leadership team. Not only do they have critical, different and often more operationally sound perspectives but this is an important act of engagement for the wider organization. There are several ways to do this in the normal running of the business, such as surveys, focus groups and specific feedback to the board. It is particularly important in significant change projects. One approach is to form colleagues from outside the leadership group into 'pulse' teams. For instance, in an eight-week exercise where a major corporate bank was framing its future vision, several pulse teams brought in the operational perspective from all levels of the bank, working on key aspects and regularly meeting with the 'Big Picture' team which was the leadership team. This enabled the project to be managed at great speed, it started the engagement process and it brought highly valuable operational perspectives into the redesign work. Peter Erskine, CEO O2, cites one of his chief executives, who put together a shadow 'board' of around a dozen people selected from volunteers from throughout the organization. On anything to do with the customer – new products, changes in pricing – leadership will put the idea to this board and their view is taken into account, based on the fact that they interact more with the customer than leadership does.

e) *Bring external voices into the process*

Similarly, use the perspective of people from outside the organization and push this beyond straightforward survey and consultation work. Include them actively in the change process. For instance, an organization responsible for encouraging the quality of design in the UK found it valuable to seek the opinion of all its stakeholders, culminating in a two-day event which brought them all into one place. A major oil company, trying to enhance its innovation process when looking to develop new oils, climaxed its efforts with an event at Silverstone, which brought representatives from dealers, mechanics, drivers and distributors to work together on new ideas.

6. **Get early wins that show the vision in action**

You need to build the winning habit that exemplifies the vision. Careful setting of goals and targets is key. For a business that is really struggling, it could be something extremely minor: the point is to identify the focus of an **careful setting of** overfamiliar in-house gripe, to declare that **goals and targets** it will be rectified, to rectify it quickly, and **is key** to underline that this has been done. For a company which is already successful, winning will involve building on that success, celebrating it, improving on it and using it to instil a confidence that can trickle down the organization.

7. **Learn the lessons of success**

Clive Woodward stresses the importance of this:

'Work hard to learn the lessons of victory and success. Don't dwell on failure. Focus on the positive.'

He points out that post-mortems are usually conducted after failures: at a time when confidence is weakest, people are encouraged to pick themselves apart to discover what went wrong. Of course, failure needs to be addressed and lessons learned from it as objectively as possible. But successes need to be dissected just as finely because success is replicable. Pinpoint what it was about your judgement that was sound, what it was about your performance that made it so efficient. Take note of these winning traits and incorporate them into your future strategies.

8. Ensure good working methods and review them regularly

Too often, leadership teams get stuck in working methods that make it very difficult to create the space to hold the deep-rooted conversations necessary to get the driving sense of vision. In particular, they often get lulled into a habit of just discussing the managerial agenda and all the various initiatives that are being implemented across the organization. As M. C. Mankins points out in the *Harvard Business Review*,[66] executives' time is too frequently wasted in poorly designed leadership team processes.

He suggests one simple way to deal with this is to separate out managerial and strategic meetings and not let them bleed into one another. Consistent with these recommendations, several leadership teams we have led or have worked with have sorted this out by insisting that good time (and different processes for discussion) is put aside for the strategic, such as one half-day out of every four meetings, an evening discussion and dinner, or more formal arrangements establishing a strategy board and an executive management board.

Make sure that you regularly assess the leadership team's process and performance.

Carriers: the perfect voice

Just as you cast a shadow as the leader of the organization (or department), so those around you have the power to magnify that shadow and to increase its effectiveness. As Peter Kilgour previously of Exxon, now Towers Perrin, puts it:

> '[The top level's] collective shadow is a much more profound thing than individual shadows or an individual leader's shadow.'

The board of an organization was presenting a new strategy to its top 200. Having had little time to develop it together, they each presented their part of it while the CEO did a good job of picking up the various threads and explaining the core thinking. Afterwards we asked various attendees what struck them most about the message. Every one of them commented on the body language of those on the board: when they were not speaking, they slightly inclined their body away from the speaker and looked distracted. It presented to the audience the tableau of a board which was not in full agreement, immediately sowing doubt about the message.

In a private-sector organization, the Head of Manufacturing stood up to give an unscripted and impassioned presentation on a particular aspect of plant productivity and on the importance of safety. He then got out his notes, turned on the overhead and delivered the core script from the top team. It was quite obvious which part of the strategy he cared about and would back and reward.

This kind of behaviour is in direct opposition to the way the top team should be behaving. Remember: taken together the team is meant to represent one perfect leader. It follows that, once the team's collective purpose is set, it speaks with one voice and one mind. To do anything else – to allow ongoing dissent to be visible – is to present a schizophrenic face to the organization.

If the change programme is to have staying power, it must be constantly reinforced by the actions and behaviour of the management cadre. The commitment of the entire leadership will be judged by the commitment of the member present in the room. Time and again, we have witnessed the truth of Schein's findings in the early nineties.[67] His evidence suggested that, above all, it is leadership that has the most direct impact on the culture of an organization and its capacity to change. He argued that 80–90% of behaviour is determined by what leadership attends to/measures/rewards/controls, their reaction to critical incidents and their role in modelling and coaching. Other factors such as criteria for promotion/recruitment, organizational design and structure, design of physical space, and stories and myths have an impact but to a much lower extent. Peter Kilgour sums this up as follows:

> 'The bulk of people's experiences of cultures and organizations is driven by what leaders attend to, what they reward, how they react in critical incidences, what they coach, and that accounts for 70–80% of behaviour in organizations by fairly consistently and rigorously tested research and therefore how a group of people behave collectively, what behaviours and values they manifest, will have a huge impact on the delivery of the organization.'

Conduits for the right purpose

In Part two we saw how effective, engaging leaders bring their vision to life through their winning ways. Our conduits need to be 'carrying' for the right purpose. They need to be crystal clear on what they are exemplifying, the yardsticks they are going to use in their decision making.

Uniqema was an ICI business that was formed from the coming together of five separate businesses, each with its own cultural norms. Self-consciously and deliberately the top level concentrated on an engagement agenda. The process of building the new Uniqema culture started with the senior leadership: they spent considerable time on the testing process of defining a new future that would surpass any of the individual company histories. They selected the best practices from each of the constituent businesses to deliver this future and so they learned to set aside their tribal loyalties. Key top team roles had been settled early in the process, thus minimizing any jockeying for position and concentrating energies towards future success. This was not a process which could be rushed: discussions, workshops and relationship building centring on this issue continued for two months before consensus was reached. Unexpected issues, such as the lack of a consistent vocabulary, had to be rectified – the team eventually introduced a formal 'business language' to aid communications.

Even more importantly, they spent much time and thought developing ten business principles (including 'nothing we do is worth getting hurt for', 'be positive and assume people are trying to do the right thing' and 'encourage calculated risk taking to improve the business'). When they looked back at the success of the enterprise, they put their finger on the leadership team's development of these principles, and the care with which they crafted them, as being the most significant contributor to success. The principles were initially developed by the top team, then shared more broadly and with key opinion formers whose views were taken into account. Once they were finalized, they were taken back to the wider organization through transformation workshops.

The organization was extremely receptive, with individuals quickly taking on board how the principles applied to their work. Quite soon people were heard to say during discussions 'that's not in line with Business Principle X'. Virtually all the workshops were deemed a success by the participants, who showed a clear understanding of the idea that everyone needed to change to the new ways of working if Uniqema was to be a success. The top team remained highly involved with the process throughout, with the principles being first discussed with the global leadership team (of about 60) and with members of the top team ensuring that they took part in facilitating and engaging in the workshops. To reinforce them, they regularly took 360° assessments of their performance against them.

Did this degree of effort pay off? It resulted in high levels of two-way engagement within the business which served Uniqema well: first in the relatively benign business environment which characterized the initial period of operation; second in the difficult market conditions which set in a couple of years later, when it became clear that raw material prices were ranged against them and that a substantial sum had to be taken out of the cost base, meaning headcount reductions of more than 12%.

Rather than a relapse into the habits of command and control, Uniqema elected to use a similar process of engagement to redesign the organization and retained the ten business principles unchanged to guide ways of working. Again, the top level was vital in this process. Simplification began at the top with a streamlining of the top team and next-level and leadership teams. New business processes were introduced. Training, particularly in the behavioural aspects of change, was emphasized. One-to-one discussions with employees on how and why their role would change were an important element of the implementation plan.

The top team took many of the training modules themselves to ensure buy-in at the lower levels. Different scenarios were practised at all levels in the organization, including the top team, before changing over to the new ways of working, encouraging a perception that 'we are all in this together'.

The second transformation was completed with savings ahead of plan and ideas for further savings of a similar magnitude developed from within the business as a next phase of efficiency and effectiveness improvements. Profits began to improve in 2005 and in 2006 the business was trade sold at a price well above market expectations.

Throughout this book, you will find a variety of examples of the members of the leadership carrying its message into the organization – the crucial point is that leadership be clear, united and collectively responsible before it begins sending messages.

Shifting behaviour

What if you have selected your top team with complete balance in mind but are then faced with the challenge of changing the approaches and behaviours of that team in order to exemplify and 'carry' a new message for the organization? Indeed, most organizations have to wrestle with this at some time, whether a global oil company trying to instil a more accountable, decisive, compliant culture, or a professional services firm that is encouraging its partners to be more client-relationship orientated.

'Carrying for the right purpose' often requires engaging the top team in some form of behavioural shift. In our experience, there are three critical ingredients in such a process:

- ❖ The primacy of leadership.

- ❖ 'Just do it': all too often, leadership communities are drawn into long debates about the types of values and behaviours they should adopt without much reference to action. Research in the nineties indicated that a strong foundation for behavioural change was the *experience* of working in different ways.

- ❖ Pay attention to the whole system (structure, processes, technology, culture, leadership, etc.). The leadership team of a newly merged global FMCG company endorsed new values of passion, trust, action and integrity. However, they soon realized that there were a number of systemic obstacles to their people being able to deliver on these. It was only when they began to tackle these institutional issues that behavioural change was accelerated.

Working with top teams, you need to pay attention to the following to support behavioural change:

- ❖ balancing the team (see 'Balance: the perfect leader', page 105)

- ❖ throwing them into action, experiencing new behaviours in responding to significant business challenges

- ❖ carefully articulating the desired values and behaviours (as in Uniqema)

- ❖ creating learning situations where colleagues see how the paradigm is shifting for them and why they therefore need to change to continue to be successful.

Do on Monday (for the perfect voice)

1. **Create a feedback culture**

   This is the start of a long journey. It requires nothing short of a new culture (in most cases), which is more important than strategy (culture eats strategy for breakfast). Rob Margetts would say it takes 5–10 years. You will be working at both the rational and the emotional level. So at the end of each monthly meeting ensure that each person in the room gives feedback to each other. This should be against agreed criteria that are relevant to this group in your organization. The feedback should be very short to allow time to explore any issues that emerge. The questions will revolve around whether we are adopting the behaviours and developing the culture that the organization needs. Peer group feedback can be extraordinarily powerful.

2. **Unify your message**

   Find ways for each member of your team to have to explain the vision and how the organization will achieve it. Give feedback: what you are looking for is that while people come across as authentic and retain their natural style, they come across as aligned and engaged and look like they have spoken to their colleagues. While it might feel repetitive, each member of the team will learn something from the others in each iteration.

3. **Harness different perspectives**

   In developing your story, see it from different angles, typically from the viewpoint of the employee, investors, the external stakeholder community and the customer. Ensure your themes are relevant to each audience but that they are consistent from one to the other. It's just that certain issues must be emphasized for different target groups.

4. **Get feedback**

   Ensure you get and listen to feedback from employees. Get qualitative feedback and quantitative feedback. You need both.

Find out whether your people think your team is visible. Take opportunities to be seen more in the organization. Track progress and set expectations. Also a bit of healthy competition can be harnessed, e.g. which part of the organization feels most communicated with, etc.

5. Foster teamwork

Give cross-team responsibilities. To encourage your team to rely on each other, to engage with each other, you should give individual members responsibility that cuts across the silos. Get them to work out what they expect and need from each other so there are no excuses for not delivering. While there will be some initial resistance, in the end you will be a more effective leadership group and speak better with one voice.

NOTES

[60] Hennessy, Peter (2004) 'Rules and servants of the state, the Blair style of government 1997–2004', OPM.

[61] Towers Perrin Global Workforce Study, 2005 – UK data compendium and also DTI booklet.

[62] Collins, J. (2001) *Good to Great*, Random House.

[63] Ricks, T. E. (2007) *Fiasco: The American military adventure in Iraq*, Penguin.

[64] Collins, James and Porras, Jerry (1996) *Built to Last*, Century Books.

[65] Towers Perrin Global Workforce Study, 2005 – UK data compendium.

[66] Mankins, M. C. (2004) 'Stop wasting valuable time.' *Harvard Business Review*, Vol. 82, Issue 9, pp. 58–65.

[67] Schein, F. H. (1992) *Organizational Culture and Leadership*, 2nd edition, San Francisco, CA: Jossey-Bass.

PART THREE

SEVEN PILLARS OF ENGAGEMENT

6 The context

Every organization has its own, often unspoken, set of issues, its own reality, born out of its history. Unsurprisingly, companies that have seen a range of management fads come and go will be naturally resistant to change programmes. In fact, human beings are generally and wisely resistant to change for its own sake. Understanding your organizational culture involves recognizing these unconscious reactions and allowing for them when drafting out your engagement plan.

In Part One we set out the top drivers of engagement in detail. The recognition of these drivers was enabled by the volumes of employee comments which came out of extensive research. However, a simple tabulation of engagement drivers does not constitute an action plan. In Part Two we examined how leaders and their teams need to interpret and respond to the drivers. In this part, we build on Parts One and Two to offer a range of actions, conceptual and practical tools that deliver an engaged workforce. We call these the seven pillars of engagement. These pillars are the product of our thinking and experience, as applied to the questionnaires, interviews, feedback and analysis we have undertaken in the past decade. The product is arranged in seven components simply for the sake of manageability. It is not a hierarchical typology, not least because it is for leaders/managers to place the emphasis where their particular organization most needs it. Our hope is that it provides a ready reference resource for busy people and that they find it helpful.

These seven pillars do not exactly map on to the engagement drivers but they do draw from them and our wider experience to help to address those drivers and effect them. They provide the stable, lasting structure of engagement. The pillars are:

Pillar One – Commitment

Pillar Two – Get to the Front Line

Pillar Three – Loudhailers to Conversations

Pillar Four – The Reservoir of Wellbeing

Pillar Five – Bring Back the Manager

Pillar Six – Harnessing Talent

Pillar Seven – Consequences

All of these pillars are relevant to every organization. But bear in mind as you read and try to apply them that you will have to apply them relative to your own context. You will have particular aims for your engagement programme depending on what kind of industry you are in. If you run a high-hazard chemical plant you may be less interested in the idea of fostering an entrepreneurial spirit throughout the organization than if you are running a dot.com start-up. The environment in which you operate will modify the emphasis you put on certain behaviours and will affect what characteristics you are trying to enhance.

You should recognize that your context also includes the trajectory that your company is on, together with a realistic assessment of where you are in that journey. Exactly how you shape your engagement programme will depend on the levels of engagement – and success – that you already have. This calls for a clear-eyed judgement of where your company stands in relation to its environment. Every company would like to think that it can reach the summit of its industry, and every company should aim high, but to pin your engagement agenda to an unrealistic expectation is bound to end in disaster.

this calls for a clear-eyed judgement of where your company stands

Tackling these seven pillars, then, will be effective only if the original assessment of the state of the company is analytical and honest. Fortunately there are research methodologies that can be harnessed to help you with this process. Quantified engagement surveys, augmented by qualitative research, can help to identify which of the drivers of engagement need the most attention in your particular organization.

Surveys and research may help you to know where to start and where to concentrate your efforts but they won't show you how to go about it. Part Three is about providing that knowledge. Read on.

7 Pillar One – Commitment

'If it is going to mean this amount of effort, this number of people, that cost, the depth, the size, the shape of the pain, then if you start on this road you have got to see it through and if you don't think you've got the guts or time – don't start.'

Alex Wilson, Group Human Resources Director, BT

The great American football coach Vince Lombardi said that everybody has the will to win; only the best have the will to *prepare* to win.

There will be times – they are inevitable – when your engagement process seems to be going backwards, when progress seems slow or non-existent, when criticism becomes ever more vocal, and the naysayers seem in the ascendant. However enthusiastically your organization has seemed to embrace your new commitment, the real test will come at around three months into the process, when you have started to make the changes but there are few tangible benefits. Every change programme is susceptible to the same emotional cycle: a period of false optimism and excitement followed by a period when morale drops away as people begin to think of objections, problems and difficulties. This is to be expected. For people to change their ways of thinking and working, it is necessary to let go of their old metrics, benchmarks and certainties, before fastening on the new ones. Not surprisingly, this is an alarming process, and will be made far more alarming if there is any sign of wavering at the top.

If you are the person driving the change, however, there is no doubt that you will be sorely tested, and if you have created an open atmosphere in your organization, you will be tested all the harder. We would go so far as to say that if this doesn't happen, your changes are not really being embraced by the organization. If you are not tested, are you really changing anything? As Machiavelli said: 'There is nothing more difficult to carry out, nor more doubtful of success, nor more dangerous to handle, than to institute a new order of things.' England's swimming coach Bill Sweetenham backs this up:

> 'Never stop selling your vision of the future. Otherwise, change can easily be reversed. A determined manager of change is rarely popular. Anyone who seeks radical change is going to make enemies of those who benefit from the current system. It doesn't matter. Excellence should be the goal, not popularity.'

Your job is to give the organization (or your part of it) the leadership it needs, not just what it says it wants.

You need to ride out the period of uncertainty: as people become accustomed to the new order they will forget their earlier objections, and the more secure they are in being confident that you know where you are going, the faster they will become comfortable. Once benefits start to be visible, enthusiasm levels will pick up. You must, however, be prepared for the downturn.

A lack of commitment on your part will result in an atmosphere where the following kinds of statements (taken from various change processes we have witnessed) can flourish:

- ❖ 'The boss is working it out, so let's just wait until he's certain.'
- ❖ 'I don't want to change my priorities and to put more effort into engaging my people only to find that it was yesterday's story.'
- ❖ 'I don't want to go out on a limb, take a risk, be at the vanguard of an engagement programme only to have the boss change her mind so there is no reward – in fact maybe even a punishment – for the things that I have given up in order to focus on engagement.'

Such a drip-feed of uncertainty can have an undermining effect. One of our colleagues once observed an American CEO, whose company had been bought, fight off the internationally minded acquiring CEO by continually and subtly feeding the latter's fears and doubts. The acquiring CEO wanted to engage the people in the new company in an endeavour to create a world-leading organization by building synergies, sharing best practice and pooling effort where sensible. The 'acquired' CEO didn't share this desire. Although it seemed that the initiative lay with the latter, it was the 'acquired' CEO who prevailed. How? Faced with a constant stream of doubts, the acquirer wasn't firm in his resolve and nothing happened. He couldn't put the grand future he envisioned into place and the company stayed static, until of course there was a massive Night of the Long Knives. Being clear, tough-minded and resolute from the outset would have saved the company a lot of unproductive upheaval.

Two things are vital during this period: first that you continue to demonstrate through all your behaviour your faith in the programme, and second that you don't lose your nerve and go into reverse. People will be watching you and people will take their cue from you. As Andy Green of BT puts it:

> 'You really are on display at every moment and I fail sometimes with my "in team". I've got a fantastic group of support people who are very rude to me and very clear to me. They will just say smile! It's very important, because the moment I wobble it's a disaster ... I think people talk about what makes good leaders and it certainly is not intellect, it certainly is about how well you choose people and manage them and it's absolutely about stamina.'

another common failing is to give up at the first hurdle
If people don't hear and see commitment from you – if they see you reading from notes, avoiding awkward questions, or seeming unsure about the central proposition – they will assume that you haven't made up your mind. Picking up on this, they will never allow themselves to let go of the past order and embrace the new one. This is a recipe for becoming stuck in the second, difficult phase of the cycle, without being able to progress.

Another common failing is to give up at the first hurdle, to dip your toe in the water and, finding it chilly at first, to withdraw. Why is this so disastrous? Isn't some move towards engagement better than none at all? No. Not once you have announced your commitment to the wider organization. You can (and should) question, test and examine it as much as possible with your team and practitioners of best practice from other organizations, but once you have made up your mind and gone wide with it, there should be no turning back. Andy Green, again, is succinct about this:

> 'If you don't change *everything* then you won't get a change. So you have to be very very careful. There are going to be big moments where this will feel like dissonance to people, that is bound to happen as we go through this process, but what I can try and do is to be as consistent as possible about it.'

What you are doing is not a gentle shuffle towards higher levels of employee engagement: you are trying to institute a new order, whereby employee productivity, based on engagement, becomes part of the fabric of the organization, and engagement metrics form part of your measures of success. This cannot be done without a top-down change in attitudes, targets and strategy. To get a little way down this road and then give up will leave people confused. In practical terms, you will be leaving your organization unsure about the measures against which performance is judged – a surefire method of getting underperformance. Psychologically, every change programme that you leave uncompleted creates doubt, tension and lasting scars – and an organization that is considerably less willing to trust you in the future.

Do on Monday

How then do you find your commitment? Where do you go to discover whether engagement is for you?

1. Look at the evidence

We have drawn together in Chapter 2 a wealth of the evidence which underlies engagement. Re-read it with your own organization in mind. Checklist against it: are you fulfilling all the categories you should, or does a majority of your workforce comprise that 23% of the working population that is disengaged?

2. Observe engagement in your organization

The next step is to try to see engagement in action. A highly engaged team or organization should be something you recognize emotionally. To know what you're aiming at, you have to see it in practice. Look first within your own organization. Is there a department that delivers all the potential of all of its members? If you find it, look closely for what differentiates them from the rest of the company. Is it simply down to charismatic leadership on the part of the manager – and if so, what lessons can you learn from that manager? Or can you identify systems, habits, protocols they have installed to keep achievement levels high without draining the employees? Spend time with them; observe what works and what doesn't.

3. Observe engagement in the external world

You can also look outside your company. Find organizations which believe they are practising engagement. There's a small but growing list of companies that believe their financial and delivery success rests on high levels of engagement. Visit them. Most organizations are more than happy to show off.

Time spent watching high levels of engagement in action is valuable, not only because it can start to give you ideas relevant to your own circumstances but because you will need to create a personal vision of success, and that vision will be far more powerful if it is based on experience. In the same way that McLauren of Tesco became inspired by a visit to the US and decided to make what he saw there the future of food retailing in this country, you are far more likely to cling to an idea with missionary zeal if you have seen it working. You need a similar kind of belief. Many people find that it helps them to come up with an analogy, or a single powerful metaphor that they can hold on fast to as they work through the complicated mechanics of what needs to be done. Allan Leighton, for instance, often uses footballing analogies – a simple, powerful theme that can bring his point alive to everyone in his organization.

4. **Network with other interested people**

Try to talk about the topic to people in other organizations. If you have any business leaders you particularly admire, read what they have to say about how they relate to their employees. It is no coincidence that the books you find on the shelves of most great leaders are biographies of other great leaders. Look at the other side of the coin: if you know people who work for a boss they find inspiring, or for a company which has brought out the best in them, ask them about how this has happened on a day-to-day level. Look outside your own industry and outside your own sector. Be alert at all times for pockets of brilliance and measure them against your understanding of what engagement is.

5. **The process of creating your commitment**

In the first stage, the commitment you are looking for is simply a visceral conviction that engagement is a vital issue and one that you want to address. There is no need to start working out specifics.

The second stage is to work through any potential problems *before* you go public with it. Even an act as simple as sending out an employee questionnaire sends a message in itself, so you will need to tread carefully. This is where, as we have already seen, the team around you becomes critical. Working with them to develop the engagement programme should have two effects: improving the quality of that programme and engendering a feeling of co-ownership among the team. By the time you are ready to go public they should feel the same kind of conviction about it as you do.

8 Pillar Two – Get to the Front Line

Tony Blair is someone who understands the power of the personal. Anji Hunter, his aide, described his approach in her interview with us about her employer, the then Prime Minister:

> 'When [Tony] was trying to drive through change in the Labour party to make it an electable body ... we literally went on the road and talked to as many of the party members as possible and then we extended it to the public, we had meetings in village halls, in town halls, in leisure centres, in cinemas, in theatres.'

There are many reasons for getting out to the front line of your business and here Peter Erskine of Telefonica O2 Europe explains why he spends as much time as he can out on the front line:

> 'I think it's three things. One, the main reason, is to be in touch. Secondly, it gives licence to everyone else to do it. And thirdly, you don't half learn a lot back. I find the best way to hear what my businesses are really doing is to talk to customer services: they'll say, "did you know three weeks ago we changed this and do you know it is really annoying people?" – and I didn't know that and I bet the person who introduced it didn't know it was irritating the customer either.'

Richard Baker of Alliance Boots tries to get into stores every week:

> 'I try and talk to the people to find out what is going on. You're also role modelling the behaviour you want of others. Very rarely do I visit entirely on my own. Normally I ring the area manager and tell them, I'm going to pop into three of your stores if you can join me. At some point in the afternoon, we can catch up as "I'd like to hear your views". When your people see you doing this, then that's how stuff gets done around here. It becomes the norm. And when I leave the store, there'll be 50 calls to other people in other stores.'

Sir Andrew Turnbull saw the value of getting out to his front line as much as he could:

> 'Over a course of three years I am pretty sure I met with every department's leadership group. They have senior leadership away-days and I would wangle invitations to go. I also visited a large number of front-line offices around the country.'

Yet again, this is an area where leaders may believe they are performing well – almost everyone will refer to the value of getting down to the shop floor – but the figures tell a different story. Research from the Chartered Management Institute and DTI found that over 60% of followers report that their leaders are out of touch with how people are feeling, and that this remoteness and distance have a negative impact on morale and motivation levels.[69] Either leaders are not getting down to the front line as they should, or, when they are there, they are not connecting with the experience in a meaningful way.

Face to face, eyeball to eyeball

When Paul Stephenson, Chief Constable of Lancashire, was appointed he had one aim: to make it into the best possible police force (according to HM Inspector of Constabulary rankings). The effort to do this took him to the front line, often when he was least expected:

> 'I am not the best of sleepers and because I knew Lancashire like the back of my hand I would get up in the middle of the night and go out and visit [the stations] rather than read a book for several hours. I would go out at two or three o'clock in the morning. I loved it. I would see people I knew and I created the impression that at any moment there's a likelihood that I was going to be there ... I spent vast amounts of time talking to the key service deliverers who were the operational commanders.'

Of course, this is extreme. But it was not the only way in which Paul Stephenson demonstrated his commitment to the front line. Some of his initiatives – a series of roadshows at which both senior and junior ranks could see him stand up and deliver his vision – were relatively conventional in concept. Others broke the mould a little more. He introduced a rule that said that everyone from inspector level above had to do at least four hours of foot patrol a month ('no matter what their job was, including Chief Constable'). It was, he says, 'a symbolic thing', but he also measured participation:

> 'I'd go into the training school and there would be an inspector there and I would say, "tell me about your foot patrol this month", and everybody knew I would ask that question so it became . . . you might as well do it because he's going to ask.'

Stephenson also implemented a system whereby chief officers visited at least two victims of crime a week. It was clear to officers that it could be their case in any given week and that this was their opportunity to show their quality of service. The officers would get a follow-up e-mail the next day, congratulating them on the job they had done, or addressing poor performance. To reinforce the significance of response times, he himself went into the control room ('in full uniform with all the braid') and asked to be given the next job on the sheet ('you don't have to do that too many times before people start taking you seriously'). He held workshops regularly and ensured that any question asked of him would be answered by e-mail within 24 hours. In all, he instituted a culture and systems whereby the Lancashire police service felt as connected as possible to their leadership. And it bore results. Across the rankings, Paul's organization achieving its ambition, to be judged at the highest level of effective police service.

Paul Stephenson's commitment to the front line seems to be almost instinctive, but it is worth analyzing exactly what he was doing here. Through the roadshows, at which he ensured there was attendance from all ranks, he made himself *visible* to his people, speaking passionately and clearly about his aims for the organization. ('I've done the mission thing, I've done the vision thing, I'm bored with all of that: I've only got the ambition thing left and that is to be the best.') But he didn't stop there. He followed it up by personally visiting his service deliverers, often when they would least expect it, and demonstrated through his own behaviour that he was really *committed* to contracting the distance between the top and the bottom of the organization. Even this might have not had the impact that it did, however, had he not also taken steps to ensure that all senior officers mimic his commitment. What could have been dismissed as an ephemeral personal crusade was backed up by *systems* that ensured that all leadership followed his lead. ('It was a question of encouraging, exhorting, doing all the things one would do but putting systems and devices in place that are saying, this is the way leadership looks around here.')

leadership became very present to the organization

The result was that the leadership became very present to the organization:

> 'The chief officers did it, this encouraged other committed leaders to do the same and we became a much more visible organization, much more visible leadership.'

The front line believed – with good reason – that the leadership was connected to them and this in turn created momentum for Stephenson's simple ambition and associated change programme: 'to be the best'.

Compare all of this to how a typical leader often approaches his front-line duties: they turn up for their communication cascade, complete with satellite links, autocues, briefings, even rehearsals. They will write or, more probably, read the keynote article for the written communication material. They will have spent days developing their mission statement. They will deliver it in a one- or two-hour theatre-style communication session. Employees attending, of course, will not have read the written material and their behavioural change is then supposed to happen after one half-day workshop before being championed by their line manager who doesn't really get it.

By using – and maintaining – a direct line to the ground floor of the organization, you are giving yourself the opportunity to make your change programme real, personal, thought about throughout the organization. As Gill McLaren of Coca-Cola says:

> 'Most employees think "I want to make a difference" but can question, or not understand, how their job fits with the broader goals or vision of an organization. A good way to drive engagement with a vision is by deconstructing it into goals that are relevant to smaller groups or individuals and secure their active buy-in to these. Without this degree of personalization there is a risk that people will switch off or not connect with a company vision and it becomes too distant from their day-to-day work. If this is the case they will carry on doing what they were doing before and the company goals will not be met.'

Peter Erskine describes the same phenomenon:

> 'I don't meddle too much, my CEOs run the business, but if I go up to a call centre it never ceases to amaze me – if you sit in groups rather than just talk to the management and you ask them a question they really love that, they really feel they have started to understand a bit more where we are headed, where we are. And I encourage all my people to do that.'

It could be argued, of course, that to take interaction with the front line to the extent that Paul Stephenson does runs the risk of making the organization overmanaged and paranoid, unable to stand on its own feet. Interestingly, Stephenson has given thought to whether what he terms this kind of 'intrusive management' can co-exist with a drive to empowerment and has come to the following conclusion:

> 'I describe intrusive management as the thing we all have a right to expect ... I have a right to expect my boss to intrude in my professional life , .. because that's the only way you can find out just how damn good I am, to say "well done". I tried to use that because I do believe intrusive management is necessary to create successful organizations.'

For him, the equation is flipped on its head: far from being stultified by scrutiny from above, the scrutiny works as a spur: the front line, in fact, has a *right* to expect this level of attention from the leadership.

Does size matter?

Of course, it is possible to argue that the Lancashire police force is only 5500 people strong and that in an organization of that scale it is easier to make your mark. Many of our interviewees agreed that finding the time to spend on the front line was one of the hardest things in their job. David Barnes of AstraZeneca makes the point even more strongly:

> 'Where I failed and everyone else will probably I think fail is that you can't get round frequently enough.'

Tony Blair took the principles of personal contact and applied them as extensively as possible. Lord King and Colin Marshall, during the famous transformation of British Airways, asked everyone in the organization to go through a customer service session. This exercise would have been useful in itself, but the point was driven home by the fact that one or other of them turned up to 90% of these sessions. To make this kind of personal appearance rams home the importance of the message. Take advantage of occasions when groups of staff will be gathered together.

take advantage of occasions when groups of staff will be gathered together

You should also be looking to reinforce your presence with systems that ensure that all your leadership is amplifying your personal voice. It is important to do this to avoid the danger that the change process becomes too strongly associated with one person, a possibility that Andy Green of BT highlights:

> 'We went out on the road and I spent a huge amount of personal time in front of groups of 30 to 200 people trying to touch as many people in as many parts of the world as possible with a sense of leadership. This is a risk in my view in a big organization as people may seek to identify the recovery story with an individual . . . but if you are in a period of high change then the importance of actually communicating in your words to people is crucial.'

In the Lancashire police force Paul Stephenson guards against his presence being overly central to his programme by making sure that his senior officers reflect his behaviour, and that all activity at the front line is systemic, noted and reacted to. In this way, he is not just reducing the height of his own ivory tower, he is reducing the height of them all.

Intelligence gathering

In a recent newspaper interview, Sir Philip Green described how he returned to the shopfloor of BHS after a dinner, because something was niggling at him. A gift product he had had high hopes for wasn't selling and he wanted to know why:

'I thought: "That's not possible." So when I went back in at 11.40, I went to find it. There was a sticker on it saying, "Buy one get one free". I rang [the manager responsible] at 12.15 that night and said: "Call me." When he called at 7.15 in the morning, I said: "Here's a clue – buy one get one free. It's a present. Nobody wants a present that's free – and nobody wants to give a present they didn't buy. You do buy one get one frees on tubes of toothpaste, not gifts." I said to him, "Take the sticker off and sales will go up 45%." He did, and they already have.'[70]

It may seem extraordinary that a businessman of such enormous wealth and power would take such pains to discover what the problem was with a product that, at best, would make him a relatively small additional profit. That is missing the point. What Green was demonstrating was an instinctive, almost obsessive, desire to be connected to the ground floor of his large organization. (He also makes it a habit to walk down Oxford Street on a regular basis, checking out his own, and his rivals', shop windows.) But here the reason is not just to be a visible leader, it is primarily to discover what is going on. This is environment scanning at its most rudimentary. Usually, this will be done not by looking at products on the shelves but by talking to people.

As Richard Baker of Boots puts it:

'You need to give your organization a damn good listening to.'

The point is to root everything you do in the reality as it is felt by all the levels of the organization. It is horribly time-consuming, but necessary. Although there are research techniques open to you, the constant problem for senior leaders is to know what is really happening on the lower levels. Adam Crozier of the Royal Mail, another great believer in the necessity of getting yourself out there, puts it like this:

'Otherwise how would you know [whether what you are saying is right] because you have never seen it for yourself? The problem with just taking management's word for it is that people talk a lot about the facts when you are on top of an organization; you get presented with various people's versions of the facts. By the time they have got through these iterations, through all the different levels, they probably look very little like what they started off as. And that is why you have to keep ducking down again and seeing it for yourself: is this really what's happening out there or is it actually completely different?'

On top of the blurring effect caused by repeated iterations up the levels lies the problem that, when you are in senior leadership, people often simply won't tell you bad news. At the time of writing, senior civil servants in the Home Office have described a culture of fear where they are frightened to relay bad news. Peter Erskine identifies this problem and suggests the seemingly obvious yet underutilized solution:

'Walk about and listen – by that I mean not just talking to your immediate reports. People are all guilty of telling you what they think you want to hear. Try and find people who are brave enough to tell you how it is – and they are there.'

People just won't take the risk to speak truth to power: and the results can be disastrous. During the First World War, aides around Field

Marshall Douglas Haig were unwilling to tell him about the serious-
ness of the weather before the battle of Passchendaele (he wasn't
inclined to encourage critical feedback), so they didn't – one of the
factors that led to the grossly high casualties of that battle.

The view from below

Personal fact finding is critical (not least because you cannot hope to
have a successful strategy without a realistic picture of the status quo).
As far as employee engagement is concerned, you must be able to
demonstrate to your workforce that you have an understanding of
what challenges they may be facing. As Adam Crozier says:

> 'You have to start by having a very adult conversation at all levels of the business,
> particularly the front line, about either the problem you are trying to address or the
> opportunity you are trying to take advantage of. You've got to state that in very clear
> language with no sugar coating at all so that people really get it because my
> experience is the front-line people know the problems long before anyone else in the
> business because they see it in front of themselves every day. And when they hear
> management saying, don't worry, the business is doing fine, rather than being
> reassured by that actually that sends nightmare signals to them because what that
> says is you don't know what you're doing. And if you try and pretend it's alright and
> sugar coat it, they just start to lose faith and lose confidence in the organization.'

Nothing crushes your followers' confidence in you more than asserting
all is well when the front line knows that it isn't.

Get ideas

Drucker said: look for the unexpected. You will almost certainly find it
at the front line rather than in head office. Think of it not as the
bottom end of your organization but the sharp end. It is those who
deal with the customers every day who know them best, as Peter
Erskine recognizes. As referred to in Chapter 5 on top teams, one of

his UK CEOs has set up a shadow board, drawn from volunteers across the organization, which the board consults on any decision which will affect the customer.

it is the people at the front line who have the closest view of their jobs

Watching the organization at a nuts-and-bolts level can sometimes bring a clarity that is lacking if you remain constantly in the realms of management. You may also pick up some ideas: it is after all the people at the front line who have the closest view of their jobs. Here is Gill McLaren of Coca-Cola on the subject:

> 'We were asking the guys on the production line about how they thought we could improve the efficiency of the line and they had loads of ideas.'

There is a well of knowledge and expertise at the front line. Make sure you are engaging with it.

Do on Monday

1. **Establish a strong internal communications infrastructure**

   You need to ensure upward/downward feedback, including regular sensing mechanisms. These can include surveys, sensing groups – regular meetings with a panel of colleagues – or for example Royal Mail's 'Ask Allan Tell Allan', an echo from Allan Leigton's Asda days, a website at the Royal Mail where employees can post queries or ideas and be sure of getting a response. The aim is to open up routes for direct employee questions, feedback and opinions. Make use of the technology available; websites on the corporate intranet which can offer accurate information on a hot or sensitive topic; use of blogs in which management participates; video diary boxes, where individuals can drop in to record their views on a particular issue, which can be effective so long as you also put in place a mechanism for responding. More low-tech, but also effective, systems might include distributing 'myth-buster' postcards to counter the negative rumours that can float around an organization – one side shows the myth, the other side gives the true facts. Letter boxes specifically for employees to post suggestions or ideas can be placed in offices or at entry points. You need to bear in mind, however, that introducing such mechanisms for communication is, in itself, sending a strong message. The message will be a positive one so long as the channels for communication are consistently attended to. If they are neglected, the message will very quickly become negative: the sight of an uncollected letter box full of unread employee suggestions will very quickly communicate a lack of interest.

2. **Remember your behavioural leadership**

   Whatever you say when you are at the front line, people are probably paying at least as much attention, if not more, to the way you act. Be aware of the subliminal messages you might be sending.

3. **Just do it**

   There are all sorts of reasons not to, particularly the pressure of time – none of them is an excuse for not getting to the front line.

4. **Amplify the effect**

   Make sure that each contact gets known about beyond the immediate area you touch.

5. **On occasion, get to the front line when it is least expected**

   Don't be predictable.

6. **Regularly visit customers with colleagues**

   Engage with colleagues at the customer interface.

7. **Insist on leadership colleagues following**

   Establish your pattern of getting to the front line and then insist that your colleagues follow suit.

8. **Find the truth-tellers**

   Identify a handful of colleagues at different levels whom you can trust to tell you what is really happening on the front line, even if it is bad news.

9. **Be straight, treat the front line like adults**

   Nothing crushes confidence more than asserting all is well when the front line knows that it isn't.

10. **Abandon any 'traditional' communication approaches for the next six months**

    If you are using lots of set-pieces with autocues and rehearsals, stop and try different approaches for a period.

11. **Make yourself accessible online to the front line**

    Make sure that you have the support to be able to reply promptly and authoritatively.

NOTES

[69] DTI/Chartered Management Institute Research. A number of quantitative and qualitative surveys outlined in the DTI publication titled 'Inspired leadership, insights into people who inspire exceptional performance'. First published August 2004.

[70] *Evening Standard,* 24 October 2006.

9 Pillar Three – Loudhailers to Conversations

Consider this: if people believe that they have a hand in creating something (co-invention), there is a much greater likelihood that they co-own it. Co-ownership of a strategy heightens the levels of engagement. An employee's feeling that they have some form of input into decision making in their departments (whether or not they actually do) ranks as the fourth highest driver of engagement.[71] If you can harness this sense of co-invention to create co-ownership with your people, you will increase levels of engagement and, by extension, profitability. It requires the mindset to move from 'me' to 'we'. It requires leaders to stop shouting louder and louder at their employees in the hope they will eventually get the message. It requires a starting point for change to come in the form of a 'conversation'.

Currently there is an overriding sense that the 'big stuff' is happening somewhere else in the business. Only 55% of the European workforce believe they can openly express their views within the organization; only a third feel that they are kept informed about how the organization is performing financially.[72] Only 35% of the UK workforce feel that their senior management effectively communicates the reasons for important business decisions.[73] Only 26% of the European workforce agreed that their organizations help employees to understand how they impact on financial importance; 62% were less than clear on this crucial point. Far from feeling any sense of co-ownership, employees are feeling shut out.[74]

There is an increasing body of evidence that 'coercion' (as in, 'if you're late again, I'm leaving without you') has a negative effect and even 'rational persuasion' ('if you continue to be late the effects on our business will be catastrophic') has little if any effect. What is most effective is 'relationship referencing' ('*we* need to help *our* business by ensuring that we arrive for meetings together, how can *we* do this?'). These conclusions are statistically substantiated in the work of Robert Cialdini, Regents Professor at Arizona State University, among others. Or as Peter Erskine puts it:

> 'My view is that with the kind of people we want, even down to the people in our call centres answering the telephone, particularly as they are British, you can't tell them what to do. What you have to do is try and make them feel a part of how you arrived at the decision and, if you can, get them bought into performance improvement.'

Cialdini argues that simply changing the terminology from 'me' to 'we' changes the mindset. The issue becomes the relationship, *not* the behaviour.

the issue becomes the relationship, *not* **the behaviour**

In one organization, we recently saw a very powerful and influential group HR director talk with his top 150 about their challenges ahead. Not once did he talk about 'I' or 'me' or, for that matter, 'you'. It was always 'we' … 'the challenges we face … we know … we need to move forward in this direction'. The audience were with him. In the same organization, we saw another leader use 'I' and 'me' and 'you' a lot and, as a result, there was a distance between him and his audience. It grated. This allies with Jim Collins's research in *Good to Great*[62] that found that high-performing leadership is without ego an absolute dedication to results, always taking the rap when things go wrong and never taking personal acclaim (i.e. giving it to others) when things go right.

Martin Sorrell, CEO of WPP, has identified this as the sense of 'emotional connection' to the organization from which engagement can be built, a connection which is perhaps relatively easy to achieve at the very senior levels of an organization, but not necessarily automatic further down:

> 'Of course, I have an emotional link to the company. Now what you're trying to do with companies . . . is to build a similar emotional connection between the people and the company, like the one you have to with a brand or product.'

An individual is far more likely to feel an emotional attachment to a course of action if they feel they played a part in its creation and are therefore far more likely to give their discretionary energy to it. A sense of co-creation fosters a sense of co-ownership, as Eric Peacock, Chairman of Baydon Hill PLC, points out:

> 'Over a period of a few months we invest about five or six days of work with groups of people from all levels of the business, debating, arguing, shaping. It is very much a cooperative effort about what we think is important around here. What we stand for, what we would like to be remembered for as an organization . . . and as a result the output has got a great sense of co-ownership'

Unsurprisingly, individuals are more likely to champion a course of action if they feel they had a hand in shaping it. Anji Hunter, of No 10 Downing Street and BP, makes the point:

> 'The really smart leader or manager is the one that knows precisely what they want but they let other people – the ones that are going to be responsible for getting it and driving it through – think it was their idea.'

Listening to the workforce provides valuable insights; more importantly for the engagement agenda, it gives the workforce a sense of control and of choice. Ian Smith, SVP Oracle UK, told us of a visit he had taken to one of his customer's call centres. While there, he fell into a conversation with an employee. The employee was dissatisfied: his boss had asked him to present at a unit meeting. He had been asked to prepare a 15-minute presentation, which he had done in his spare time at home and practised in front of his family so that he would be completely ready. When he got into work that day he discovered the unit meeting had been cancelled because of a call centre being down in another part of the region. When Ian asked the call centre manager about this afterwards, the manager was surprised:

> 'He said it was obvious – "there was a call centre down, we had to cancel all the team meetings." I said, "why didn't you get the people together and say, here's what happened, what do you think we should do? What would they have said? Would they have said, oh we'll go ahead with the unit meeting and sod the customers? Or would they have said, no let us reschedule our unit meeting some other time? Do you think the people would be more motivated or less motivated if you let them make the decision, if you trusted them? If they didn't make the right decision, so be it, that's learning for you. But my guess would be that they would say, let's defer the meeting so the customers are served, but it would be their decision."'

We sometimes hear the reaction 'I haven't got time for all this buy-in stuff', 'I'd like to pay attention to it but I don't have the hours in the day to do it'. But if you recognize the power of engagement for success you are going to have to take this aspect seriously. It forms the basis of the employee's emotional connection to their work, a connection which cannot be faked or bypassed.

However, it is also clear that there is a time when the debate and dialogue must stop and the conclusions must be clearly set out to everyone – loudhailered – in order to create alignment.

How do you set about creating this co-ownership?

Story telling

The power of the narrative to engage people's attention is universal and timeless. Come out of management jargon and make your aims and your strategy understandable. Define the narrative with enthusiasm and emotion and you have the most effective internal communications tool an organization can mobilize.

Consciously take your narrative back to the roots of the organization. David Bell (DCSF), one of our interviewees, recalls the power of story telling:

'I try to draw on the traditions of the organization. The history of school inspection goes back to 1839 and I often say, do you realize that in 1905 the then senior inspector was saying this. And it's partly about myth making, story telling within the organization. And celebration of almost-icons of the organization. People who have just made such a difference. People who are doing a fantastic job and that sense of passion and enthusiasm.'

Terry Smith of Microsoft emphasized the way that his organization perceives itself as follows:

'At the start it was Bill and a bunch of bright people saying, we're going to set out to do something different that you can chart right the way through our history, that is what actually keeps people in the company and drives and fulfils people.'

James Crosby, CEO HBOS 1999–2006, also talked about stories, this time projecting them into the future:

'So your strategy is an ever-changing series of hypotheses which change by virtue of a story and you tell a story . . . that is what we said six months ago and of course this has happened and therefore this is what we now say. It's not a u-turn, it's a story. And you're also working from it and I think that is very important as well.'

Make it personal

As Alex Wilson, Head of HR at BT, says:

'If you can't make this thing personal to you you're dead . . . you've got to make it personal to every one of them . . . they've got to know why it is important to them, they've got to do something, them as an individual, not as units of 5000 or 10,000 but one by one by one.'

The way you make it personal to your workforce is to start by showing that it is personal to you (which you do by revealing yourself, and also by behavioural leadership: you need to live your commitments).

Lucian Hudson, Chairman of the Tavistock Institute and Director of Communication at the FCO, sees it like this:

> 'You need to pepper what you say to teams and individuals with some element of self-disclosure which then makes them feel more relaxed about realizing that they have had to prop themselves up, and can therefore focus on what strengths to lever.'

By revealing something of yourself, your persuasion becomes more powerful. We were present recently when a Chief Constable took his top team through their business plan for the next three years. He had spent a lot of time

by revealing something of yourself, your persuasion becomes more powerful

on it. It was very clear, full of evidence and targets. But there was little reaction in the room. The CC was disappointed. Then, one of the participants asked, 'That's all well and good, sir, but what do you really care about in this?' The Chief Constable paused, thought about it, and what followed was spoken with passion – 'I hate the effect the criminals have on young people, how they role model ways of life that steal people's futures and destroy the possibility of a positive and worthwhile life.' You could feel the buzz coming back into the conversation as his colleagues responded and the discussion took off.

You need to find the metaphors and the stories that touch people. Expose your values. Sir David Varney emphasized the importance of this:

> 'I think you can tell, you have a horse-sense of whether somebody connects with you. I see people whose presentational skills I would say might rank pretty low, but who convey a sense of integrity that they have thought very deeply about the issue and they have something to say which affects the lives of the people they are talking to.'

Draw on the values of your organization

Tap into the 'purpose beyond profit' that you have identified. It is about meaning, about the difference to be made beyond the mere production of goods and services. For instance, Unilever has recently built its internal and external brand around 'vitality', a sense of purpose beyond the manufacturing and sale of consumer goods. The mission of the Healthcare Commission in the UK is 'to inform, inspect, improve', with the underlying purpose of helping improve healthcare and thus the wellbeing of UK citizens. These are simple but powerful values around which people align.

Relationship referencing

Share issues within small groups. Listen to the next meeting you are in, particularly a leadership team meeting. You will probably be listening to a debate in which opinions are traded and points of difference set out. Try to shift this to a genuine dialogue in which there would be more listening, less advocacy, more inquiry, more determination to explore differences and find common ground.

Be a winner

We know that winning and engagement are closely connected.

If your organization is not 'winning', then set milestones on the path to become a winner and achieve your milestones, however insignificant they might be. Create the organizational habit of delivering on promises, of climbing up a winning ladder to an overall sense of 'winning'.

Do on Monday

1. **Watch your language**

   The words 'I' and 'me' need to be banned from the lexicon. Use 'we' and 'us' instead.

2. Learn the basics

Step back a pace and make sure that you understand the capabilities that underpin the conversations you have with your workforce. In terms of the Myers Briggs dichotomy of thinking (constructing the logic, seeing the argument, looking at the data) and feeling (stepping in the shoes of others, orientation to values, empathy, etc.) types, there is a huge preponderance in senior teams towards the former. There is usually very little 'F' in the room, with the result that leadership teams frequently pay insufficient attention to the key questions of 'where do our people stand on this, what would be their reactions, how do we engage them effectively?'. You need actively to counteract this. For example, one leadership team actually created an 'F' stick which was waved around at key decision points.

Getting from 'me' to 'we' requires skills of dialogue. Too often in leadership teams the predominant style is that of trading 'points of view' loudhailering, rather than just displaying the skills of advocacy and inquiry. You need to develop conscious practices to build in more 'F'. Senior management meetings might start with questions such as 'How is the mood out there?', 'What do we need to do about it?'

3. From rational to emotional

Find ways to expand the space in your conversation so that there is more emotional content; ensure there is more than just a rational sequence of required action. Plan to use a mix of the emotional chords such as personal disclosure, demonstration of values, sense of personal esteem, growth, development, excitement and passion in people's roles, winning – and then combine them all in a story.

4. From debate to dialogue

Identify the subjects when you need your team to think deeply together to get to the root of the issue, to shape and explore common ground. Challenge them to avoid the mere trading of different points of view. Encourage lots of inquiry, accompanied by measured advocacy. Model this yourself.

5. **Plan from the audience's perspective**

Adopt some simple disciplines when planning your conversations with your people. What is the desired result? What will be on the audience's minds? What messages are critical? What style do you need to adopt to convey these messages? As Stephen Covey[75] says: 'Seek first to understand, then to be understood.'

6. **Get out to the front line**

Time should be spent 'out in the field', connecting with the workforce in their environment and observing at close hand the challenges they face. See Chapter 8, 'Get to the front line'.

NOTES

[71] Towers Perrin Global Workforce Study, 2005 – UK data compendium.
[72] Towers Perrin Global Workforce Study, 2005 – UK data compendium.
[73] Towers Perrin Global Workforce Study, 2005 – UK data compendium.
[74] Towers Perrin Global Workforce Study, 2005 – UK data compendium.
[75] Covey, Stephen (2004) *The Seven Habits of Highly Effective People*, Simon & Schuster.

10 Pillar Four – The Reservoir of Wellbeing

The employment deal

Catering to an employee's overall wellbeing, creating goodwill, is one means by which we enter into a 'deal' with our employees. It sends a message: we are attending to your needs so that you can attend to ours. Around three out of ten employees work for organizations where they know what is expected of them and what in return they can expect from their organization. But that leaves seven out of ten employees feeling less than good about this relationship.[75] The employee should feel fulfilled, appreciated and developed and cared for; in return they are encouraged to respond in kind and invest their discretionary energy.

Financial remuneration plays an important part in the employment deal, but you should be wary of thinking it represents the whole of the employer's side of the bargain. If you are familiar with London, picture yourself standing on High Holborn. If you were to go one mile in an easterly direction, you would find yourself in the City, a work environment where the pace is hectic, the hours are long, the job security is low, but the pay can be enormous. If you walked one mile towards the south, you would find yourself in Whitehall, where the pay is considerably lower, but job security is better, the pension is safer and the sense of contribution to society is far stronger. What drives people is a continuum that varies sector to sector, job to job, person to person. People may take jobs to polish their CVs, to climb higher on the ladder, to make as much money

what drives people is a continuum that varies sector to sector

as possible. So, from an employee perspective, what are the components that they can expect from their organization in this 'deal'? There is a full list of engagement drivers in Chapter 2.

However, in the constantly busy world of management, ten drivers are too many to focus on. In order to bind them into a cohesive strategy for engagement we can synthesize them into four key statements:

1 I believe rewards are fairly distributed.

2 I feel respected and listened to.

3 I am improving my skills.

4 I believe my organization has a sincere interest in supporting me.

The theme that runs through this synthesis is that of employee wellbeing. Employees naturally have a reservoir of energy and goodwill with regards to their job, a reservoir that is vital to the harnessing of

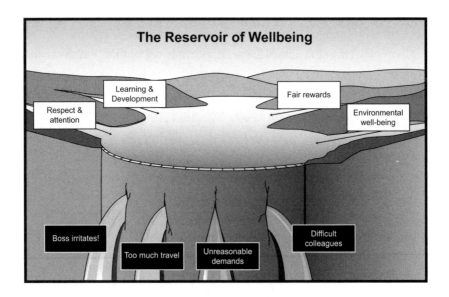

Figure 10.1 Reservoir of Wellbeing

engagement. The normal day-to-day demands of the vast majority of jobs tend to drain away this resource: rushed deadlines, faulty IT, difficult colleagues and all the other stresses of the workplace sap away both energy and commitment, so it is vital that the 'wellbeing reservoir' is continually topped up. It is hard to put your all into the next big marketing push, say, when your last pay increase seemed rather harsh, you have not had systemic help with your development (there are no funds and no management time), your last idea was rejected out of hand and your PC keeps crashing. A central component of the engagement agenda involves paying attention to the different ways in which the reservoir can be refreshed.

1 Fair rewards

As we have said, remuneration does not comprise the whole of the employment deal. Indeed, as we pointed out in Part One, salary and pay issues come surprisingly low on the list of overall engagement drivers: usually ranked about sixth or seventh. However, this is generally because the pay of such respondents is within an acceptable bandwidth and becomes, to a certain extent, a hygiene factor. As Ian Smith of Oracle UK says: 'Money is a satisfier or a desatisfier, it is not a motivator.' Nevertheless, we come to it first, partly because it is perhaps the first part of the engagement deal that employers naturally think of, and partly because it is a hygiene factor that, if you get wrong, will constitute a significant leak in your wellbeing reservoir. A general theme in rewards is that financial rewards are there for you to avoid getting wrong (demotivating through a lack of perceived fairness) and non-financial rewards are there to get right (to really motivate people with).

It doesn't sound remotely revolutionary to propose that a perception of *unfair* rewards will cause employees to withdraw effort. Most employers would consider this to be no more than common sense. Why, then, did only 27% of the employees surveyed across Europe react favourably to the statement 'criteria for determining salary and wage levels are fair and consistent'? This means that 73% of the work-force *do not* see a direct link between the performance they deliver and the rewards that they will be given. Similarly, only 32% consider they are compensated fairly compared with those around them.[76] In the UK, 46% of respondents always or frequently found decisions relating to promotions or pay policies frustrating, and a huge 67%[77] of people surveyed believe that their company tolerates poor performance by not removing the poor performers. Even allowing for the natural human propensity to be dissatisfied with one's lot, these are worrying statistics.

We are not saying that all of this is easy: matching employee desires in this area with their employers' capabilities is a perennial problem. And it is becoming increasingly difficult. Look around. A maelstrom of change, driven by economic and regulatory forces, is taking place and there are no signs that this will abate. Remuneration in the form of equity compensation, retirement plans and benefits is likely to suffer, and employees worldwide are highly tuned in to this.

Employees can see, and are experiencing, the downside of the low financial value, higher risk or greater effort required to manage their current or future wellbeing. These factors combine to give a huge potential danger of diminished commitment to the organization and less engagement in work. However, organizations that take a thoughtful, thorough approach to such change can emerge with an improved financial position which is generated by an engaged work-force. It need not be an either/or equation.

Remuneration packages, and organizations' approach to them, will of course vary enormously, a fact demonstrated in the different approaches we heard from the business leaders we interviewed.

> 'Discretionary effort is garnered through the achievement of social esteem. However, monetary bonuses make it real and thought about.'
>
> Sir Rob Margetts, Chairman, Legal and General

'People frequently reflect upon "Does the business recognize and appreciate the job I've done? Am I getting the support, thanks and praise for the contribution I'm making?" Giving positive recognition to individuals has a major impact on their overall job satisfaction and actively celebrating success is a key driver of a positive work culture.'

Gill McLaren, Coca-Cola

'I used to like bringing people on quite low pay and advance them very rapidly. Because if they are really doing well, the incentive effect of stepped and rapid pay increases as they learned and as they got better was intoxicating.'

Martin Taylor, Syngenta

'The best thing is shares. The best thing we do is when we hit our profit in a year, and the next 25 million goes to the employees. So last year we hit our profit plus 25 million so all our employees, me included, got £350 worth of shares. When you hear your driver talking about the share price rising and why has the share price gone down today, you know he is involved. I found shares the best motivator.'

Mike Turner, CEO, BAE Systems

'I don't think it [financial reward] incentivizes people a great deal, at least with the size of bonus we were offering, but it has a beneficial side effect. It gives more purpose to the process of performance appraisal. If there is some money at stake, however small, people will make the process much more thorough.'

Sir Andrew Turnbull, head of the Home Civil Services, 2002–2005.

'I wanted a scheme that motivated everybody from top to bottom, there could be some bells and whistles but essentially one that was the same ... You could have half your bonus in cash but you were mandated to put 50% into shares. If you held the shares for the four years or the three years, the company would match and put another one for one. Buy one get one free. And that worked spectacularly well . . . that was for the sake of argument 25% of their annual salary and with a rising share price it could well become 50% or 60% and did, of their annual salary. And wherever we had places where people had to log on to the intranet, the first thing they saw was the share price. They watched that share price like a hawk and it worked spectacularly well.'

Sir David Barnes, AstraZeneca

There is clearly no hard and fast rule that can be applied across the board. However, almost all the feedback we received from business leaders confirmed what we already suspected: as far as engagement is concerned, two principles have emerged as vital:

❖ first, that rewards are perceived as fair, and

❖ second, that they provide the employee with a kind of 'emotional equity'. That is, they strive to tie the employee into the success of the company as closely as possible. To achieve this, we must think in terms of all aspects of reward and not just the pay and benefits side.

Fairness

It is not enough that rewards *are* fair and consistent; what is necessary is that they are *perceived* to be so.

'It's got to be fair: if people think they're being underpaid that's no good because you start with disgruntled employees. But as long as they think it is fair, you're ok. We try and be flexible. We have people working from home, we have job sharing. We do extended hours. I've got people working four days a week but they do nine-hour days on four days, then take the Friday off and they've got a long weekend. We're very flexible like that and those are the sort of things that make Camelot a great place to work.'

Dianne Thompson, CEO, Camelot

As noted in Davenport and Roberts' article, social scientists might separate out this 'fairness' into three categories:

❖ **Procedural**: the perceived equity of the processes by which rewards are allocated or reward systems are changed.

❖ **Distributive**: the degree to which the outcome conforms to the individual's sense of worth.

❖ **Interpersonal**: the consideration, respect and sensitivity that people receive when rewards are delivered or changes made.[78]

As Ian Watmore, former Head of Accenture in the UK and now Head of the Delivery Unit at the Cabinet Office, points out:

> 'I have seen people get really upset by relatively large amounts of pay rise/bonus/reward of some description because they find out that somebody else got more and it ceases to have value as an amount of money and starts to become a number . . . so money is about absolutism and relativism and actually the relativity is almost more important than the absolute once you get to a certain level.'

It is highly demotivating, not to say destructive, if employees feel that they are being penalized while a colleague – or a superior – is cashing in.

Note: fairness does not necessarily, or even usually, mean equality. Do not be scared by the prospect of injecting differentiation into the deal, i.e. earmarking the greater propor-

fairness does not necessarily, or even usually, mean equality

tion of your reward for the high performers. The research shows that high-performing companies are more likely to differentiate. Employees actually recognize, accept and need to see differentiation – it helps to manage scarce resources and it sends a powerful message about performance. Rewards Change and Challenges surveys indicate that the percentage of organizations which differentiated rewards significantly increased from 15% in 1999 to 39% in 2003 and continues to rise. As we shall see in more detail in our Consequences pillar, if you care about engagement, you need to yoke your reward schemes to engagement metrics. It is very demotivating to see the timeserver at the next desk reaping the same rewards that you do for half the effort.

Emotional equity

Beyond a sense of fairness, which should probably be the minimum measure your employees can expect from you, rewards can help to engender that sense of emotional investment in the organization which is so crucial to engagement. This is what David Barnes and Mike Turner were doing when they ensured that all their employees had shares in the company. This is not necessarily an approach which will be appropriate or desirable for every organization. What should be distilled from it is that the ideal remuneration package connects the employee to the organization's success. What is primarily required for this from an employee point of view is a measure of choice, engendering a feeling of competence and control.

Davenport and Roberts, citing social scientists such as Eisenberger, point out that employees view their reward portfolios holistically, forming generalized impressions about how much the organization values their contributions and cares about their wellbeing. In a sense, they make a rational assessment of reward value and then bridge to an emotional conclusion about how the organization demonstrates concern for their welfare. They also note that there is an employee willingness to make trade-offs in their portfolio of rewards. The organization, therefore, needs to gather data about how employees trade off the different elements of the rewards portfolio. The data will indicate the relative importance of changes to that portfolio and allow preparation to be made for employee reaction. Consequently, decisions can be made about both the optimum *level* and *allocation* of investment across the whole portfolio of rewards (base pay, variable pay, health benefits, paid time off, retirement benefits, learning and development, etc.). The engagement impact can be established by asking the trade-off questions.

The 'recognition' element of any rewards package is undoubtedly a valuable tool. The human need and desire for respect and appreciation can be harnessed to focus energy and commitment. Spot bonuses or other unexpected rewards can be used to incentivize performances, so long as they always obey the principles of fairness and objectivity. Vodafone's 'Legends Programme', whereby a group of 30 employees, nominated by their colleagues, are selected each year for a holiday, combines reward with peer recognition. Personalized rewards can have a perceived worth far higher than their financial value: a key employee of Sir Digby Jones at CBI whose children were eager rugby fans was rewarded with a set of tickets for a match, a gesture that far outweighed its street value in terms of gratitude earned.

If carefully designed, a targeted remuneration approach can raise the levels of engagement in the organization. For instance, our global workforce study shows that well-crafted elements of the pay package (competitive base pay, base pay increases tied to individual perform-ance, bonuses tied to individual performance, bonuses tied to company performance) can have a positive impact on employee engagement to the tune of 22%; adding successful management of line of sight elements (managers helping employees understand their impact on company success, managers providing clear goals and direc-tion, the provision of challenging and achievable performance/bonus goals) can raise this to 35%; and the further provision of an empow-ering work environment (employees having appropriate decision-making authority, employees having resources needed to perform high-quality work) can raise this further to 50%.

The fallacy of leadership

When constructing pay structures, organizations should consciously strive to look at the question of remuneration (and all other questions in the wellbeing reservoir) from *the point of view of the employee*. There is a tendency in senior management to assume that everybody in the organization wants the same things that they do. It is often not true. People will have different expectations depending on a host of things:

their personality type and thinking preferences, their values and the stage they are at in their career. To an extent, organizations can anticipate the various stages that a typical employee might go through, for instance:

- ❖ 'I'm 24, single and loving it!' (Give me cash, I want a cool car, I don't want insurance/long-term savings, etc., I want it all and I want it now)

- ❖ 'I'm 32 and about to tie the knot' (I need to start boosting my pension savings, I need disability insurance and life insurance, I want to get my spouse some medical cover too, we could use a computer at home)

- ❖ 'I'm 45 with two (hyperactive) kids' (I'm putting loads into my pension now, we are spending a fortune on child care, I need more holiday).

A company which recognizes these demographic groups and tailors rewards accordingly would certainly be helping its employees towards engagement. However, we would argue that the truly engaging organization does more and recognizes people's *individual* needs and preferences. What of the father who has his children early? He may be 24 yet *very* concerned with life insurance and the ability to work from home, and by the time he reaches 45 might well be ready for that cool car and some cash. Clearly, no system in the world can allow for all the possible variables and no sane senior manager would be able or willing to keep track of all the different demands of his employees. This is where middle management comes in. As we shall see in more detail in the next chapter, empowering the middle management is a vital component of engagement. This is just one aspect of that. The key here is to set up a framework that promotes fair rewards and to engage managers to work with it and within it.

Managers need to be part of the process: both listened to and empowered. They need to be provided with the appropriate information and build their skills to be an effective conduit. Success involves providing managers with a thorough toolkit (backed up by training) to understand and then convey new arrangements, anticipate and answer employee questions and know where to go for detailed process and design information. Davenport and Roberts argue that managers can contribute to a successful reward change effort in three significant ways:

❖ Participating in reward system design and restructuring. For instance conducting a series of focus groups to obtain managers' input about employees' likely responses to changes in their benefits packages.

❖ Re-establishing an energizing deal in all their interactions with their people – this entails understanding the relative nature of the way in which reward systems are viewed.

❖ Demonstrating individual fairness, particularly in their interaction with individual employees. To implement this last point it is necessary that the line manager demonstrates (i) consideration of the individual's viewpoint, (ii) consistent application of criteria, (iii) justification for any changes, (iv) truthful communications, and (v) courtesy in delivering the message.[79]

In other words, within an overall structure that is fair (and one, as we shall see in the final pillar, whose metrics are linked to engagement), managers should be given levers. Their voice should be heard and should be seen to be heard by the levels below them. Clearly, this means investing a level of trust in the managerial cadre – something that, as we shall see in Pillar Five, is vital for the engagement agenda on many levels. The challenge is to build a system which is institutionally fair, but which allows managerial discretion: managers must be able to use all managerial levers – spot bonuses, non-financial rewards, advancement and praise – to help tailor each employee's rewards package as closely as possible to their needs and to bind their interests as closely as possible with those of the organization.

Do on Monday (for fair rewards)

1. **Lead by example**

   Deal with poor performers in your office and among your direct reports. Have the tough conversations. Give clear feedback and set improvement targets where required. Be clear about what you think and set it in a positive context (this can be done). Be very clear how you define the successful outcomes you require.

2. **Set the tone**

   You can give one-off financial bonuses and/or other rewards. Let your direct reports know you are doing this.

3. **Acknowledge success**

   Make a special effort to acknowledge success in public. Acknowledgement is best directed towards teams but can be directed towards individuals.

4. **Link performance and reward**

   Ensure your annual bonus and recognition systems are built into the performance management systems. Most companies say they are and most employees don't believe it. Constantly challenge your people to ensure the link is clear.

2 Respect and attention

'Social animals seek recognition. Engagement is from the point of view of the organization, recognition is what it is from the point of view of the individual.'

Geoff Mulgan, Head of the Young Foundation

But rewards and reward packages are only the first of the streams by which we replenish the wellbeing reservoir. The second element that an engaged employee requires is a dose of respect. As we have seen in 'Loudhailers to Conversations', a sense of co-ownership is a vital part of the deal if you are looking for employee engagement and an engaged employee will remain engaged only if they believe that their input counts and they feel respected. Richard Baker of Alliance Boots feels extremely strongly about this:

> 'I banned the use of the word "staff". I had a year where if anyone used it in a meeting, they had to put £1 in a jam jar. People thought this was mad but I said, we are in the personal care business, we are not in the retail business. We are in the personal care business where we look after people's health in a meaningful way. People come in and ask us all sorts of questions about why my hayfever tablets aren't working, etc. So we are in personal care, therefore we employ people and not staff. It's an attitude of mind.'

Quite clearly nobody will continue to invest their discretionary energy if it is routinely ignored. In the UK, the fourth highest driver of engagement is the employee's perception that they have input into decision making within their department. People want to know they count. The majority of the UK workforce doesn't feel that way.

The engaged employee has a sense of competence and of control. Interestingly, the most highly engaged employees tend to feel that they have an influence on products, services and finances, *whether or not this is true*. See Figure 2.6.

Fewer than four in ten followers see their leaders as affording them respect. More than 60% of employees cannot agree that their leadership makes an effort to be accessible to them, more than 70% cannot agree that their leadership communicates with them openly and honestly. Only 25% could agree that their leadership is aware of the issues they face in their day-to-day work. All of these are facets of respect and attention, and at all of them, UK leaders are failing.[80]

The responsibility of the employee is to present their opinion cogently and concisely; the responsibility of the employer is to demonstrate that it is taken into account. Research shows that around only one third of employees feel that they are consulted before decisions affecting them are taken. Input into decision making in any department is the fourth highest driver of engagement. It is critical to co-ownership. A word of caution: consultation does not mean consensus.

Why is it so important to recognize the workforce? The benefits to the employer of promoting a culture of recognition and appreciation can be split up into three interlinking areas:

- ❖ It is vital for effective team management and therefore success.

- ❖ It encourages a higher quality of individual contribution.

- ❖ It increases the employee perception of co-ownership and encourages loyalty.

effective management is not autocratic but harnesses knowledge and feedback

Effective management is not autocratic but harnesses knowledge and feedback, drawing on expertise up and down the levels of the organization. This obtains at both the micro and the macro levels – as Jurgen Grobler, Britain's senior rowing coach, concisely puts it:

> 'Listen to what your team is telling you. If you don't you won't understand them, and if you don't understand them, you can't manage them.'

Admiral Sir Mark Stanhope, who is Deputy Supreme Allied Commander Transformation, after years of experience and with a senior role in the Navy, echoes this sentiment:

> 'First of all listen to what they've got to say. Listening is a critical feature of leadership in my opinion. Anybody who thinks leadership is standing up there and giving orders to everybody has got it all wrong. Indeed the orders you give will be a feature of the feedback you've got in terms of what people have told you. You have also got to be able to respond to some of the things you are listening to. You've got to be ready to take criticism, you've got to be ready to take advice and if you're not going to take it, be ready to explain why . . . back to the why: why it is you are not or why it is you are.'

The second reason for implementing a 'listening' culture – because it encourages a higher quality of work – speaks directly to the engagement agenda. 'Of course people come to work for the money, but they want to do something useful. And therefore if you give them the hint that they are listened to, the quality of their ideas is significantly enhanced,' as Peter Erskine puts it. If you want to encourage people to give of themselves, you have to demonstrate that you will take notice.

The organization should pay attention to establishing routines in which people at all levels are actively engaged in understanding and shaping the direction of the business; this is highly important in days of increasing complexity, speed and 'emerging' strategy. At Legal and General all staff are engaged in sessions on the annual business plan. In Dresden Bank a few years ago, at a time of changing strategy, 9000 employees at three different locations were engaged at the same time in sessions that brought to life the new strategy through well-crafted Root Learning pictures. At Coca-Cola in a strategy called Mindset for Growth, 2000 people were involved in strategy development. These policies recognize that harnessing input, listening to people across the organization, can aid problem solving and enhance innovation. At Asda, a system called 'Tell Allan' encouraged everyone in the organization to put forward innovative ideas. All ideas were responded to; if they were implemented, the individual would win £50 and the chance of a weekend break for two.

Other organizations take the same principle and apply it in a more focused, top-down way, by establishing routines for engaging with the leadership group and managerial cadre in intense, intimate sessions on a regular basis. In Shell's Exploration and Production business, the top 150 gather every six months to reflect on business progress, their collective and personal leadership, and their change programme. At Sainsbury's, CEO Justin King meets with all 1000 'leaders' over a period of six months in groups of 30–50. All of these policies recognize that by the simple expedient of listening to employees you can enhance the quality of your output.

The final reason for employing a respectful and listening policy towards your people concerns the harnessing of commitment. Engagement is easier to achieve if the employee believes that they in some sense 'own' the strategy. While there are limits to the practice of consensus and co-invention, the organization should nevertheless go as far as possible towards implementing them.

Do on Monday (for respect and attention)

1. **Formal and feedback**

   After your communication cascades set up a series of one-hour group discussions (maximum of 30 per session) to listen to people's views. Don't fall into the trap of giving another presentation.

2. **Really listen**

   Set up informal communication sessions whenever you visit sites. Listen more than you talk. Even half-hour sessions at lunch or mid-morning/afternoon are important.

3. **Involve people and communicate your conclusions**

   Consult and involve people at the major steps of the strategic development process. Always give feedback and summarize your conclusions – having heard theirs.

4. **Involvement groups**

   Involve pulse teams and shadow boards to garner people's views. Recognize people by inviting them to join such groups.

5. **Cascade your commitment**

   Ask your direct reports what their reports are saying and feeling. Get into this routine so it happens naturally and encourages managers to ask as a matter of course.

6. **Blogs are here to stay**

   Take part in Blogs. After the initial bloodletting which sometimes occurs, it normally becomes positive and then can be an important part of understanding what is going on.

7. **Be authentic**

   Always let people know what you are thinking (you almost certainly will through your body language and expression whether you like it or not), but beware of cutting people off and especially of challenging people in a hostile way in public. You will cut off anyone else from exploring that issue further. (Unless of course you are tackling a behaviour you abhor.)

3 Improving skills

The reservoir is also topped up by demonstrating to an employee that you care enough about them to develop them. Here, at least, organizations are doing rather better: 72% of employees thought they had improved their capabilities over the preceding year. But it is still worth recognizing how seriously employees take this issue.[81] Learning new skills and improving abilities ranks as the second highest driver of both engagement and retention, and similarly highly (fifth) as a driver of attraction.[82] The reason for this, from the employee perspective, is twofold: it gives confidence in performing the job they currently fulfil, as well as equipping them for future, perhaps more senior, roles. As Stephen Covey has said: 'Security lies in the power to produce rather than in what you own'.[83] The opportunity to shore up this security – the knowledge that they are developing their own worth in the market place – is understandably a concern for employees. From the perspective of the employer, there is no reason why this should not be a mutually beneficial exercise: it is clearly in an employer's interests that the employee should hone their abilities to do their job as well as possible.

The best people – who tend to flock together – are likely to be switched on to the needs of their own careers as well as the needs of the organization; acknowledging this fact and trying to cater for it is simply good sense if you want to retain and develop a high-quality workforce. This is not to say, however, that there will not be a short-term cost: employers need to recognize that they must invest in their people. Organizations grow and develop as their people do.

Employability is the new loyalty

Gone are the days when the young saw a career for life with their employer. People have been shocked out of complacency. Bird's Eye was arguably at the heart of Unilever; now it has been sold off. ICI was the bellwether of British industry; now it is proportionally small in comparison to its heyday. Parts of the Civil Service have gone to the private sector and its character is now very different to its old image. We can no longer count on a secure job in a secure organization. So every sensible employee will have a loyalty to themselves, their development and their skills. This is where security now comes from.

Apprenticeship

A large part of the development of skills and abilities, of course, happens within the job itself. Motivation can come from the work itself: it is generally true, and especially in an age when most people are devoting a large proportion of their life to their job, that work helps define the individual and shapes their sense of self-worth. A key driver of engagement is the feeling that the work provided is challenging. Even more important is a sense of control over that work, both in terms of being taught the necessary skills – yet another driver of employee engagement – and being given a degree of autonomy. It may not be possible in practice to give every member of your organization interesting work that is fulfilling in itself, but by involving them as far as possible in decisions that affect both them and the final product, a greater level of engagement is likely to be perceived. It is not possible to provide challenging jobs for every member of staff; neither is it desirable to try to ensure that every task assigned to every employee represents a learning opportunity. However, it is important that employees at all levels are given the opportunity to develop and are monitored to ensure that progress is being made. This can take the form of a personal development plan, as it does at Oracle and Serco. Typically this might be reviewed by the employee and their line manager regularly. An example of how it can work comes from Mike Turner CEO at BAE Systems:

'We need processes. We don't want too many – we don't want to knock the entrepreneurial out of people. We put about three major processes into the company. One of them was called Performance Centred Leadership and that requires every person in the company to have a PDP – Performance Development Plan – and in there you've got some very simple things. You've got your objectives as an individual, which are lined up with the business unit's objectives, and twice a year you have your interview with your manager against those objectives that you set at the beginning of the year.

You get what is called a spectrum rating: you're either red, orange, green, light gold or deep gold. If you're orange, you're on your way out unless change occurs and every year about 5% to 6% of our people are told they are orange and they are either managed into a different job or they are managed out of the company. If you're green, like I am, which is 70% of the company, you are in the right job, you're at the right level and you're probably going nowhere but we love you. Don't be disappointed if you're green. If you're light gold, you've certainly got at least one more promotion in you, in our view. You could do more, and if you are deep gold, you've got two more promotions in you. So everyone knows what colour they are and why they are that colour.

Then we have what is called the management resources review where everybody looks at the light golds and deep golds in their business unit and we do in the centre for the top 300 people in the company and see how long that person has been in their job – is it time to move him? – and we move about 20% of the people, the light golds, every year. That is the process where people feel as though they are engaged and encouraged to contribute to the business and know where they fit in the business.'

The Personal Development Plan must be connected to the performance management process and should be tailored by balancing the needs of the organization with those of the individual. It should take into account the principle that as far as is possible within the needs of the business, employees should be given the opportunity to excel at tasks that challenge them. As David Barnes puts it: 'All of us work better with a little bit of stretch in the system; we don't want a totally benign system.' Several of our interviewees identified this as one of the main duties – and pleasures – of the leadership role: 'There's nothing more exciting in the business than giving somebody a job that they didn't think they could do and watching them do it,' as James Crosby of HBOS puts it.

Sir Digby Jones, perhaps, expressed the possibilities of this role most forcefully:

> 'I know this is cliché stuff but I love being the wind under the wings, I love seeing people fly. I absolutely adore watching people set free and maximizing talent. You'd be amazed what people can achieve if they do it knowing they're not going to get into trouble. And I often say to them, you know, if you have a go at this I will defend you, I really will, I'll take the flak and I will defend you, but please understand that the only thing you'll upset me with is if you don't maximize the chance that I'm giving you. Now get on and do it – go for it!'

All of these leaders are pinpointing the value to the organization of stretching and developing their people. They also pinpoint the emphasis that must be placed on support during this process ('if you stretch people but don't support them you create stress,' says Sir David Barnes of AstraZeneca).

the role of the line manager throughout this process is critical

The role of the line manager throughout this process is critical: the confidence that the manager shows in the individual's ability to develop is encouraging in itself. It is demonstrated by assigning challenging work – an area that currently organizations are falling behind on: only 44% of respondents to a Workforce Study[84] could agree that their line managers provided performance goals that were challenging but achievable. Good managers are just as important while the task is being carried out. Without their encouragement, guidance and, if necessary, help, the learning opportunity will be outweighed by the stress to the individual and the potential cost of error to the organization. Finally, the line manager is there to guide but also to assess and to give feedback: the route to learning is through honest, though constructive, criticism of performance. While the company culture should be as blame-free as possible, performances still need to be assessed. The method of delivery here is key. Jurgen Grobler, Britain's senior rowing coach, explains:

> 'For your people to improve, they have to know where they are going wrong. Criticizing others might not be pleasant, but having a nice, cosy life should not be your goal. Make sure that any criticism of individuals is sensitively handled. You need to get across that you are not criticizing them personally, but are criticizing a specific technique or way of doing things.'

It is also important for the organization to understand that, within realistic parameters, this in-job learning may hold costs for the organization. This is one reason why it is critical that line managers are careful about the more challenging assignments they allocate: there must be, to some extent, the freedom to fail. Eric Peacock, Chairman of Baydon Hill PLC, has an interesting approach to this:

> 'In all of my businesses I have a line in the P and L account which is always negative, which we call the learning account. We try to capture the cost of where we have made a screw-up and that's a line on the accounts and we're looking to see a negative figure there because that's where the learning takes place. My role as the chairman is to make sure that the errors we are making we can learn from, but that financially these errors are not life threatening to the firm and out of that we share the learning from the costs of screw-up.'

Ideally then, the job itself should provide learning opportunities, within a framework of boundaries and of support. This will be effective as a method of learning, however, only if the work is objectively assessed and feedback is honestly given.

External learning

Alongside the development an individual should expect to receive within the job there should be a periodic infusion of more formal learning. Again, this should be implemented in conjunction with an effective HR department and should form part of the employee's development plan. This can take the form of courses, professional exams, or the creative use of secondments. Asda, for instance, has a 'Flying Start' programme aimed at helping undergraduates develop management skills. Virgin has a policy of 'relocation with holiday', a reward for exceptional work combined with an opportunity to develop. Employees who make an outstanding contribution are offered a relocation to a Virgin Group office of their choice anywhere in the world for two weeks, thereby combining a career development opportunity with a holiday. For more junior employees, even the chance to visit customers can be a worthwhile exercise.

Attending to the development of the workforce pays off by increasing their capabilities in their current role and by encouraging them to stay. Your most switched-on – and therefore valuable – employees will be operating with one eye on their career progression. Ensuring that by staying with you they are constantly developing is sound business practice if you want to build a workforce that is strong, stable and forward-looking.

Do on Monday (for skills development)

1. **Personal development**

   Set an example. Set the tone. Can you own the idea that if your people are growing, developing new capacilities, learning skills then so will your organization? Check that you formally and informally are developing your own skills and capabilities.

2. **Organization skills and capabilities for the future**

   Be clear what capabilities and skills the organization needs to be successful into the future. Assess these against those which your organization already has. Challenge the organization to fill the gap. Be seen to pay personal attention to these areas.

3. **Get inspired**

   Get your people to visit other organizations in the form of

benchmarking visits, secondments and people exchanges. Instruct HR to enable this exchange of best practice and benchmarking. Have them report back to you on how well you are addressing the skills and capabilities gaps the organization needs to fill.

4. **Reward people**

People should be rewarded formally and informally for acquiring the relevant skills.

5. **Monitor progress**

At least once a year people in the organization should formally address their skills and capabilities development plan. This can be tied into the appraisal process. Allow space for each person to address their personal development needs so each plan addresses both the top-down organizational needs and the bottom-up individual needs. Monitor and report on progress.

6. **Check the leavers and joiners**

Are those joining the organization bringing in the right skills or are they just generally competent people? For those who leave, are they being poached for their skills which the external world believes you have (and may be underexploiting) and/or are the leavers leaving through frustration associated with a lack of skills and capabilities (either in them or in the organization)?

If you are big enough as an organization, set up periodic alumni events. (McKinsey is an exemplar in this regard.) You get feedback at such events and you stay in touch with people who directly or indirectly offer recruitment opportunities. (There is a growing trend for people to leave organizations for a few years and then return.)

4 Employee support

Finally, the engaged employee needs to be able to feel that their organization is interested in their overall wellbeing: this means you must be seen to be supporting them. The nature of the specific employee 'deal' may be particular to each organization, but there is always an underlying principle – reciprocity. The organization cannot be allowed to be characterized as 'inhuman'; to ignore the day-to-day realities of employees' lives weakens the employment deal by dehumanizing it. It is tempting for organizations to ignore what they consider to be the 'soft' issues that surround this area. It is easy, in fact, to dismiss environmental support and to consider that it consists of nothing more than pleasant cafeterias and nice offices: side issues that can be taken care of later. But the notion of employee support goes deeper than this because management's genuine interest in employee well-being is the *top* driver of engagement. Only 30% of the UK workforce can agree that they see it in action. Not only that, but employees also want to work for organizations that have a *reputation* as a good employer: this is the third highest driver. Cafeterias and comfortable chairs *are* important, at least insofar as they send a consistent message. Put simply, it is hard to offer discretionary effort when your chair is broken and no one will fix it, it's 85° and no one has thought to bring in an air conditioner, or your PC keeps crashing and no one will help. The signal is clear.

Providing for environmental wellbeing and support concerns ensures that everything is in place for employees to do their job well. For example, regarding the job itself, it is no more than common sense to ensure that everyone has proper access to the information that they need for their job and that the tools they work with – whether they are computers and telephones or industrial equipment – are up to the job and well maintained. Ensuring that IT systems are up to date, appropriate and properly supported is an obvious part of your responsibility as an employer. A dodgy system costs the organization in down-time and worse sends an implicit message to front-line people that their jobs and time are not important enough to invest in. Economies in these basic areas are almost always false ones. Small investments – they do not always need to be expensive computer systems – demonstrate to your workforce your ability to see things from their point of view.

Systems which allow for flexible working **respect and space** practices reinforce the employer's side of the **should be given to** employment deal and encourage employee **personal issues** loyalty. Respect and space should be given to personal issues. Flexibility and understanding in times of personal crisis will be remembered. Company crèches demonstrate that the organization is alert to childcare needs. If you talk a lot about the need to employ women – and you probably do – you should make sure you back this up in the practicalities and demonstrate clearly that you have a non-discriminatory stance in your hiring and promoting policies. It is not enough simply to have policy statements in place. A 2006 employment tribunal found against the Hertfordshire Police in a gender discrimination case. They are now using this example in an upgraded training programme to ensure that actual practice reflects the policy guidelines.

For similar reasons, you need to pay attention to the practicalities of employees' lives. Nationwide ensures that at lunchtime shuttle buses run into town to allow employees to take care of errands, as does Camelot, which has also installed a shop on its premises with facilities for dry-cleaning, film printing and buying groceries. Cost-saving measures must therefore be carefully weighed. Economy is good, driving new efficient processes to take cost out of the system is good. But drive to reduce costs should not mean 'second-class travel and no biscuits', as James Crosby of HBOS phrases it.

The employment deal can similarly be reinforced by giving your employees different opportunities. At one of his companies, Stevenage Packaging, Eric Peacock has what is referred to as the SPL 'breakfast university'. Once a month they organize for a visiting expert to bring in stimulus in areas not necessarily related to their job – a professor will come in from Cambridge to talk about memory and learning, for instance. The same company runs a weekly book club which encourages shared learning, and the personal development plans include some aims and goals for their lives outside the company. Eric Peacock is convinced that such activity signals that the organization views the employee as a whole person.

Sending these signals is not an altruistic gesture but a performance enhancer.

At Coca-Cola, for example, each employee is given a learning allowance to go and do a course on something that they find interesting – be it business learning, windsurfing or cookery. They also make sure that the values the company espouses – in particular a sense of community – are encouraged by allowing people to volunteer for charities, for instance coaching local schoolchildren or supporting the Special Olympics, and giving them work time to do that. Gill McLaren pinpoints the reason that this benefits the company:

'Creating a sense of community is becoming far more important. Many people want to feel that they are making a decent living and are successful in their job but they also strive to have balance and to do the right things in life. The "do the right thing" bit increasingly impacts on the companies they choose to work for, actively choosing companies based on whether they feel that their culture and policies fit what they personally believe in.'

The environment must be thought through and appropriate both to the employees and to the business, something Terry Smith of Microsoft realized when analyzing the culture of his organization:

'Probably the best example is our MSN business in London where we employ a lot of people with media and advertising backgrounds. They are not technologists in the traditional Microsoft sense but . . . there was a real stress problem there and ironically there was a real culture of presenteeism that had grown up. So we did a piece of work around work–life balance and one feedback we got back was, "well, I know I have the technology to work from home and people say it's ok to work from home but it doesn't feel that way". So we then put a lot of time and effort into that, but what then came out of it was interesting . . . You talk to a 26/27 year old, one of the reasons they actually want to work for MSN is because it's in London. And this whole thing of work and life merges into one. So they didn't all want to sit working from home all day, they wanted to be with other like-minded people . . . it was how do you find a balance? The social side is very, very significant.'

A company should therefore pay attention to the physical environment in which its employees work, both from the point of view of their comfort and because the office itself can be an expression of what the company stands for, as Eric Peacock points out:

> 'I've always been inspired by those organizations which use their physical environment to reinforce their culture and values. Southwest Airlines in the States; the values around the business proposition there is the freedom to fly, point to point, cheap, value for money offer. The premises out of which they operate is the Lover Field at Dallas which is a glorified hangar. It's one of the most cost-effective buildings but within that they have mirrored the culture which they want in the organization, one of fun, one of value for money so that the whole area is personalized as a tribute to their belief in the people who work for Southwest Airlines who provide in their words "positively outrageous service". So you'll find all of the open areas in the buildings are covered with individual memorabilia from every employee.'

At SWA, the 'positively outrageous service' is mirrored internally: they make the space personal. They explicitly recognize the demands that the organization makes not just of the employee but of the families of the employees. They explicitly try to reflect the value of it being a cost-effective freedom to fly. So instead of having grandiose marble palaces and oak tables they demonstrate that they are a company which is about value for money.

Similarly at IKEA, when you sit in a conference room, there is a strong feeling that anything they can save they can put into the creative development of their product. This comes right down to the pen you get there which has a sticker on it saying 'One Krona'.

The offices themselves are part of what the organization is, a fact recognized by Dianne Thompson when she came into the CEO's job at Camelot. Before she arrived she said:

> 'We didn't have the name of the company on the building because they were worried that we might be a target for violence, terrorism, theft, whatever. How can you create a company that you want people to be proud of working in if you don't put its name on the outside? So you've got Camelot plastered everywhere now.'

Lord Currie, Chairman of Ofcom, identified how attention to the physical environment pays off by translating it into financial terms. He defends his decision for Ofcom to occupy upmarket premises on London's South Bank. When journalists, for example, criticize Ofcom for the building they refer to palatial offices. Lord Currie points out that 'actually we paid £25 a square foot here which is a good bargain and the fit-out was not an expensive one. The point is that it actually works extremely well and I speculate sometimes about what it's worth in terms of the payroll. I think in terms of motivation and engaging your staff, it is worth probably 10% or 20% on payroll. So I think physical space matters a lot more than people often appreciate'.

Space sends messages. It can also be used to create an environment tailored to encourage particular tasks or roles: creative spaces can be set aside for people to work together in teams or quiet areas can be established for research. It may be most sensible, in fact, to delegate the budgets and authority to the teams themselves so that they can craft the working environment to their needs.

Health and wellbeing

Health and wellbeing are affected by both the physical environment and individual's physiological and psychological states. Therefore, strategic management of health and wellbeing needs to address a wide range of issues, including workplace infrastructure, working conditions, employee lifestyles, health programmes and health-related benefits. This potentially affects everything from climate control of the office to travel reimbursement policies for cycling, to the provision of private medical insurance.

addressing several factors in concert can significantly enhance health and wellbeing Addressing several factors in concert can significantly enhance health and wellbeing. One effect is to reduce absenteeism – for example, PerkinElmer[85] implemented a comprehensive wellbeing programme that is expected to lead to absentee reductions worth 3% of the business's annual costs.[86]

A second effect of concerted health and wellbeing management is increased productivity. For example, Unilever found a 400% return on investment in its pilot wellness programme, based on 8% greater productivity.[87]

Health and wellbeing programmes focus on proactively preventing ill-health and empowering employees to improve their personal health and wellbeing. This means removing unnecessary risks and stressors and supporting employees to resist the unavoidable ones. This can have a significant effect: in the Towers Perrin 2007 (USA) Healthcare Cost Survey, companies with low employee healthcare costs were more likely to provide health risk assessments and health coaches than companies with high costs. Not only did low-cost companies maintain their cost advantage despite their expenditure on the additional support, but there was a 50% difference in those costs between the best and worst groups of companies ($7,080 vs. $10,584 per active employee).

As important as material support, companies with low healthcare costs are more likely to take steps to actively communicate and engage their employees' attention as part of their health and wellbeing programme. For example, low-cost companies are 58% more likely than high-cost companies to communicate with their employees about what it means to be a better healthcare consumer and how they can benefit.

You need to make sure that you are not dealing with your workforce as a homogenous entity. Employee concerns and interests will differ across the generations, across levels of seniority, and will change throughout an employee's tenure. Ian Smith, SVP Oracle UK, for example, realized that the younger members of his organization were far less interested in hierarchy than in flexible roles, and structured the company accordingly. The preoccupations of people in their fifties are going to be different to those of people in their twenties. In short, let each individual know you support them and they will take care of supporting the company.

Do on Monday (for employee support)

1. **Keep checking**

   Check that your people are getting the right support – IT help, office space and equipment, etc.

2. **Set the example**

   Set an example if someone around you is in clear need of support. This doesn't take time. Just ask, demonstrate concern and offer even small bits of practical help.

3. **Harness diversity**

   To harness diversity, couldn't you do more to make it easier for your people with particular needs; crèches or transport to local crèches, rooms that can be used as prayer rooms, etc.?

4. **Be imaginative**

   Have your HR department bring in speakers on health and wellbeing. Arrange lunchtime or early evening sessions on the topic. Better still, tie it in with absentee programmes and so turn this into a cost saving! Arrange discounts from local gyms.

5. **Just ask!**

   As you go round, check how people feel about their support and wellbeing. Promise only what you are certain you will deliver.

The purpose of all of the above, the purpose of paying attention to your employment 'deal', is to ensure that the engagement 'reservoir' remains topped up. It is a systemized way of examining the organization from the employee perspective – to ensure that the good work you are trying to do in aligning and engaging your workforce is not undermined by negligence or sloppiness in the basic areas.

NOTES

[75] Towers Perrin Global Workforce Study, 2005 – UK data compendium.

[76] Towers Perrin Global Workforce Study, 2005 – Ten steps to creating an engaged workforce, key European findings.

[77] Ibid.

[78] Davenport, Thomas O. and Roberts, Darryl R. (2005) 'Managers – the missing link in the reward change process.' *Journal of Organizational Excellence*, Spring.

[79] Ibid, p. 142.

[80] Towers Perrin Global Workforce Study, 2005 – UK data compendium.

[81] Ibid.

[82] Towers Perrin Global Workforce Study, 2005 – Winning strategies for a global workforce.

[83] Covey, Stephen (2004) *The Seven Habits of Highly Effective People*, Simon & Schuster.

[84] Towers Perrin Global Workforce Study, 2005 – UK data compendium.

[85] A global technology company.

[86] *Personnel Today*, 17 April 2007, pp. 30–31.

[87] *People Management*, 5 April 2007, p. 10.

11 Pillar Five – Bring Back the Manager

Of all serious academic management literature and research effort, 90% has been expended on two areas: leadership and the development of strategy. Yet both are rendered ineffective if middle management is disengaged.

The cult of 'flattened organizational structures' had a major casualty – middle management. In the rush to downsize, organizations stripped out the layer of management which dealt most directly with the workforce and carried out the monitoring function essential to the smooth running of any system. It was a failure of this function, for example, which was ultimately responsible for the collapse of Barings. Nick Leeson was able to evade accountability because no single individual was held responsible for actually managing him.

This restructuring generated by the 'flat organization' proponents happened despite the fact that there is general agreement about the importance of management. As our research demonstrates, significant enhancement of managerial capability will raise the levels of engagement in the organization. This is hardly surprising since anecdotal evidence and our own experience tell us that a department manager has almost unrivalled power to engage – and, of course, to disengage. Gripes about work all too commonly begin with the words 'my boss ...' as in, 'my boss doesn't appreciate me', 'my boss likes to play favourites'. Just as powerfully, the manager can be seen as a mentor, a figure who inspires, or who holds the keys to more interesting assignments. Either way, the 'boss' is often the personification of the organization: they represent

gripes about work all too commonly begin with the words 'my boss ...'

both authority and opportunity. And 'boss' almost always means departmental head or line manager rather than any senior leadership figure. For any organization interested in engagement, the middle management level is a vital layer to target because it holds the keys to the rest of the workforce.

Traditionally the view of the middle management level is that they are the 'permafrost' of the organization: frozen into their behaviours and impossible to influence, a deadening layer into which most change programmes will disappear.

It is perhaps not surprising that middle management behaves in this way, given the degree of unsettling change in the last 20 years. Rationalization, mergers, downsizing and delayering have all taken their toll most heavily on this management level. The result of this has been a kind of ostrich effect: if middle managers are going to represent an obstruction, then their leadership has found that the easiest thing is to ignore them, to go round the obstacle rather than deal with it. The knock-on result has been that middle management becomes considered as relatively unimportant compared with the significance of a dynamic senior leadership. To take this approach, however, is to ignore a powerful, in fact indispensable, tool.

To reverse this trend and really invest in management capability, assumptions must be challenged and questions asked. Why is it, for example, that middle management is traditionally so hard to move? For Sir David Omand, this process starts with looking at the organization from their viewpoint:

'If you just remember for a moment what it felt like to be in the middle management group, there's a very powerful feeling that the whole enterprise rests on your shoulders because it's the people in the middle who are connecting it all up. So for most of them there is a very strong sense of responsibility and that is why they are so resistant to most change.'

David Spencer, CEO, NSG, echoes the point:

'The middle manager had a pivotal and transitional point in the organization: sometimes, if the senior management is poor and has a modus operandi of barking instructions which aren't fully understood, they quite naturally instinctively say, "what a load of rubbish: they don't know what we do" and then go into a kind of anti-establishment mode where they see their role as protecting the workforce from the crazy senior management.'

The middle manager knows that the actual work of implementing change processes lies with them. In their view, it is they who take the risk of the programme not working and they who will be left to pick up the pieces. All too often they see change as something visited upon them from above without their input, and as something which has the potential to make their task and the tasks of those below them harder rather than easier to perform.

The challenge then is to turn them from unwilling participants into champions. The solution is to invest in this often neglected layer. Allan Leighton is clear about the significance of middle management. 'Give me two to three outstanding leaders, no more,' he says, 'and invest in a cadre of excellent managers, and I'll guarantee performance.'

The manager's view

The truth is that middle management is more likely to be characterized not by an obstructive attitude but by a frustrated one. Our research indicates a desire by managers to achieve outstanding results, engage their people and secure deep personal satisfaction, which is often frustrated by the mundane and other bureaucratic demands of their jobs. Typical statements from managers on the subject of engagement taken from focus groups include: 'I would feel overjoyed [to engage those around me], not only because I accomplished the impossible but because I improved myself, the business I work for and possibly the lives of the people I manage', or ' My team would be productive and happy themselves. My goal is to enable my team to be satisfied with their jobs and efforts'. This reveals not a cynicism about engagement but if anything a desire to harness such a tremendous tool.

Increasingly, we see organizations beginning to understand the need to improve the bureaucracy that so frustrates middle management. However, they are more often than not doing so in a piecemeal way, identifying one or two pressure points and implementing initiatives to improve the specific situation. This is an inadequate response – firstly, because improvements in managerial capability need a multi-faceted approach and secondly, because these responses seriously underestimate the potential return (and thus the levels of investment worth making) that can be secured in fundamentally tackling this issue.

If organizations wish to genuinely engage the workforce, this situation cannot be allowed to continue. If middle management are not at the core of your efforts to improve levels of engagement and hence performance, they will become an obstruction to it. Organizational change is too complex to handle without being able to rely on managers who can address people's rational and emotional needs. Managers are the 'distribution network' for people programmes and processes, the key link in the performance management process. We have already seen how invaluable they are in the presentation of the employment deal. In short, the high demands placed on employees cannot be met without a team of excellent managers who create engaging, rewarding and resourceful environments.

> **managers are the 'distribution network' for people programmes and processes**

The power of the manager

What intuition tells us, research confirms. It shows irrefutably the power of the immediate supervisor level in harnessing engagement.

David Spencer, again, articulated this vital point:

'When somebody says to me there is low morale in the team, I bounce up and say, "whose responsibility do you think that is?" It is important that middle management understands their roles and that the motivation of the workforce is their responsibility. It isn't the chief executive standing on the stage once a year and doing an annual review. It's the person you see every day.'

While Peter Erskine puts it more simply:

'A good manager is somebody who can take their people with them – that's probably the most important skill.'

The consistent results of the talent/engagement studies in the last few years have shown that manager behaviour, and the work environments they create around them, have a more profound and direct effect than any reward programme on the ownership feelings, engagement levels and behaviours of employees.

It is the manager who can best inspire enthusiasm for work (ranked number one among desired manager behaviours by employees), empower their people to take the initiative and encourage them when they do (ranked third) and guide them both in understanding their role and in carrying it out.[88]

Good managers have the power to create the conditions within which ownership/engagement behaviours can flourish. For instance, effective managers outscore ineffective ones in addressing both emotional factors (willingness to put in extra effort, personal motivation on behalf of the company) and rational factors (the understanding of individual and departmental roles). Of respondents who rated their managers as effective, 87% said that they had opportunities to provide input on how things are done in their departments – a sense of control and of course co-invention – as compared with only 32% who said that they had relatively ineffective managers.[89]

In particular, the role of the manager as a means of communication is vital: as we can see from Figure 11.1, employees are prepared to hear the truth, but they believe that their organizations are not always

Managers' comments about the importance of their communication role – and the key part that they play as a filter and source of credibility – are consistent with recent research on the communication environment in large organizations.

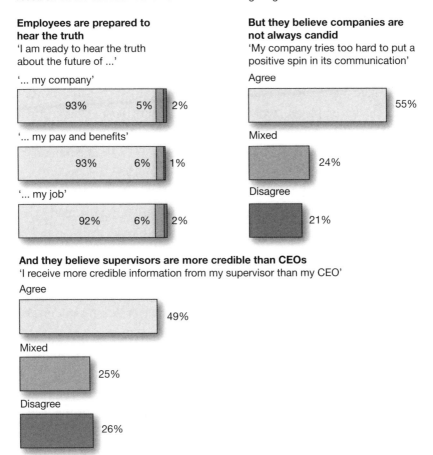

Employees are prepared to hear the truth
'I am ready to hear the truth about the future of ...'

'... my company'

93% 5% 2%

'... my pay and benefits'

93% 6% 1%

'... my job'

92% 6% 2%

But they believe companies are not always candid
'My company tries too hard to put a positive spin in its communication'

Agree

55%

Mixed

24%

Disagree

21%

And they believe supervisors are more credible than CEOs
'I receive more credible information from my supervisor than my CEO'

Agree

49%

Mixed

25%

Disagree

26%

Figure 11.1 **Managing the information environment**[90]

candid. Supervisors, however, are regarded as more credible than CEOs, and employees would therefore prefer to receive information from their line managers in person. The manager, not unreasonably, represents a 'real person'.

So, middle management has the real power to engage those below them. Yet the capability has been lacking. While good, and improving, at process and the tools that enhance rational alignment (goal setting, quality improvement, process management), managers are not so good at using the tools that would enhance emotional engagement (values, involvement, dialogue, etc.). Only 35% of the UK workforce could agree that their immediate manager 'understands what motivates me';[91] only 30% of the European workforce agreed that their manager 'inspired enthusiasm for work'.[92]

Perceptions of poor managerial performance contribute to a largely negative employee work experience; indeed concerns about their immediate management represent the second largest negative factor in the current employee work experience. There is a feeling among employees that to a certain extent they are placing their future security in the hands of their managers, and therefore it is an understandable concern if they feel that management competency is lacking.

Managers, then, are 'stuck in the middle'; they have a key influence in improving overall engagement results but are not particularly good at it, being perhaps only moderately engaged and mostly untrained themselves. Once again, it is David Spencer who articulated this: 'Good middle management is where they have had their minds slightly broadened and good management development, and this is a really key element of employee engagement. If the manager doesn't understand that engagement delivers value added, they have missed a part of their own development.' As a result, they have become a huge source of frustration, both for the employees beneath them, who tend to see their failings as a major negative aspect of the work experience, and for the organizations, which see them as barriers standing in the way of the drive to high-performance culture. Meanwhile the managers themselves are resentfully carrying a full day-to-day workload and therefore squeezing people management into the margins.

But let's be clear, this is not about mobilizing and re-invigorating the classic approaches to management; these will no longer cut it in our increasingly complex world. We are talking about 'engaging management', capability that is equally adept at harnessing the rational and the emotional sides of those around them.

Simons and Davila[93] point out that managers need to understand what drives productive energy and need to know how their time contributes to it. This will enable them to exercise their time and resources towards pushing up productive organizational energy, and to

'Classic' management	'Engaging' management
❖ Managers direct and deploy human assets to produce output and increase shareholder value	❖ Engaging managers recognize that employees are not assets – they are owners and investors of human capital. Engagement brings about productive investment of human capital
❖ Managers dislike broadened spans and greater complexity of tasks managed – they cause stress but are necessary evils	❖ Engaging managers don't mind broadened spans of greater complexity – but they need help with priority setting and the removal of organizational/political obstacles
❖ Managers exercise direct control over people who in turn develop and deliver products and services	❖ Engaging managers don't 'manage' people – they manage the environments in which people develop and deliver products and services
❖ Managers care about people as productive units	❖ Engaging managers create personal bonds with individuals, while not creating personal dependence
❖ Managers faithfully administer the organization's reward and performance management programmes	❖ Engaging managers deliver a customized, individual deal to each employee and give honest feedback, communicated sensitively

understand how to use their managerial resources and authority to delegate and empower others to release productive energy in situations where the marginal returns on time invested are greater. They argue that to estimate their return on management, managers can apply the following five 'acid tests':

- ❖ Does your organization know what opportunities are out of bounds?
- ❖ Are your company's critical performance measures driven by a healthy fear of failure?
- ❖ Can managers recall their key diagnostic measures?
- ❖ Is your organization safe from drowning in a sea of paperwork and processes?
- ❖ Does everyone watch what the boss watches?

Do on Monday – four-point plan

There are four key areas in which organizations need to focus their attention if they are to raise the capability of their managers to deal with both the rational and the emotional and create outstandingly engaging environments for their people.

1. **Redefine the concept of manager**

   Current management needs to be differentiated both from 'leadership' and from 'classic management'. In order to break

   managers need to be elevated in importance

   free of the sometimes negative management stereotype, managers need to be elevated in importance and emphasis placed on the particular competencies relevant to the job of engaging those below them:

   ❖ **Embodying values** – reinforcing organization and team values through the manager's own behaviour (goes beyond 'communicating').

   ❖ **Empathizing** – understanding and taking an interest in others, showing concern for perspectives, goals, feelings (goes beyond 'active listening'); listening.

   ❖ **Catalyzing action** – causing effective performance, being concerned with what people and their behaviours are achieving (goes beyond 'action-oriented').

   ❖ **Inspiring learning** – creating a climate in which people have both the desire and the means to learn and develop themselves (goes beyond 'coaching').

   ❖ **Navigating the organization** – comprehending the company's landscape and forging connections (goes beyond 'team building').

   ❖ **Mediating differences** – surfacing and addressing issues and helping to resolve disagreements in a way that builds productive relationships (goes beyond 'collaboration').

   ❖ **Improvising** – using initiative to harness opportunities, not falling back on 'process' to solve all problems (goes beyond 'adaptability' or 'flexibility').

Redefining the concept of the manager means bringing to the fore a focus on engaging management and avoiding a one-size-fits-all approach. A more strategic approach to the nurturing of this echelon in your organization, it involves:

* ❖ **defining** what is meant by engaging management including minimum standards

* ❖ **deciding** which management jobs require outstanding engaging management skills and abilities and investing in these

* ❖ **simplifying** as far as possible these jobs and some of the work processes running through them, in order to liberate the people-management focus

* ❖ **ensuring** that leadership does an excellent job in engaging colleagues in these roles (we are convinced that a strong engagement experience for managers is an absolute prerequisite for them delivering an equally strong experience to their people). This requires, among other things, regular measurement of their engagement levels as a group

* ❖ **investing** in the appropriate ways, over the long haul, to build up the required engaging management capability (source, deploy, engage, reward, develop)

* ❖ **measuring** regularly the progress you are making.

At the core of this is the establishment of expectations, the measurement of performance against these, the management of positive and negative consequences and the provision of wide-ranging developmental support.

2. **Clarify the deal and simplify the job for engaging managers**

The 'deal' for engaging managers entails the distillation of what is expected of the manager and what the manager can expect of the organization in terms of alignment and engagement.

What is expected of me	What I can expect of the organization

❖ Upper quartile performance	❖ Outstanding engagement by leadership
	  – respect and attention
	  – sincere interest in my wellbeing
	  – development of my skills and abilities
	  – fair rewards

❖ Compliance	❖ Clarity of alignment
❖ Alignment of my people	❖ Strong development to support my downward alignment and engagement processes

❖ Engagement of my people
  – respect and attention
  – sincere interest in employee support
  – development of their skills and abilities
  – fair rewards	

It is important to simplify the job of the engaging manager so that their energies can be more effectively diverted to the management of their people.

Robert Simons in his article 'Designing High Performance Jobs',[94] states that 'improving the performance of key people is often as simple – and as profound – as changing the resources they control and the results for which they are accountable'.[95] He points to four 'spans' or characteristics: control, accountability, influence and support. It is by adjusting the scale of these four spans from narrow to broad in the right combination that you can unlock the employee's capabilities. If they are configured incorrectly, the individual can find it very difficult to play an effective part in the organization.

3. Secure senior leadership involvement in manager engagement

'For someone who works in a delivery office, the person that runs the Royal Mail is their delivery office manager. That's actually their leader. So in many ways the ultimate leader's job is to make sure that those people are just as motivated, just as focused and doing it in the right way as themselves.'

Adam Crozier, CEO, Royal Mail

Organizations have focused significantly more on the development of their top leadership cadre than their middle management group. Consequently, so have they focused their engagement activities more on the leadership cadre and the first line rather than on the 'forgotten' middle management layer.

While companies tend to be effective at giving managers roughly what they require in terms of autonomy, they are not backing this up with mentoring, coaching, feedback or leadership development plans.

Here are two particular themes for middle management:

❖ Firstly, find ways for you and the leadership group actively to engage middle management collectively. For instance, at Sainsbury's, the 1000 senior and middle managers are divided into groups of 36, each sponsored by a member of the board, and targeted with workshops and other exercises to improve and maintain their engagement levels. Jeffrey Immelt at GE always has sessions with middle management on his visits to businesses and sites. And in a global professional services firm, the CEO engages all 750 partners in a series of conference calls every quarter.

❖ Secondly, insist that your leadership group actively engages on an individual basis in the necessary alignment and engagement activities with middle managers – removing obstacles, guiding priority setting, providing performance feedback, mentoring, coaching, creating development opportunities. Increasingly organizations are supporting their leaders with training and development in coaching and mentoring. For instance, one FMCG company recently took all its leaders through a three-day coaching course.

4. **Pay rigorous, patient attention over time to the development of the required managerial capability**

The recruitment, promotion, deployment, development and rewards of managers should be orchestrated over time into developing a strong cadre of managers whose strengths lie in handling both rational alignment and emotional engagement:

❖ *Promotion, recruitment*: All too often arrangements encourage the promotion of people with the requisite technical know-how, without necessarily taking into account the requirements of the people side of the job. The rational side is covered, but not the emotional one. When hiring or promoting, the primary criteria must be managing skills, engaging skills. Other than for very specialist areas, technical skills can be taught.

❖ *Development*: Specific cases with which we have personal knowledge illustrate the value of development:

A global electronics company needed help with design and implementation of a modular line management development programme. In Europe, the company was facing distinct performance pressure. Its strong focus on the sales and dealer network meant that other core processes in support of the sales organization were unconnected and seen as less important, and there was a need across the business for a widespread shift in behaviour. All the organization's line managers went through a development programme that focused on the 'hard' aspects of business planning/management and the 'soft' aspects of self-awareness, emotional engagement and coaching. The programme was underpinned by improvements in performance management, involvement in teams/task forces, etc. and coaching; and support by improved behavioural role modelling by senior leaders, strong external/internal expert contribution and effective project management/delivery by the HR function.

Another company had the need to build managerial capability very quickly as part of an outsourcing initiative where a new management cadre was being established. Their performance was critical to the success of the new venture. A programme was designed for them to enhance the critical manager responsibilities of interviewing, onboarding, managing performance, career planning, communicating, facilitating teams, recognizing efforts, engaging others, linking to leadership and initiating problem solving over a period of 6–9 months. This programme consisted of a context-setting session, followed by skill-building modules on leading through change, managing performance, the role of the manager, building and sustaining employee engagement, establishing and leading effective teams and communicating for impact.

Nick Reed, whose first ten months as Chief Executive of Vodafone UK coincided with a rapid turnaround in the company's fortunes, said business success lay in spotting and nurturing talent rather than scrutinizing sales figures. 'And I question whether many businesses I see are doing that.'[96]

Many organizations introduce training courses for supervisors which focus simply on 'inspiring our people'. A recent example was a major organization which took all its 6000 salespeople through a course on 'empathizing' – 20% decided to leave, but sales results rose significantly, powered by greater skill in forming relationships with customers.

❖ **Deployment**: At Nationwide, attention is paid to the needs of the management level under a programme called Resource Management. A series of fire-fighting teams is set up throughout the organization in order to deal quickly and effectively with any pressure points that build up. If a branch manager, for example, finds his branch temporarily over-busy, help can be manoeuvred in quickly. In this way the organization avoids leaving people exposed under pressure for long periods of time – something that experience has taught the organization is a key disengager.

This is a practical example of deployment to meet particular work needs, easing the burden on middle managers.

Additionally, as you take a more strategic approach to the management and deployment of the middle layer, you will wish to be carefully planning the deployment of people to management jobs. Which jobs require the highest levels of engaging management? Who needs to be doing these now? What is our talent pipeline for these jobs and how do we give them the necessary experience?

❖ **Rewards**: At RBS, where a strong emphasis is placed on engagement, managerial promotions and bonuses are partly linked to the in-depth analysis of the department's performance in what might be termed the 'soft' issues of motivation – questions are included to elicit information about engagement levels and management is evaluated accordingly.

NOTES

[88] Towers Perrin Global Workforce Study, 2005 – UK data compendium.

[89] TP Research USA.

[90] Source: 'Is it time to take the 'spin' out of employee communication?' Towers Perrin, 2004, USA.

[91] Towers Perrin Global Workforce Study, 2005 – UK data compendium.

[92] Towers Perrin Global Workforce Study, 2005 – Ten steps to creating an engaged workforce, key European findings.

[93] Simons, R. and Davila, A. (1998) 'How high is your return on management?' *Harvard Business Review*, January–February, pp. 70–80.

[94] Simons, R. (2005) 'Designing high performance jobs.' *Harvard Business Review*, July–August, pp. 54–62.

[95] Ibid, p. 55.

[96] Davies, Gareth Huw (2007) *Sunday Times*, 1 April.

12 Pillar Six – Harnessing Talent

We are told that we are in the middle of a 'war for talent'. Ed Michaels, Helen Handfield-Jones and Beth Axelrod famously identified this in their *Harvard Business Review* articles of 1999–2001 and their subsequent book.[97] Our contention is that, while talent is crucial, it is nowhere near so scarce as we are led to believe. We are not diminishing the importance of talent – on the contrary, engagement is critically concerned with enabling it to flourish – but we believe that the way to win the 'war' is not to treat talented people like counters on a draughts board that have to be captured, but to discover and use the latent talent you already have. In other words, to engage it. Put simply, the 'war for talent' is the wrong mindset.

almost certainly there is a huge amount of talent under your nose

When we say you should pay attention to harnessing talent, we mean by this *all* the talent in your organization. Almost certainly there is a huge amount of talent under your nose. Why, then, is there a perception that talent is so rare? Largely, it is because organizations have become too lazy to look within themselves, discover it, then develop it. It is the easy, overtrodden path of identifying and corralling off a small number of high-potentials that leads to the myth that talent is hard to come by. Instead, you should consider your whole organization to be a source of able people, and ensure that you develop everybody as far as their ability and willingness allow. Skills aside, people's thinking preferences (assessed, for instance, through Myers Briggs) – personal preferences, behaviours and psychological make-up – clearly mean that different people will flourish in different situations.

Matching the role to the person therefore is a critical part of the development of the organization, and this delicate process is one of the dominating features of the current era of management.

Some of your people will have the desire and ability to aim for the most senior executive positions in the company from the moment they step in the door. But this is not the exclusive definition of talent. Far too often 'talent management' is regarded as synonymous with an elite echelon being pointed towards the most senior positions. Instead, talent management should be a mindset, underpinned by organizational processes, which develops everyone *including* those destined for the top.

Talent matters

Certainly, successful organizations and successful chief executives worry about talent. Almost all our interviewees stressed the importance of finding the right people. The following quote from Martin Sorrell, CEO of WPP, is typical:

> 'It's very simple: this company has to be the place where the best talent in the business resides. The best motivated and aligned and engaged people in the business. Don't make it complicated: just the best people ... Businesses will be differentiated on the basis of quality of people.'

Research demonstrates that companies with enlightened talent management policies and programmes generate higher returns on assets, investments and sales.[98] 'CEOs of successful companies are ... twice as likely as CEOs of less successful companies to cite the "availability of managers/executives" as an issue to concentrate on'.[99] Jack Welch, GE's legendary boss, spent half his time on 'people development'.

Why is this so important now?

Peter Drucker has suggested the confluence of a bulging aged population and a shrinking supply of youth is unlike anything that has happened since the dying centuries of the Roman Empire.[100] *The Economist* also highlights the significance of the ageing population:

> 'This will be most dramatic in Europe and Japan: by 2025 the number of people aged 15 to 64 is projected to fall by 7% in Germany, 9% in Italy and 14% in Japan. But it will also make a difference to China thanks to the one-child policy. And even in America where the effect will be less marked, the retirement of the baby boomers which has just started means that companies will have lost large numbers of experienced workers over a short period. RHR International, a consultancy, claims that America's 500 biggest companies will lose half their senior managers in the next five years or so when the next generation of potential leaders has already been decimated by the re-engineering and downsizing of the past few decades. At the top of the Civil Service the attrition rate will be even higher.'

Simultaneously, structural changes are making talent issues ever more important. The deepest such change is the rise of intangible but talent-intensive assets. Professor Baruch Lev, the Philip Bardes Professor of Accounting and Finance at New York University, argues:

> '"Intangible assets" – ranging from a skilled workforce to patents to know-how – account for more than half of the market capitalization of America's public companies. Accenture, the management consultancy, calculates that intangible assets have shot up from 20% of the value of companies in the S&P 500 in 1980 to around 70%.'[101]

So the trend is clear: good people have always mattered, but as we go forward into the twenty-first century, they will matter even more.

Are we paying attention?

The Corporate Executive Board (CEB), a provider of business research and education based in Washington D.C., conducted a poll of senior HR managers: three quarters of them said that 'attracting and retaining' talent was their top priority. Actually their top priority should be being smarter about acquiring talent but also about *developing* the talent they already have. Talent development is the best way of retaining it, as well as ensuring you get better value out of your existing workforce (reducing the numbers of 'working absentees'). Employees want to be developed. Career advancement opportunities, and learning and development opportunities, rank third and sixth respectively as drivers that attract the European workforce to jobs. Together with the second highest driver of engagement ('able to improve skills and abilities in the last year') these speak directly to development issues. Not only that, but people want to work with other talented people.

The highest overall driver of retention is that organizations are employing and retaining other high-calibre people. In other words, by developing your workforce, you automatically are making your company more attractive to other high-quality employees. If you are complacent on this issue, it may well be misplaced: only 23% of the respondents in the UK survey agreed that their organization did this.[102]

Yet what percentage of leaders actually manifest a commitment to developing their talent? In A.T. Kearney's 2004 survey on the effectiveness of corporate governance, participating board directors acknowledged the importance of leadership development and succession planning. However only one in four respondents believed the board of directors was very good at these activities. Cohn, Khurana and Reeves in the October 2005 *Harvard Business Review*[103] found that almost half the corporations they studied had no succession plans for VPs and above. Only one quarter of CEOs in these organizations had talent pipelines that extended at least three managerial levels below them.

Why aren't we looking harder?

Why are leaders, concerned as they are with the talent issue, over-looking seemingly obvious areas for improvement? To a certain extent it is simple laziness of thought. Many companies are still clinging to the myth that Collins and Porras so effectively exploded in *Built to Last* – that the best change agents come from outside.[104] And some are just letting the issue slip down their list of priorities. Martin Sorrell of WPP, having highlighted the importance of talent issues, went on to describe how tricky they are to implement:

> 'The issue for us is monopolizing talent, what we have to do is monopolize talent. That's the best way to put it. It's the talent issue. It's the people issue … finding really good people, it's very difficult. We might have very good people under our noses that we probably don't know because our people spend more time on the $350 million capital expenditure decision as compared to the $6 billion investment in people decision … The trouble with the HR function is that everybody uses it as a crutch … what you shouldn't do is ring up your chief talent officer and say, "we've got a hole here, fill it". That's a disaster. You should have five people in mind to fill any job, it's being aware of what's going on in the market. Everybody who runs our company should be the chief talent officer.'

When it comes to succession issues, there also seems to be a psychological unwillingness to look beyond one's own tenure. Cohn, Khurana and Reeves again:

> 'Many people from the CEO down consider the word "succession" taboo. Planning your own exit is like scheduling your own funeral; it evokes fears and emotions long hidden under layers of defence mechanisms and imperceptible habits. Perversely the desire to avoid this issue is strongest in the most successful CEOs.'[105]

All of these may sound like reasonable explanations – after all, time is always at a premium, and concerning yourself with talent issues sounds like an enormous outlay of time for little short-term benefit. However, to fail to hunt out and pay attention to talent in your organization is not just to fail the people who work for you but to fail the organization itself.

Grow your own

Nevertheless, there is some cause for mild optimism given this finding from a recent Chartered Institute of Personnel & Development (CIPD) report: 'It seems there is now a widespread acceptance that organizations need to grow their own future talent rather than simply relying on the wider market place to provide it.' Some companies are specifically tackling this area. At Starbucks, for example, the board oversees a formalized succession planning process for 2500 positions. Its goal is to make sure the company always has the right people with the right values in the right places at the right times. 'From the board of directors on down, senior executives are deeply involved and line managers are evaluated and promoted expressly for their contributions to the organization wide effort.'

To grow your own talent makes sense, not just for strategic reasons but because it saves money. Jeff Pfeffer, a Professor at Stanford University, has estimated that attention to high-quality talent saves SAS US $60–80 million annually. It is very expensive to recruit someone from the outside. Moreover, a study of investment banks found that when imported from elsewhere stars cannot necessarily sustain their performance in the new organization, on top of the cost and energy expended in inducting them.

Where do you look for talent?

Given that our broad definition of talent is *everyone*, our broad answer to where you should look for it is, of course, *everywhere*. If you suspect that, in your organization, inertia means that talented people are often left languishing, seek it out. For instance, IBM from time to time insists that its leadership team actively goes out into the organization to identify the talent needed to freshen up the talent pools constructed by the normal processes. This executive reachdown process recently identified another 126 people willing and able to set their sights on a more senior role in the organization in the future. Without such a programme, these 126 people would constitute 126 missed opportunities. One part of Shell apparently in reviewing its talent issues found that it was recruiting just 25 Chinese graduates!

This kind of approach is clearly not sufficient. As Sir Andrew Turnbull says:

> 'Bringing in people with a wide range of backgrounds, skills and experience enables you to understand better the needs of your customers, to develop innovative solutions and to tap into a wider pool of talent.'

Harnessing diversity

Ian Dodds, Managing Director, IDC Consulting, who has done a great deal of work on diversity issues, sees the harnessing of diversity as being a response to a perceived talent shortage. Dodds explained that around 30 years ago increasing international competition led to many employers beginning to engage their non-managerial employees in helping their organizations succeed. This was the first step in fostering an inclusive culture to increase innovative business thinking and productivity and performance.

Where it was done well it delivered significant business dividends. ICI's Huddersfield Works was transformed over five years from one of the worst performers in the group to one of the best. This was achieved by involving factory floor personnel and their first-line supervisors in project teams and task groups to turnaround the Works' performance. However, this was about only two affinity groups, i.e. managerial, middle class and university educated, and non-managerial employees, lower-middle or working class and having left school at 16 or younger.

It was some ten years later when some employers (driven, admittedly, by equal opportunities legislation and by the need to manage risk by avoiding costs arising from discrimination claims and the possibility of negative publicity) began to look at the causes of so few women and people from ethnic minorities achieving middle and senior level manager status. It was in the early 1990s that Louis Platt, then CEO of Hewlett-Packard, when challenged by HP's employees to justify their efforts on diversity, defended it on the basis of the value added from having and understanding diverse employees, customers and suppliers. Many organizations have successfully pursued the Diversity Dividend as first articulated in HP.

However, Bitc's FastForward 2003 research 'lifts the game' because it demonstrated that talented and diverse employees, irrespective of their affinity grouping, see the ideal employer as being one which has managers who are able to recognize and understand each employee's unique qualities and help them apply them for the betterment of their work and their careers. This is no mean managerial challenge, but we believe strongly that employers who can meet it will have a clear, competitive edge in developing a talented and diverse workforce.

And no, this is not just about conventional, basic, good management. It requires, in a diverse business environment, that managers **it is commonly assumed that people of high potential will be fast trackers** are cross-culturally aware and sensitive in their practice of these skills and that they recognize that talented individuals can have different career track preferences. (We are back to the manager again.) It is commonly assumed that people of high potential will be fast trackers and want rapid promotion and the rewards that go with it. Research by Towers Perrin and The FutureWork Institute, both in the UK and the US, has shown that there are at least five different career archetypes, as illustrated in Figure 12.1. Hence, in helping their team members develop and leverage their talents for their personal career advancement, the inclusive manager has to recognize each individual's career track preference to mentor and coach them most effectively.

Free agent
Moving quickly between/within organizations where your skills are in highest demand

Experimenter
Trying many things, building a portfolio of skills

Fast tracker
High involvement, high reward, quick advancement

Organization-dedicated careerist
Long-term skill development

Balanced careerist
Work–life balance is priority

Figure 12.1 UK career diversity profiles: individuals have different preferences[106]

The messages are clear:

1. Being an effective diverse business increases profitability.

2. Diversity has evolved from a simple managerial/non-managerial difference to embracing every way in which individuals are unique from one another.

3. Businesses which have managers who are skilled in harnessing diversity by fostering an inclusive work environment are likely to enjoy a competitive advantage through their ability to recruit and retain a diverse range of talent and the profitability this adds from more effective and innovative business problem solving and development.

Who will rise to the top?

There is no doubt, assessing who is willing and capable of going to the top is difficult. Requirements will alter over time, as markets change, or as your position in the market changes. But this fact merely reinforces the value of looking throughout your organization for talent, rather than contradicting it. To impose a caste system that differentiates high-fliers from the rest at an early stage is to limit your opportunities. Even more importantly, to allow a culture of 'the anointed' and 'the rest' is a surefire path to two negative outcomes: a demotivation among the lower group and complacency among the higher. The wall between the two groups needs to be perceived as permeable. The lower group should be able to lift their eyes upwards and the 'elite' should certainly not feel cushioned by a comfortable floor below which they cannot fall.

There is, moreover, a risk in playing this limited-numbers game. As Boris Groysberg, Ahshish Nanda and Nitin Nohria state, company 'stars' are the first to be approached by competitors and are the least likely to stay.[107] The potential effect of this is that you are choosing your future leaders from an ever-diminishing pool, or being forced to look elsewhere, diluting your painstakingly nurtured organizational culture in the process.

We are not suggesting that you do away with systems that spot potential early, just that you make them more pervasive throughout the organization and garner your group of high-potentials from as broad a base as possible. Make sure your talent management programmes are permeable – when was the last time someone left the programme? When was the last time someone joined it mid-career? Send a clear message that high-potential talent is not a clique – the organization is a club and players will be selected and deselected for the first team on the basis of their skill, fitness and teamwork. As Jose Mourinho says: 'He performs, he plays; he doesn't perform, he doesn't play.' Visit your existing talent pool members, engage with their aspirations and give them your help to climb out of settled positions and into the type of experience they will need to advance their goals.

Under a more permeable system it becomes doubly important that those who do want to aim for the top, and have the ability to do so, will be guided by talent management programmes that ensure they get the experience and development to make them well prepared for future senior roles. Focus your effort on designing attraction, recruitment, incentive and retention strategies that are specific to people's different roles and flexible to accommodate the diversity of roles in your organization.

For example, Joerres and Turcq ('Re-thinking the value of talent', *Strategy & Business*, 2006) identify four types of roles (creators, ambassadors, craft masters and drivers) on the basis of their value and cost impacts. Each type has different talent management requirements, but in general talent placed in a position where it has a high strategic impact needs to be secured more permanently and succession planning undertaken more carefully. Great talent cannot flourish independently of helpful organizational systems (even if it thinks it can). As *The Economist* concludes: 'Talented people may think that their brainpower allows them to walk on water but in reality many are walking on the stones that their employers have conveniently placed beneath them.'[108]

The nectar-carriers

Who is it, then, that you move towards your most senior positions? Of course, they must have the necessary skills – that goes without saying – but it is not enough. What you are looking for are those who can engage and align others in the organization – those who will pass the nectar. People should not be regarded as 'high potential' if they can't engage those around them. Too often people get on by focusing exclusively upwards. They say what they think senior management wants to hear, they create short-term successes, but around them they leave a trail of destruction and demotivated people.

Eric Peacock, Chairman of Baydon Hill PLC, is very used to the questions surrounding the talent issue. He sees it like this:

'Building an internal dream team who have similar beliefs in the human spirit, who want to see people grow, who clearly want to see their organizations grow because that is a very rich privilege to be able to participate in watching people grow. And that way I have momentum in each of these businesses.'

You are looking for energy-givers. Pay attention to how well people manage and engage those below and around them, not just how good

you are looking for energy-givers

they are at managing upwards. This is important because people, by and large, learn from other people. A MIT study found that people are five times more likely to ask a co-worker for information than to consult an internet database or company computer system.[109] A Lexis–Nexis sourced report asked in which situations people learn most. The answers – 66% when working together with a colleague on a task, 22% when doing own research, 10% when a colleague explains something personally and 2% through a manual or textbook.[110]

People affect those around them, acting either as nectar-carriers or as potentially harmful viruses. As Ian Smith of Oracle UK explains:

> 'The values and behaviours of the individuals you choose go through the organization like a rifle shot; they can be felt at the line level within months. We can't afford to hire or promote people with the wrong values. It's a path to mediocrity.'

Finally, remember that time spent developing talent, at every level, is eventually time saved. The great thing about a talented workforce working within processes that align them is summed up by Dianne Thompson of Camelot:

> 'The better the people beneath you, the easier your job becomes and what you can do is be a nurturer of great talent. And it took me a while to understand this. When I did, my management style changed and I realized I didn't need to keep on proving that I was so bloody good at everything in order to get respect. Actually what was important was developing a great talent and have it to come through the organization.'

Not only is developing people so that they reach their full potential valuable to the organization, it is an experience that a large number of our interviewees identified as deeply satisfying. The following comment from James Crosby of HBOS was typical:

'The most exciting thing is bringing people into certain roles who will just change your view of how the job can be done; change your thought processes as to what can be achieved in that job. But there are thousands of people behind them.'

The real competitive differentiator between organizations lies in how well they harness their talent. In the end product differences won't last, somebody else will copy you, the market will change, the edge will be lost. Your reputation and the people in your organization are the things that make the critical difference.

Do on Monday

1. **Stake out your position and commit to managing talent**

   This means understanding what talent means, nurturing the talent in the organization and hiring the right people in the right places to do the right jobs. It also means that you personally should actively drive this area. It would be sensible to have someone else on the leadership team with oversight of the talent agenda, but you must have presence and energy in this area.

2. **Establish a framework for managing talent**

   This needs to have the following ingredients:

   ❖ Systematic identification of the critical, strategically important areas within your organization. Map the roles according to their value impact (the value at risk if the job is not performed properly) and cost impact (the investment in training and development required to perform the job). Focus your priority talent management efforts on the strategically critical jobs.

   ❖ A strategic workforce plan, driven by the business plan, which gives a roadmap to the workforce that you need in five, ten years' time, taking account of your future capability requirements, demographic trends, etc. Tie the talent management process into the business planning cycle so that it is not regarded as something separate.

❖ Establishment of clear talent pools that enable you to orchestrate the strategies that will source, engage, deploy, reward and develop your talent.

❖ Clear definition and communication of your talent objectives and process.

❖ Senior leadership team time devoted to the process, renewing the workforce plan, being on top of the succession plans, actively identifying and engaging talent.

❖ Strong levels of interaction and dialogue with colleagues in your talent pools.

❖ Insistence that the basics are in place throughout the organization. Set out a programme for every employee to have a talent plan, based on their abilities and needs. Budget specific time for managers to review plans with their staff.

3. **Make your talent management programmes permeable**

In one company, a talent identification programme that was put in place gave every one of the 140,000 staff the opportunity to put themselves forward for leadership development. Previously, talent identification had just been in the hands of the top team and a narrow talent pool was being selected.

4. **Make sure that the talent approach is aligned**

Large organizations face the danger of lapsing into the (sometimes) bureaucratic rhythm of the talent management process and losing the sharpness of the changing business drives. For instance, make sure your talent programmes align the business imperative with individuals' needs.

It is also important to tune your talent management process to the culture of the organization. This will not be the same for a large construction company as for a creative industries company.

5. **Put talent management at the top of your priority list**

   And move it to the top of your expectations for senior managers.

   ❖ Personally chair all the key talent management meetings.

   ❖ Always review talent with your business leaders when you visit their parts of the organization.

   ❖ Take a walk around the business with your human resources adviser and share your perspectives.

   ❖ Visit your existing talent pool members, engage with their aspirations and give them your help to climb out of settled positions and into the type of experience they will need to advance their careers.

   ❖ Start setting up a mentoring network by matching yourself (or asking your HR adviser to match you) as a mentor to a few individuals whom you think you can support in a meaningful but confidential way.

   ❖ Have conversations with your direct reports to plan their assignments. Demonstrate the processes you expect every manager in your organization to be fulfilling.

   ❖ Challenge your leadership colleagues to follow your example. Partly, this is about modelling good practice. Partly, it is about setting challenging goals – for instance, the IBM executive reachdown effort was based on the CEO's challenge that members of the leadership team should personally go out into the organization and find talent that was being missed by the normal processes.

6. **Begin to think of your talent management process as an eco-system**

   Stop thinking of your organization's boundaries as the limits of your talent management process. Your employees certainly do not – they are thinking in terms of their careers, the development of their skills and abilities, their employability. Think about seconding people in and out of your organization. Stimulate your people with new thinking and challenges.

Notes

97 Michaels, E., Handfield-Jones, H. and Axelrod, B. (2001) *The War for Talent*, Harvard Business School Press.

98 Caudron Shari, (2001) in 'How HR drives profits.' *Workforce Management*, December.

99 Successful companies have higher average returns on assets. Source: 'CEO Challenge 2004', The Conference Board, August 2004.

100 *The Economist*, 1 November 2001,'The next society'.

101 Wooldridge, Adrian (2006) 'The battle for brain power.' *The Economist*, 7 October.

102 Towers Perrin Global Workforce Study, 2005 – UK data compendium.

103 Cohn, Jeffrey M., Khurana, Rakesh and Reeves, Laura (2005) 'Growing talent.' *Harvard Business Review*, October.

104 Collins, James and Porras, Jerry (1996) *Built to Last*, Century Books.

105 Cohn et al. (2005) 'Growing talent.' *Harvard Business Review*, October.

106 Business in the Community, FastForward Research, 2003.

107 In 'The risky business of hiring staff.' *Harvard Business Review*, 2004.

108 Wooldridge, Adrian (2006) 'The battle for brain power.' *The Economist*, 7 October.

109 Allen, Tom (1977) *Managing the Flow of Technology*, Cambridge: MIT Press.

110 Lexis–Nexis, March 2004.

13 Pillar Seven – Consequences

People need to feel accountable. Engagement will never happen on the necessary scale unless there are consequences attached to it.

> 'We're very simple as human beings and we want to be recognized, rewarded, cheered on.'
>
> Howell James, Permanent Secretary Communication, Cabinet Office

Engagement will remain a background issue until you make people believe it is a pressing one. And the way you do that is to demonstrate it to them. Ensure that the level of their engagement has tangible results. For the managerial level, you need to make sure that doing the things that lead to engagement pays – and that not doing them hurts. People-based issues in the form of engagement scores should form part of the metrics on which you judge an individual's performance.

It is perfectly possible to measure whether managers are doing those things that lead to higher levels of engagement – or not! It is also perfectly possible to measure whether employees are feeling engaged (see Part One). The former can be measured using 360° feedback and the latter using an engagement survey. So having undertaken these two types of survey you know which groups are engaged and which managers are engaging, for instance, which managers are perceived to be listening to their staff, which managers are communicating clearly, which managers are rewarding their staff for extra effort and in a fair way. You can also check whether managers and their staff have understood the strategy, i.e. are aligned.

A note of caution: the word 'consequences' can carry rather doom-laden connotations. Too often businesses regard it as synonymous with punishment: this should not be the case.

the word 'consequences' can carry rather doom-laden connotations

While the whole point of this book is that engagement issues should be approached in a rigorous, hard-headed, result-based way, we use the word consequences as a neutral term – comprising admonishment, if necessary, but also reward. The currency should be one of fair and just reward for effort, and also of appropriate action for lack of effort.

We explore the broader issues of rewards packages and how they contribute to overall engagement levels in the Reservoir of Wellbeing pillar; here, we focus on the specific ways in which you reward engagement and engaging behaviours themselves.

This process should comprise four stages:

1. Clarity

2. Measurement

3. Types of consequences, financial and non-financial

4. Performance management.

And HR support, for the whole process.

Clarity

First, the organization needs a clear strategy that people can get aligned to. Lack of clarity makes evasion very much easier. Lack of clarity in people's objectives nearly always starts at the top with an unclear strategy. When you don't know where you are going, any route is good enough. People make up their own mind, or worse still organizational inertia sets in. Once the roadmap is clear, organizational energy can be directed to achieving progress in the market place, rather than being dissipated on internal wrangling and misaligned objectives.

It is dangerous to attempt to enforce consequences unless you have made it absolutely clear what is important to you. Define what constitutes success. Define what constitutes failure. And then communicate these definitions. Implement processes that will ensure alignment, make sure you keep repeating your aims, your narrative, your strategy. Never accept that your people have 'got it' until your conclusions (after a process of co-invention) have been rigorously promulgated, until you can give your stump speech in your sleep. (President Reagan reportedly once asked his adviser: 'Say, how many times have I got to make this speech?' His adviser replied: 'Well Mr President, when you feel physically sick you've probably made it enough times.')

Bear in mind, you seek to create aligned and engaged employees and you define goals in terms of achieving certain outputs – the what – and having done this, utilizing certain behaviours – the how. *Both* performance and individuals' behavioural goals are essential to engagement. They are closely related because the process goes as follows:

❖ You have defined a strategy.

❖ You have identified behaviours which will help you achieve that strategy.

❖ You now want to encourage those behaviours by measuring and rewarding them.

However, tilting your goals too heavily towards people-based metrics will, in the long run, be counterproductive. How you balance the two sides is for you to decide given your unique context. Gill McLaren of Coca-Cola identifies the balance in her company as follows:

> 'We focus on the "what" and a "how" in our objective setting in Coca-Cola. There's still a strong focus on what you achieve which accounts for 60% of an individual's rating. However, the remaining 40% is rewarded for how you achieve it. This enables us to recognize skills such as team working, collaboration and strong project management alongside strong business results delivery.'

In order to implement the strategy, in other words, certain behaviours will be required. If, for example, the strategy is vastly to increase the rate of innovation, then the behaviours must include tolerance of mistakes, encouragement of experimentation, respect for people's ideas. If the strategy is to expand into Asia, then the support functions must be aligned around delivering the infrastructure to do this by prioritizing it, giving extra attention to Asian leaders, being respectful of Asian culture and requirements. Adam Crozier of the Royal Mail describes his perception of the process as follows:

> 'Align all the rewards at all the levels of the organization around the achievement of the strategy. Make sure that you don't have sort of conflicting signals – where people actually are rewarded for something that is against what you are trying to do.'

The definitions should be set by prioritizing what is most important for *your* organization: the standard and typical ten drivers of engagement referred to in Part One have been well tested and developed throughout many organizations, but which are most lacking, or most present, in a particular organization will vary. Research can easily identify which are the prime drivers of engagement in your organization (through regression analysis) and assess how you are doing against each criterion.

The drivers which you choose to concentrate on will reflect the realities of your business as it stands, what its history is, what its trajectory is, where it stands in the market and what market it is in.

Measurement

The behaviours you have isolated as necessary for the implementation of your strategy have probably already been identified. It is quite likely, in fact, that at some stage your organization has already discussed the need for them. But such good intentions usually end up as nothing more than that and just a list on a meeting room wall. The middle manager will agree that listening to those below him is something he should do, but somehow in the day-to-day running of his team other things will seem more pressing and he will continue in his command and control habits. A member of the top team will agree that empowering those below him is a good idea, but in the hurly-burly of his busy life it will seem easier – or less risky – to continue to micro-manage. Lofty aims will fall prey to the old, usually unconscious, trick of 'consent and evade'.

To prevent this, key behaviours must be measured. Sir David Varney highlights the importance of this:

> 'Highly successful companies, which have been successful over long periods of time, are characterized by internal cultures which focus on those things that deliver business success and have measures and metrics around them.'

Richard Baker of Alliance Boots believes measuring the attitude of your employees is one of the key ways of assessing the quality of the local management. In part, this is practical because you can't set goals for the future without assessing where you stand in the present. But it also has a psychological effect; the very act of measurement sends a message and affects how seriously people will take the engagement agenda. At Nationwide they ensure that their performance management system assesses employees against the PRIDE values. Individual performance is assessed against PRIDE, and it is even built into the recruiting and assessment of every employee so that at every level individuals are clear about what PRIDE means to them.

Alex Wilson of BT has seen a similar process in practice in his organization:

> '... [in this organization] the environment was always there: engagement and the belief in it is a huge cultural thing. [And then] we hired a Chief Exec who has got a fundamental value set around this stuff. He came in and said, "Well it feels good, but instead of it feeling good, let's actually drive it, make it make a difference and measure it and check it." So he brought in a real discipline and drive to this as a concept rather than it just being a fuzzy feelgood thing. And suddenly the only problem in this area for me and my people is the size and the shape and the speed of delivery around that sort of agenda. Honestly, the great thing is that I don't have to prove it ... I have worked for five companies and this is by far and away the most structured, serious, emotionally engaged company I have ever seen.'

checking must involve the measurement both of performance goals and engaging behaviours

But note, this checking must involve the measurement both of performance goals (which you should already be doing) and engaging behaviours. This 'temperature-taking' allows you to compare your organization against an industry standard, identify areas of particular concern and, crucially, set engagement goals. These overall goals can then be translated into specific objectives for individuals or departments, and a process for monitoring them can be put in place.

We have seen in Chapter 2 how seriously RBS as an organization takes the issue of engagement levels. Here we see how it went about harnessing consequences to implement it. It took seven months to create the human capital toolkit, which involved a policy and employment team, an HR-specific web design team, and focus groups from the business units. This identified the key diagnostic areas for the system, including call centre performance, organizational development, employee surveys and competitor benchmarking. Internal performance for each of the businesses was given a colour code according to the 'traffic-light' system of red/amber/green to highlight areas for HR staff to attend to.

The human capital model was designed to focus HR managers' efforts on identifying and measuring the things which add most value to the organization. This contrasts with approaches that simply account for activity or performance. Therefore, the RBS approach requires the collection of information on leading indicators such as those around employee engagement. The model supports business decision making by predicting future business performance instead of simply matching historical human resource information to historical performance. However, this insight in the model is made possible only by rigorous analysis of large volumes of data collected from disparate sources to identify the key drivers of engagement and high performance.

Data on employee attitudes is gathered via an annual anonymous survey which is directed at all staff and has an 86% response rate. The survey is conducted online or on paper and run by an independent firm. Surveys are also carried out with joiners and leavers, as well as to take the 'pulse' on particular topics and with newly acquired businesses. The raw survey responses are stored so that managers can compare data directly as well as at the aggregate level for business units and cost centres at different levels. Qualifier data collected includes demographics, length of employment, position, geography, gender and benefits preferences – this allows segmentation and analysis on these lines. This survey data has been combined with pooled data from RBS's 30 systems across the world as part of a data warehouse. An important part of this process was standardization of the data and standardization of employee research across the RBS group.

An important aspect of the way RBS collects data is its standardization. This comes from having the single data warehouse (bringing together the 30 global HR systems) and from altering all groupwide surveys to have consistent questions. Not only does RBS have a good number of surveys that go out to the whole group (annual employee opinion surveys, new joiner surveys, leaver surveys), but it also uses questions aimed at measuring engagement from joining to leaving, and questions to identify the drivers of engagement changes. Since all the surveys are run through the same human capital model, RBS can extract extra longitudinal information and compare survey results directly with each other to identify the differentiators in each case.

You might, at this point, feel that there is an inherent contradiction in all of this. Isn't engagement meant in part to be about creativity, about empowerment? And don't all these processes, all this measuring and calibrating and tracking, stifle that creativity? Isn't this just another layer of bureaucracy that inhibits empowerment? In fact, the most creative companies tend to be those with a limited number of well-managed systems. Similarly, an innovative culture can really be successful only if that innovation operates within a rigorously managed system (usually some form of stage gate process). Empowerment, in fact, can flourish only within a defined framework.

Sir Andrew Turnbull sees it as follows:

'Strategic purpose leads to structure, it leads to something about the kind of people you employ. And then you immediately have to ask yourself, "are our reward systems supporting those strategic aims and the strategic staffing requirements or are they not?"'

Metrics and measurements, then, are both practical tools and psychological weapons. Think of them as a flag in the ground: a marker of where you are, but also a message about what you are trying to achieve.

Do on Monday (for measurement)

1. **Measure your organization against others and benchmark the scores**

   A supplier with an already existing database can enable you to make measurements from a questionnaire which can then be compared with the industry standard. You may have to add questions to ensure you get the data on behaviours specific to you. Relate the findings to your opinion surveys and include other HR data in your analysis. The types of questions you need answers to could include:

   ❖ Are you losing the kind of people you'd rather keep? If so, how many?

   ❖ Are members of your workforce enhancing their skills? Do they consider that this is happening?

   ❖ Is salary/bonus determination being applied in a fair and consistent way across the organization? Is it perceived as such?

   ❖ Do people feel respected and listened to?

   ❖ Are people engaged or cynical?

   ❖ Are people up for change improvement or worn out and disengaged?

2. Understand why you got the scores you did

Such a questionnaire will give you the broad data, but you will also want to understand *why* people have rated their levels of engagement as they have. For example, conduct qualitative surveys on leavers and joiners. Also conduct pulse surveys on specific topics that need exploring. These can be related to your critical business metrics.

3. Consistency of data collection

In large-scale organizations, ensure that as much data as possible is consistent, so you can make cross-group checks. Remember, however, that comparisons across companies, though helpful, sometimes fail to take into account the context or the in-built assumptions appropriate to each different organization.

4. Accessibility of information

Make the information gathered easily accessible, not held behind closed doors. Make sure people can access the findings on the company intranet together with your narration, your interpretation and what comes next.

5. Integration of information

Engagement objective setting, tracking and improvement action should be an integrated part of the wider HR processes. Recognize that even in the measurement processes, different parts of the organization will be at different levels of readiness to understand, use and embrace the measures that will become available.

6. Commit to operational reviews

You need reviews of engagement levels, and levels of commitment to the particular behaviours required to deliver the strategy, ones that are as rigorous as those conducted for ongoing business performance. RBS uses its employee opinion survey to drive improvement. The EOS (Employee Opinion Survey) targets are set and incorporated into the people section

of the business balanced score cards, either as an overall target
or percentage rise from the previous year.

❖ Analysis, in the form of 360° questionnaires, pulse surveys,
   etc. should be carried out at levels in the organization where
   managers can be held accountable for the findings and
   responsible for any required improvement actions.

❖ You can use 360° feedback to get much richer data about
   individuals' behaviour. For those parts of the organization
   which are customer facing, get customer feedback.

Consequences, financial and non-financial

Having made the measurements and set the goals, you must now act
on them. On the simplest level, all you are aiming for is that each
employee perceives a basic cause-and-effect connection between
quality of work done and the outcome for them. Extra effort, in other
words, is rewarded, lack of effort is punished. The attitudes you are
trying to promote are encapsulated in the following kinds of statements from our research:

> 'I didn't think I could achieve this outcome, I did, I feel good, my confidence is
> growing and I feel rewarded.'

> 'I want the rewards I know I will get from delivering my promises.'

It sounds simple. It is, in practice, hard to achieve. There are no short-
cuts: this needs to be a constant, consistent process. The systems of
the organization must be set up to show that the organization is
paying attention, and this can be achieved only if consequences ensue.
What do we mean by consequences? How do you use the resources
you have to make engagement real? The levers are various and particular to individuals. Two alarming statistics have emerged from the

Towers Perrin global workforce surveys: only 53% of UK respondents agree that their 'immediate manager holds people accountable for performance goals'; only 43% believe that their 'immediate manager manages performance reviews fairly and effectively'. These are crucial statements that should be scoring far more highly. *And* these are largely results based, alignment measures, which are by and large easier to measure and easier to reward against.

Financial consequences

Will more pay be rewarded with more engagement? In some environments, for instance in the trading floors of the City, motivation for extra effort – a bonus linked directly to performance – is fairly obvious. The equation is clear and compelling. It probably won't lead to loyalty to a specific company, but it can certainly be an effective incentive for high-value performance.

However, there are few jobs where the effort/money equation is, or can be, so simple, or the bonuses so large and so potentially life changing. Financial incentives will vary from job to job and from sector to sector. As we have noted already, it is fairly evident that those working for a charity, or in the NHS, are likely to have different attitudes to levels of pay than an investment banker. Moreover, in most jobs it is difficult to correlate performance and reward neatly. Simply issuing bonuses based on overall company performance might seem fair, for instance, but is not necessarily evenly weighted. Money in most instances is a blunt instrument, though there are ways to sharpen it. However, as we pointed out in Pillar Four, what is universally accepted as being important is that financial rewards are perceived to be fair and consistent. Mike Clasper, CEO of BAA to 2006, reinforces the point:

> 'Money is important but you'd better have a whole load of other things that are rewarding around it . . . the reward system has got to be perceived to be fair and aligned to the strategies.'

Unless you use your financial incentives carefully, they may not be buying you the engagement you think they are. Money is better used as a tool to reinforce the messages you are sending your workforce in other ways. Rob Margetts, Chairman of Legal and General, explains that 'discretionary effort is garnered through the achievement of social esteem'. But he adds that 'monetary bonuses make it real and thought about'.

Notwithstanding, pay does play an important role because it is a simple metric related to how the organization values you, both absol-utely and relatively. Financial reward, used wisely, will therefore form a key part of your portfolio of consequences. However, pay is unlikely to engineer change, unless the bonuses or salary rises involve life-changing sums (which they rarely do). Pay will not, on its own, act as incentive enough to change the habits of a lifetime. As Rob Margetts points out, 'bonuses, for good employees, do not change the work ethic'.

pay will not, on its own, act as incentive enough to change the habits of a lifetime

Lucian Hudson, Chairman of the Tavistock Institute, sees it like this:

'So I think depending on the context, you need a range of incentives and reinforcing messages and signals and basically the package will be appropriate to a situation or an environment over the course of time. I do think you need to make links quickly, immediately, directly between a piece of work and recognition ... But I find one of the things I do more successfully as time goes on is this whole issue of when things go wrong ... there is no substitute for trying to hold someone or a group of people to account over time. So that real learning emerges.'

If the carrot of money is not going to be a catch-all incentive, what about *the stick* of potential unemployment? In a fear-driven culture, you tell people what you want them to do and then pay them or sack them. It should be fairly obvious that this is at best a crude control, and while it may keep everyone's noses to the grindstone, it is hardly guaranteed to ensure engagement. It is likely to lead to short-termism and will constrain any effort beyond what is easily visible and overtly required. Employees are likely to concentrate only on a very narrow spectrum of their job. Tasks that employees can see need to be tackled will be left undone. It will drain the employee's reservoir of wellbeing.

Non-financial consequences

'For example, a key finding from the initial phase of the development was the importance of non-financial recognition in improving employee engagement. This information has now been shared within the HR function to highlight its importance'

Issue 3 November/December 2003, Strategic HR Review of RBS case study

Don't neglect this truth. The aim is to build a culture of recognition for achievement. This sounds rather formal and fancy, and indeed it can take the form of internal awards ceremonies or affirmative job titles, as we shall see. All that, however, represents a second step. The first step is more simple, but perhaps more difficult to achieve. In Lucian Hudson's words, 'you need to hold people to account over time'. This is a daily, constant affair, which should permeate every level of your organization. It involves simple things, done on a wide, thorough and rigorous scale: following up goals set in meetings, acknowledging success, reprimanding lack of effort.

In one organization, a drive to get senior leaders to spend more time on communication was having scant success. It was only when a decision was taken to include a question to all staff in the annual staff survey that results were seen. The results of this survey could be grouped by department and were shared openly at the top team meeting. This seemingly simple change made an enormous difference. Suddenly all the leadership started to expend effort on communication cascades. Why? Because none of them wished to be identified as being responsible for a department that scored badly.

The Prime Minister's Delivery Unit set out to monitor and assist in the delivery of the Government's public service agreement targets. Its job was to track progress and share it at regular meetings between the Prime Minister and the relevant Secretary of State. The regularity of the Prime Minister's stock-take meetings was a powerful incentive for departments and their Ministers to deliver on the agreements made. Why? Because the Secretary of State did not wish to be in charge of the department that was lagging behind.

This is why constant monitoring of progress must form an integral part of any change programme. Simple lists of targets and achievements met can be powerful tools: nobody wants to be the person in the room who is responsible for the only red crosses in a sea of green ticks. In most programme management teams there are normally two or three people whose major responsibility is to map progress and share this progress widely. The purpose of this is not purely about keeping up to date: it is about keeping the programme in the forefront of people's minds, and forcing both successes and failures into the public arena.

People react to acknowledgement, which is why, for instance, you should not underestimate the power of a genuine and heartfelt thank you and acknowledgement from the boss. An enormous number of organizations do. (Someone in one government department, when morale was not great, responded to the question 'when were you last praised?' with a dreamy look in her eye and the answer '1998'.) Organizations have quantitatively discovered just how important these non-financial appreciations can be to people's level of engagement.

Career advancement

Most employees (and especially the good ones) will want to know that they are progressing in their career, as we have seen in Pillars Four and Six. Research shows that advancement opportunities are the third highest factor in *attracting* people to a company, and the communication of career opportunities is the sixth highest factor in *retaining* them.[111] However, just as with financial incentives, the way in which this manifests itself will vary from company to company; notwithstanding, it is essential that promotions are perceived as fair and based on performance.

These factors can be bundled under the heading of genuine recognition of efforts provided. Crucially, however, the effectiveness of the method of recognition is about the employee, not the employer. Mary Kay, a cosmetics entrepreneur, encapsulates this neatly: 'There are two things that people want more than sex and money – recognition and praise.' So, public acknowledgement, career advancement, financial and non-financial incentives signal that efforts invested have consequences. As Sir David Varney says:

> 'I think one of the most important incentives is peer group recognition and colleague recognition ... saying that is a good piece of work and I am going to do something as a consequence of it and then do it ... that sort of recognition is very powerful.'

The potentially uncomfortable truth allied to this is that, for true engagement to occur, poor effort must also be appropriately recognized and sometimes this may involve brutal decisions. Nothing alienates high performers more than the spectre of poor performers not being held to account. 'You have to reassure, through behaviour, your deliverers and take action on the non-delivers', as David Barnes of AstraZeneca puts it. Dianne Thompson recalls how, when she first came to the embattled Camelot, her predecessor had always told everyone in the company that there would be no redundancies. So when she made 10% of the company redundant, at first there was shock and horror. It was an action, however, that sent a clear signal: from now on underperformance would be noticed and acted on. Further, the company was going to turn into a lean and streamlined organization designed for success. In the end, that is far more engaging than a security based on nothing really meaningful.

Value consequences

People, when reasonably treated by their organization, tend to feel a sense of obligation to their boss, department or colleagues. There is often a wish – particularly strong in the public sector, but not to be disregarded in the private sphere – to benefit the end user/customer. Interestingly, a bank found a stronger correlation between engaged employees and sales growth than that between satisfied customers and sales growth. The reason identified was that engaged employees who authentically really believe in their services are the best way to grow sales. This, perhaps, is why an organization's values are such important drivers of engagement: the latent need to invest yourself in your organization will be fulfilled happily only if you believe the organization is worthy of that investment. A truly engaged employee will be willing to invest themselves: the desire to feel that they have played their part well in reducing hospital waiting times, raising educational standards, or becoming the world's best can be a powerful driver for delivering your promises.

Do on Monday (for types of consequences)

1. **Clarity of direction**

   Ensure that positive and negative consequences are directed towards encouraging the development of the skills and behaviours that will allow the organization to go on being successful in its marketplace.

2. **Set the tone**

   In your dealings with people be honest, fair and unstinting with praise (be very unBritish!) and fearless in giving feedback (of course positively framed). Almost certainly increase your organization's focus on non-financial rewards.

3. **Encourage small acts of recognition**

   Dinners for employees plus partners, flowers, notes (handwritten if possible), positive feedback to employees in the moment or shortly afterwards – these are all important. Offer people the opportunity to represent the organization to external stakeholders and to deputize for you.

4. **Promote the exemplars**

   Don't promote the 'clever clever' types but those who really commit to the 'what and the how' which you have defined for your organization and who truly engage others in so doing.

5. **Show interest in the performance management process**

   Ensure the performance management process is transparent, rigorous and fair. Demonstrate your interest. Ensure the process is both tough and tender. The kinds of issues you should pay attention to include ensuring that the objective-setting process is as rigorous as it needs to be so that everyone is clear what is expected of them; people need to know what they will be judged on. Make sure talent management, rewards and the capability development processes all tie in, with a minimum of bureaucracy.

6. **Creating value**

   Keep articulating your purpose beyond profit or if you are in the public sector the public value that you are creating. People must feel that a consequence for their efforts is manifested in something worthwhile.

Performance management

While there are some organizations that do performance management well, the most common story is one of disappointment. Here are some of the indicative comments from previous reviews we have undertaken:

❖ 'We have too many weak performers.'

❖ 'Conversations are taking place between line managers and their people but not of sufficient quality.'

❖ 'We are not getting the levels of performance differentiation we want.'

❖ 'The data that is generated by the performance management

process is not sufficiently robust to support other key people processes such as talent management.'

❖ 'Our arrangements are much too complex. For instance, we have a range of different competency models. People have to work too hard to navigate them.'

❖ 'The problem is that our arrangements are much more geared to finding fault than celebrating and encouraging success, growth and development.'

❖ 'It's too static. Not stretching enough, not encouraging colleagues to focus on the future, what's needed for future success. Just not dynamic enough.'

❖ 'Our leadership brand is weakening because we don't do this well enough.'

Research corroborates this. For instance, most companies rate their current performance management programme in improving business results as 'somewhat effective' at best. The least effective aspects include creating line of sight, equipping managers to identify/develop/reward high performers and deal with low per-formers, communicating the company's mission vision and values, and giving employees more control over their contribution.

In order to raise the effectiveness of performance management and thereby improve your levels of employee engagement, there are two critical things to do – ensure that the design of your performance man-agement arrangements is fit for the purpose and take steps to improve the quality of performance management conversations between all your managers and their people.

❖ Do you have a robust performance management process that takes people through the stages shown in Figure 13.1 and focuses on both the 'what' (e.g. clarity of goals) and the 'how' (e.g. competencies)? Is it as simple as you can possibly make it? Does it fit your culture?

❖ Does your performance management process link in effectively to the budgeting and planning process? Can you track the goals

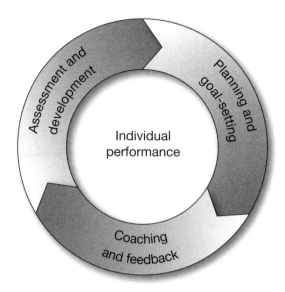

Figure 13.1 Individual performance circle

and objectives being agreed in your performance agreements to the overall goals and drivers of value in your business?

❖ Are you calibrating effectively? In other words, are you ensuring that performance goals, performance markings and rewards are being reviewed for consistency across the business?

❖ Ensure you have a reasonable distribution of ratings across your organization which reflects the performance of your business. However, beware of forced rankings, unless you do it for clearly defined, short-term reasons.

❖ Have you built in incentives to encourage leadership accountability for effective performance management?

❖ How clear are you on the roles and responsibilities of line managers and other people in this area?

These considerations are important. But don't be beguiled by the thought that the secret lies in effective design. These are the basics. Success lies much more in the culture, spirit and winning ethos that's developed. It is not

success lies much more in the culture, spirit and winning ethos

enough to design a new reward system and then just communicate it. This is why the next area is vital.

Quality of implementation

At a recent seminar about the challenges of implementing effective performance management and, in particular, appropriate differentiation of performance, this quote summed up the mood: 'It is not about the intricacies of the design of the system, it is about building the skill and, particularly, *the will* and determination of managers to make the appropriate judgements and hold the right conversations ... conversations that celebrate success, clarify performance focus, differentiate

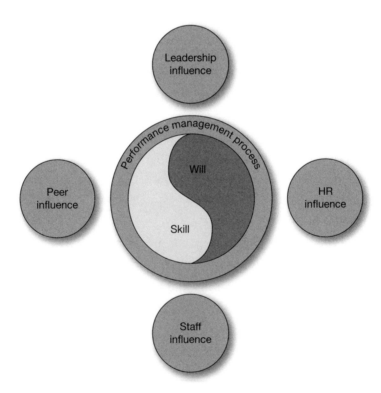

Figure 13.2 Performance management process

performance, give clear feedback, identify development needs and agree action plans.'

The HR Director of a major oil company recently said: 'We need to get much, much better at the tough conversations. It is not that the conversations are not happening. It is that they are not of the right quality. And we owe it to our people – as a right – that they have the appropriate conversation with their supervisor.'

If you can lift the quality of the performance management discussions in your organization, you will raise the levels of engagement because these discussions strike the chords of both alignment (goals, objectives, key performance indicators (KPIs), value drivers) and emotional engagement (career plans, development plans, values, the quality of relationships with line managers). Figure 13.2 is a frame that has been helpful in steering a course to improving the quality of performance management discussions. It is about bringing to bear a series of influences (leadership, HR, staff and peer) to improve the levels of will and skill needed to do this well (and, in our view, it is above all the will of managers that needs to be addressed). The priority between issues of skill and will should always be with will.

Leadership influence

Leaders have to be seen as being behind this, and leadership influence has to be visceral, from the gut – it can't be 'I've read about this stuff and I think it's quite important'.

So, in your leadership role, display visceral commitment to the performance management process; engage personally in the discussions about its improvement; take great care over the quality of the performance management discussions that you have with your immediate subordinates; intervene personally in the reviews of the performance management outcomes of different parts of the organization; and communicate the importance of the process to your people.

HR influence

Clearly the HR function has an important role to play in raising the will and skill of your people to implement performance management well. Indeed, this is a critical part of the function's ability to play an improved role as performance coach. There are four areas in particular where the function should contribute:

❖ *Working with the leadership team to stimulate the leadership role outlined above.* The HR function needs to be highly active in working with the leadership team to help them see the business case for effective performance management, coach them into strong personal practices and stimulate the purposeful reviews of performance goals/ratings/rewards that are needed at key junctions.

❖ *Boosting line managers' knowledge of all the possible outcomes from the performance management process.* Line managers can be inhibited from engaging fully in the 'tough conversations' with their people because they are simply unsure of their ground on issues such as redeployment, early retirement, redundancy, promotion, etc. They feel that they need to be on top of all this before setting out into the troubled waters of a 'tough conversation' and, because they are not, they do not set sail at all. The HR function needs to boost colleagues' confidence by providing the appropriate knowledge through just-in-time briefings, knowledge databases, etc.

❖ *Instilling discipline and attention.* HR can use a range of tools to ensure that performance management gets the attention it deserves. For instance, in one organization, performance management goals are locked on a certain date and the leadership team are given a readout on how well different parts of the organization are doing on this stage in the performance management cycle. In another organization, the HR function runs an annual dipstick survey collecting staff views on the quality of performance management that year.

❖ *Providing the coaching and development needed to raise the levels of skills.* Our survey data indicates that the provision of improved coaching for managers is the top priority for organizations in the performance management arena. There is a whole host of training interventions available. HR functions need to help their line managers move from being unconsciously unskilled (I don't know what I don't know) to being unconsciously skilled. Much of this is about language. Without a common language of performance management, conversations can remain shallow, but with training they can become much deeper. Many organizations are training their managers in effective coaching.

Staff influence

This is about bringing the voice of staff into the process. To what extent are they getting value from the performance management process? What are their line managers doing well/less well? What improvements are necessary? A range of survey and sensing tools is available.

Peer influence

At key steps in the performance management process, peer influence needs to be brought to bear – at the beginning of the cycle when goals are being developed, towards the end of the cycle when performance ratings and reward decisions are being formulated.

Do on Monday (for performance management)

1. **You need data!**

   Ensure your HR people provide you with the data and who is behaving in the way required to drive engagement and who is not. This should be a simple tracking process; it does not require an administrative industry.

2. Assess difficult issues

Do not duck difficult issues in your team. Address issues but frame your feedback positively (it can be done). Remember you are addressing a behaviour or task, not telling someone whether they are a worthwhile individual or not.

3. Be prepared to be tough

Prepare yourself to give tough feedback. If you do not it will come out wrong and you will end up making promises you can't keep or aiming off in your feedback. If negative consequences are appropriate, don't hang back. A metaphor is a jab in the eye and a walk in the park, i.e. be clear you mean business but support the person in addressing their shortcomings. Be ruthless about stamping out office politics and address those who can't, don't or won't take the time to engage those around them. No one can be in the high-potential group if they can't engage.

4. Be clear

If you are at the stage before firing (which should always be a last resort), then be clear what needs to be addressed. Offer training, coaching, mentoring, advice, etc. as required.

5. Be decisive

Fire any real blockers. If they are subject experts and you need them, then just move them out of the line. (You can compensate with titles and salaries, etc.)

6. Be positive

Don't be half-hearted with your praise. If financial recognition is appropriate, use bonuses or salary increases or small gestures such as dinners for employee plus partner, etc. If non-financial recognition is appropriate, give extra responsibilities, ask for important tasks to be undertaken. Offer the employee the opportunity of representing the organization externally or representing you at some internal event. Offer full- or part-time development secondments. Some people like attending conferences, for instance. Enable peer group recognition for special effort, preferably team based, but individual is ok. Offer them the opportunity to present success stories at conferences, etc., especially if this typifies the kind of working practice you seek to have emulated throughout the organization.

7. **Make it public**

   Ensure there are 'award ceremonies'. You may recoil, but they will be effective. They can be anything from award dinners at one end of the spectrum through to public acknowledgements at the end of meetings.

8. **Be involved**

   Constantly reinforce the skill aspect and the will aspect of rewards by energizing the system, i.e. by asking questions to ensure the system is working (the skill) and constantly checking outputs of the system (to encourage the will).

Support

HR support

Once you've measured achievement and consequences have followed, it's time to offer the support required to turn good performance into great performance and also to address poor performance. If people get things wrong it should not be assumed they

virtually everyone has a contribution to offer

are therefore inherently incapable or unable to change. Virtually everyone has a contribution to offer. Your job is to set the conditions so that many more people are able to offer more of their potential.

For many organizations this requires not much short of a revolution in HR. Too often HR has been in effect the 'uniformed' branch, focused around telling managers what is legal/not legal or in line with policy, rather than acting as a true partner to the line managers in the quest for better performance. This has been a much discussed and generally unresolved problem. Engagement offers a language which can change this. Because a significant building block of engagement is alignment across the whole organization, it requires HR to understand, and indeed co-own, the strategic direction of the company; to move from policing to facilitating. It also requires that HR concentrates on the behaviours which are required. They should aspire to nothing short of being the Chief Executive's main support function. Jack Welch took his HR director – rather than his Finance Director – to visit companies with him because he believed that people were the fundamental assets in his business. If this is true, and it manifestly is in almost every organization, then it is the head of HR who is the 'star', to put it in Jack's words.

This is not the approach that most companies take at the moment, and if HR wishes to achieve this elevated position, its best chance is to make a visible, clear and measurable improvement in performance. Their responsibility here is to perform the measurements – to ensure that engagement metrics are registered and that good performance tracks to bonus, salary, promotions, and that managers whose engagement scores are low receive coaching and support in this area. If the HR function can successfully support plans that turn good performance into excellent performance, or that turn poor performance into acceptable performance, they can make an enormous contribution to the organization. HR people, then, need to be business-based professionals. They should be experts in their fields with the capability of developing the talent in others; they should be coaches, not administrators. The administrative activities can be outsourced.

RBS considers its human capital to be so important that it has set up a human capital board with businesses and HR executives. The group uses data to prioritize human capital initiatives according to their business impact. A range of human capital measures are published as a part of the annual accounts and benchmarked to competitors' performance. The key internal outputs of RBS's human capital model are 'impact diagrams' which illustrate the impact of different human capital factors on engagement and highlight the opportunities for concentrating on particular issues which could boost or threaten engagement.

This support needs to be efficiently offered. Your support people are a cost and they need to be leveraged effectively. RBS's human capital toolkit provides tools and information on internal and external benchmarking, external best practice and research. Managers therefore are supported in understanding how they perform and how and what they need to do in order to improve. A clear dialogue between the manager and his boss can ensue so that improvements are made and monitored. Honest conversations are vital and yet happen so infrequently. Honesty is not about becoming nasty. It's not about criticizing the person – 'you are a failure'. It's about recognizing behaviours and performance that fall short while instilling confidence into people that they can – and must – improve.

If after all the support that a dedicated HR person can give it is not solving the problem, you will need to move people on. As Sir David Omand says, it is unfair to all parties not to act in these circumstances:

'I do agree with Jack Welch that the cruellest thing the organization can do is to be too soft and not tell people that actually this doesn't look like it's the career for them. Much better as early as possible to work out who is going to fit and be able to grow in the organization. And those for whom this is really just not the kind of work they ought to be doing. Now sometimes there'll be opportunities in other parts of the organization, not everybody is a good case worker, not everybody is good with the public, not everybody will find the frustrations of sitting behind a desk trying to do financial planning to their liking. So in a big organization I think you can accommodate quite a lot of different kinds of people, but I say the worst crime is to just be frightened to tell people and then they are stuck.'

In the end, all of these consequences come down to the following: a need to show your workforce that your organization *cares* about engagement. The employee who comes in and finds that his lackadaisical colleague's efforts have been rewarded in the same way as his own; the manager who realizes that for all the talk about communications, nobody realizes that he has been at pains to engage his department in dialogue and no one is tracking the results; the employees who realize that all the engagement questionnaires they have filled out have been filed away without any particular action being taken – all of these people will end up being disengaged. You have an obligation to those who invest their effort on your behalf, and that obligation is to take note of their efforts. Sometimes this will mean rewarding them, sometimes it will mean taking steps to correct them. But the critical point of consequences is to show that the organization cares about all of this. Because if you don't care about engagement, if you don't engage yourself, then you cannot expect that your workforce will.

Do on Monday (for HR support)

1. **Integrate HR and line management**

   Set up a business group of HR and line managers to ensure that the key focus for HR strategy is routed in delivering the business plan.

2. **Focus on added value**

   Outsource as much rote HR as you can, to leave the HR people to become true business partners, not dominated by the non-added value process side of HR.

3. **HR as examplars**

   Drive HR hard to be a role model in aligned and engaged working as a department. Work within their metrics and be seen so to do.

4. **Establish the facts**

   Ensure HR has set up a simple 360° feedback process which when added to other HR data (leavers, joiners, general employee surveys, performance management data, etc.) paints a clear picture of who is behaving in a way that supports the strategy (engaged and aligned).

5. Support

Ensure consequences are in place for those in the line who do and do not support the plans for engagement and alignment. HR needs to develop a toolkit of online support to help individuals who are achieving low scores and also to help diagnose any issues in the organization which are getting in the way (targeted research, benchmark data, internal and external, simple processes that have helped other people in the same situation, etc.).

Set up one-on-one help through coaches for those who need more focused support. Very carefully select and brief your coaches, whether they are internal or external. Ensure they understand what the strategy is so they are better able to focus their support.

NOTES

[111] Towers Perrin Global Workforce Study, 2005 – Winning strategies for a global workforce.

CONCLUSION

Conclusion: the extra mile

What kind of employees do you want? What kind of organization do you want? The two questions are inextricably linked.

The kind of organization you want can probably be summed up in one word – successful. You may quantify this success in various ways – market position, increased profit, share value, public value – but however you look at it, success is the goal towards which we all strive.

What kind of employees you want may seem to be a more complex question: some organizations may look to the entrepreneurial spirit, others to the safe team players. For some roles you will be looking for born networkers or salesmen, for others a steady hand on the tiller or an eye for detail is necessary. Every organization is a complex ecosystem.

But there is one characteristic that should be universal: engagement. Wherever they are in your company, whatever their role, you want to employ people who care, who bring all their efforts and brainpower to bear on your behalf.

How do you generate this elusive quality? It is something that is difficult to single out as part of your recruitment process. Every employee has the capacity to be engaged, but it is up to you to institute a culture which encourages them to invest that engagement on your behalf. Engagement levels are your responsibility: something to be worked on, not simply hoped for. You need to decide to make the investment in it. The good news is that the reins to this powerful tool already lie in your hands.

This is the extra mile that your organization should go in order to reap the rewards of engagement. The strands that make up engagement are various and interwoven. Notwithstanding, in the end, the answer is relatively straightforward: you need people both engaged and aligned. You need the strong foundations of good, inspiring leadership that looks outward as well as inward, allowing the organization to place its faith in the people who are steering it. Once these things are in place you need to be committed, visible and communicative. Your organization should construct a fair deal with its employees, exploiting their talent as imaginatively as you can and using the managers to the full. And you need to make sure that everyone knows that engagement matters, to them and to the organization. Above all, the various foundations and pillars come down to one overriding principle: mutual trust.

your organization should construct a fair deal with its employees

Every organization wants to be successful. The leader's primary duty is to ensure that it is. But this success should not come at the expense of its employees. It is not necessary to break the backs of the people who work for us in order to get to the top of the mountain. Involving them, harnessing their talents and enthusiasms and building a culture whereby they are encouraged to invest all they can of themselves is the way to build a more solid, enduring type of success – the way to build resilience in hard times and to garner the rewards in good ones.

Pay attention to your people: the rewards are great when in turn they focus their attention for you.

Annex A: Research linking engagement to performance

Linking engagement to performance: a review of the literature

Much of what we understand about employee engagement and its links to business performance comes from extensive work done by such organizations as RBS, Nationwide, ISR, Towers Perrin and various others described in Chapter 2. In this annex we look at relevant contributions to the space.

The term 'employee engagement' is a collective which incorporates many traditions within the human capital space. The evolution of the term stems from many relevant ideas and we have broken these down into the following categories:

1. Linking organizational behaviour to productivity.
2. Linking organizational culture to organizational performance.
3. Linking satisfaction, attitudes and performance at the organization level.
4. Linking individual job satisfaction to organizational performance.
5. Connecting the links in the service-profit chain.

1. Linking organizational behaviour to productivity

Organizational behaviour and its links to productivity were reviewed by Schneider in 1985. He looked at, among other things, the monetary value or 'utility' of management interventions such as improved selection methods, training, job design and job satisfaction. Taking into account the costs associated with any of the various interventions (e.g. consultant fees, lost production time, etc.), the literature going back up to 45 years from the time of the study demonstrated measurable benefits and in one study an increase in productivity was evident in 87% of over 200 cases examined.[113]

Another review looked at management interventions and their effects on productivity. This meta-analysis demonstrated a significant causal effect in that organizations which utilized intervention programmes were significantly more productive than those organizations which did not or did to a lesser extent. The strongest productivity increases, which were statistically significant, were seen in response to training, goal setting and the socio-technical interventions.[114]

2. Linking organizational culture to organizational performance

Following a similar theme and impetus, studies of organizational culture and its impact on business performance were given much attention. Denison studied 34 companies across 25 different industries with survey data taken from 1966–1981. A standardized 125-item questionnaire was completed by 43,747 respondents from 6671 work groups in the 34 companies. It looked at cultural issues, participative decision-making levels, human resources emphasis and behavioural aspects of management. Denison described culture as being 'the set of values, beliefs, and behaviour patterns that form the core identity of an organization'.[115] Cultural aspects of the companies were compared with their incomes and other financial performance data (ratios derived from S&P financial data) for five years starting in 1981. Correlations between emphasis on human resources, high levels of participative decision making and financial performance were established and the strength of the correlation increased over the five years. The results indicated that companies with a participative culture performed nearly twice as well as firms with less participative cultures. Denison concluded: 'The data presented here provide hard evidence that the cultural and behavioural aspects of organizations are intimately linked to both short-term performance and long-term survival.' Gordon and DiTomaso reported similar findings and supported Denison's conclusions.[116]

Kotter and Heskett looked at 200 companies trying to answer the question: 'Is there a relationship between corporate culture and long-term economic performance of an organization?'[117] They concluded that corporate culture impacts financial performance. Firms that emphasized all key managerial constituencies – customers, share-holders and employees – as well as emphasizing leadership at all levels (versus the ones that didn't):

- ❖ increased revenues by 682% (versus 166%)
- ❖ increased workforce by 282% (versus 36%)
- ❖ increased share price by 901% (versus 74%)
- ❖ increased net income by 756% (versus 1%).

Another study done by Denison and Mishra published in 1995 presented a model of organizational culture based on four traits: involvement, consistency, adaptability and mission.[118] The results show that involvement and adaptability (which indicated flexibility, openness and responsiveness) were strong predictors of growth. Consistency and mission (which indicated integration, direction and vision) were better predictors of profitability. All four traits were strong predictors of return on assets and sales growth, but this was only for larger firms.

3. Linking satisfaction, attitudes and performance at the organization level

Worker attitudes and satisfaction are important factors in determining individual behaviours and collectively will impact an organization's overall performance. In a study involving schools, the link between satisfaction, attitude and organization performance was investigated by Ostroff.[119] A sample of 364 schools in the United States and Canada (including 364 school principals and 13,808 teachers) participated in the study. Teacher satisfaction was measured using surveys that asked questions relating to satisfaction with co-workers, supervision, pay, administration, career advancement opportunities, student discipline, school curriculum, community and parental support, physical facilities, and communications. Attitudes and commitment, stress levels and adjustment (around feelings of confidence, comfort with job and sense of belonging) were also measured. Organizational performance was measured against the following criteria: student academic achievement, student behaviour, student satisfaction, teacher turnover and administrative performance. Significant correlations were found between most performance measures and satisfaction and attitude measures. Strong correlations were observed, among others, between satisfaction and attitude and turnover intentions, between satisfaction and test score results, between administrative performance and adjustment.

Increasing achievement in reading and maths, higher student satisfaction, lower teacher turnover rates and even better student behaviour all increased with growing positive teacher satisfaction, attitude and adjustment scores at an organizational level. It followed that organizations with more satisfied employees tended to be more effective than organizations with less satisfied employees and these relationships were shown to be stronger at an organizational level versus at the level of the individual. Ostroff admits that the weaker results at the individual level may suggest that the relationship is in fact weaker at the individual level, but she also argues that the interplay within an organization, its salient features such as attachment and citizenship, inter-dependencies and work processes may account for the differences seen at the organization level. These findings suggest that at an organizational level, management and organizational processes, culture and behaviours can be altered to improve overall performance.

4. Linking individual job satisfaction to organizational performance

In reviewing the literature up until the late 1960s, Lawler and Porter discussed how the evidence described a low and consistent relationship between individual job satisfaction and individual job performance. Further they characterized the conventional wisdom as having always been that managers should be concerned about raising the satisfaction of their employees; the idea that more satisfied workers would be more productive workers. They looked at the relationship between job satisfaction and job performance using surveys which asked about the individual's job satisfaction and about the performance of their peers and subordinates in the organization. Data was gathered from 148 middle and lower-level managers in five organizations. They demonstrated correlations stronger than a previous study by Vroom,[120] with correlations of 0.32 when superiors ranked performance and 0.30 when peers ranked performance. Their study has limits (similar to Vroom) in that the sample size is small and the scope is narrow. They conclude that it is important to consider satisfaction because it will affect turnover rates and absenteeism.

They also present a different explanation on the perplexing satisfaction–performance relationship – that the directionality is not what has been the conventional wisdom. They claim that better worker performance is not the result of more satisfied workers, it is actually the opposite: they argue that when workers perform well, they get rewards and then that leads to satisfaction. They looked at how an individual's needs were being satisfied by the job. They looked at Maslow's hierarchy of needs and tested how these needs were being met correlated to job performance. Going from lower-level to higher-level needs, five needs were considered: security, social, esteem, autonomy, self-actualization. All of these showed positive correlations to job performance, but the strongest correlation was with the highest-order need, 'self-actualization' ($r=0.30$). Extrinsic rewards (organizationally controlled things like pay, promotions, status and security – these correspond to the lower-level Maslow needs which deal with physiological needs, survival needs, the basic needs to live, etc.) were imperfectly linked and had a weak connection to performance. Intrinsic rewards (internally mediated things like feelings of accomplishment) were more directly linked to performance than the extrinsic rewards.[121]

A more recent review consisting of 312 samples with a combined $N=54,417$ demonstrated a job satisfaction–job performance correlation of 0.30.[122] It challenged the findings of Iaffaldano and Muchinsky who wrote a seminal paper on the issue in 1985 and argued that the link between satisfaction and performance was tenuous at best.[123] The case against linking satisfaction to business performance was refuted by showing that the overwhelming amount of research that had been conducted between 1985 and 2001 (which had taken into account previous errors) had shown significant and strong correlations between performance and satisfaction.

Another study, published in 2003, provides a look at the link between organizational performance and employee attitudes.[124] The results showed significant directional linkages from financial and market performance to overall job satisfaction, employee attitudes to return on assets (ROA) and earnings per share (EPS), and ROA and EPS to better employee attitudes (stronger causal directionality than the reverse). The following reciprocal relationship was suggested: satisfaction with pay increased when organizational and financial performance decreased, and satisfaction with pay decreased when organizational and financial performance increased.

Other employee attitudes (e.g. satisfaction with empowerment, satisfaction with job fulfilment) were thought to be too far removed to impact financial performance. These other attitudinal variables could not be directly linked to organization and financial performance, but it is suggested that these factors most likely show their impact indirectly via absenteeism and turnover. The notable contribution of this study is that a reciprocal relationship between the factors is presented.

Other studies related to employee satisfaction

An additional study measured employee satisfaction and then organizational effectiveness (using customer satisfaction surveys) and strove to demonstrate a directional relationship between the two. The question posed was: 'Which comes first – positive employee attitudes and behaviours or positive business outcomes?'[125] The results showed a positive average correlation of 0.33 relating HR outcomes to business unit outcomes. The directionality was from HR outcomes to business performance. Other results demonstrated that organizational citizenship behaviour (conscientiousness, altruism, civic virtue, sportsmanship and courtesy) influenced profitability. The study also demonstrated that employee satisfaction significantly influenced customer satisfaction.

Results from another study showed a strong lagged relationship between high-performance work practices (employee involvement, total quality management and reengineering programmes) and later business performance.[126] The directionality was from practices to financial performance.

5. Connecting the links in the service-profit chain

Perhaps the best established directional link is found in the literature which describes the service-profit chain in retail businesses. In the service-profit chain, the chain represents a set of strongly held convictions and applies to any service organization – financial services, professional services, retail, restaurants, hotels, etc. According to the work done by Heskett, Sasser and Schlesinger: 'Simply stated, service-profit chain thinking maintains that there are direct and strong relationships between profit; growth; customer loyalty; customer satisfaction; the value of goods and services delivered to customers; and employee capability, satisfaction, loyalty, and productivity.'[127] Service-profit-chain companies have outperformed their competition by significant margins. Share prices of such companies increased 147% from 1986–1995, compared with a 110% increase seen in the S&P 500.[128] Here the value of customer loyalty is foremost. Market share is important, but nothing is possible without customer loyalty. From that rests the thesis that customer loyalty is the result of committed and satisfied employees. Significant supporting data suggests that the strongest linkages are between profit and customer loyalty, employee loyalty and customer loyalty, and employee satisfaction and customer satisfaction (where customer satisfaction is a pre-requisite of and leads to customer loyalty). The linkages found were substantial.

The service-profit chain was examined in a large department store by Borucki and Burke.[129] The focus was a large US national retail store chain in 1985 and 1986. In 594 stores the authors surveyed over 60,000 employees and the same number of customers (a limitation here is that data came from just one company). They tested a model which illustrated the service-profit chain:

1. Importance of service to management.
2. Concern for employees and customers.
3. Sales personnel service performance.
4. Store financial performance.

The data showed causal and/or predictive links between all points in the chain. The importance of service to management related positively to concern for employees and customers which was predictive of sales personnel service performance which was predictive of store financial performance. But the strongest correlation to store financial perform-ance was the importance of service to top management.

Gelade and Young define the service-profit chain as 'satisfied and motivated employees produce satisfied customers and satisfied cus-tomers tend to purchase more, increasing the revenue and profits of the organization'.[130] Here they looked at four national retail banks (three in the UK and one in Ireland). In total they surveyed 55,200 employees and 37,054 questionnaires were completed, giving a 67% response rate. One limitation that can be mentioned here is that the survey questions were not always the same. The results showed that favourable employee attitudes and work climate led to increased cus-tomer satisfaction and sales.

Sears and the employee-customer-profit chain[131]

Sears in the mid-nineties underwent a significant change to its approach, to its philosophy. The tradition of the service-profit chain was followed with a particular focus on the customer. Preliminary results showed that there were hard linkages in the chain – that increases in positive employee attitudes drove increases in customer impressions which drove increases in revenue growth. These measurements were taken during the fourth year of the transformation programme. The company's efforts showed a 4% increase in employee satisfaction and a nearly 4% increase in customer satisfaction – and by extending the model, these numbers translated into increased revenues. The most remarkable point of this analysis is that Sears claimed that the increase in revenues was driven solely by the efforts of the managers and employees and their focus on the customer. These results were impressive with regard to increases in employee and customer satisfaction, but the linkage of these numbers to revenues was not proven.

Shortly after these measures and results were reported, Sears decided to abandon the plan, get a new CEO, close stores and initiate other finance-driven moves aimed at cutting costs, improving the supply chain and increasing profit margins. It would be much easier to subscribe to the great-turnaround theory regarding Sears if it had persisted with the programme for longer.

A recent article about Sears, mainly describing its takeover by Kmart and speculating about the future of what now is the third largest retailer in the US, rehashes the turbulent times of the nineties when Arthur Martinez was CEO.[132] Martinez said that he would have been tougher and used more of a 'throw the bums out' approach. Back then the turnaround effort fizzled fast and the efforts to focus on the customer were essentially abandoned. How Kmart and Sears will perform as a merged company remains to be seen.

Conclusion

We have reviewed the research that has previously looked at employee engagement and its relatives and link them to business performance. As outlined above, much work has been done under various guises and the body of evidence supports the idea that the success of a business is absolutely linked to the engagement of its employees.

NOTES

[113] Schneider, B. (1985) 'Organizational behavior.' *Annual Review of Psychology*, Vol. 36, pp. 573–611.

[114] Guzzo, R. A., Jette, R. D. and Katzell, R. A. (1985) 'The effects of psychologically based intervention programs on worker productivity: A meta-analysis.' *Personnel Psychology*, Vol. 38, Issue 2, p. 291.

[115] Denison, D. R. (1984) 'Bringing corporate culture to the bottom line.' *Organizational Dynamics*, Vol. 13, Issue 2, Autumn, pp. 5–22; Denison, D. R. (1990) *Corporate Culture and Organizational Effectiveness*, New York: Wiley.

[116] Gordon, G. G. and DiTomaso, N. (1992) 'Predicting corporate performance from organizational culture.' *Journal of Management Studies*, Vol. 29, No. 6, November, pp. 783–798.

[117] Kotter, J. P. and Heskett, J. L. (1992) *Corporate Culture and Performance*, New York: Free Press.

[118] Denison, D. R. and Mishra, A. K. (1995) 'Toward a theory of organizational culture and effectiveness.' *Organization Science*, Vol. 6, No. 2, March–April, pp. 204–223.

[119] Ostroff, C. (1992) 'The relationship between satisfaction, attitudes, and performance: an organizational level analysis.' *Journal of Applied Psychology*, Vol. 77, No. 6, pp. 963–974.

[120] Vroom, V. H. (1964) *Work and Motivation*, New York: Wiley.

[121] Lawler, E. E. III and Porter, L. W. (1967) 'The effects of performance on job satisfaction.' *Industrial Relations*, Vol. 7, Issue 1, October, pp. 20–28.

[122] Judge, T. A., Thoreson, C. J., Bono, J. E. and Patton, G. K. (2001) 'The job satisfaction-job performance relationship: a qualitative and quantitative review.' *Psychological Bulletin*, Vol. 127, No. 3, pp. 376–407.

[123] Iaffaldano, M. T. and Muchinsky, P. M. (1985) 'Job satisfaction and job-performance: a meta-analysis.' *Psychological Bulletin*, Vol. 97, No. 2, March, pp. 251–273.

[124] Schneider, B., Hanges, P. J., Smith, D. B. and Salvaggio, A. N. (2003) 'Which comes first: employee attitudes or organizational financial and market performance?' *Journal of Applied Psychology*, Vol. 88, No. 5, pp. 836–851.

[125] Koys, D. J. (2001) 'The effects of employee satisfaction, organizational citizenship behaviour, and turnover on organizational effectiveness: a unit-level, longitudinal study.' *Personnel Psychology*, Vol. 54, Issue 1, Spring, pp. 101–114.

[126] Lawler, E. E. III, Mohrman, S. A. and Ledford, G. E. Jr (1998) *Strategies for High-performance Organizations: Employee involvement, TQM, and reengineering programs in Fortune 500 corporations*, San Francisco: Jossey-Bass.

[127] Heskett, J. L., Sasser, W. E. and Schlesinger, L. A. (1997) *The Service Profit Chain: How leading companies link profit and growth to loyalty, satisfaction, and value*, New York: Free Press.

128 Ibid, p. 16.

129 Borucki, C. C. and Burke, M. J. (1999) 'An examination of service-related antecedents to retail store performance.' *Journal of Organizational Behavior*, Vol. 20, Issue 6, November, pp. 943–962.

130 Gelade, G. A. and Young, S. (2005) 'Test of a service profit chain model in the retail banking sector.' *Journal of Occupational and Organizational Psychology*, Vol. 78, Issue 1, March, pp. 1–22.

131 Rucci, A. J., Kirn, S. P. and Quinn, R. T. (1998) 'The employee-customer-profit chain at Sears.' *Harvard Business Review*, Vol. 76, Issue 1, January/February, pp. 82–97.

132 Berner, R. (2005) 'At Sears, a great communicator.' *Business Week*, Issue 3957, 31 October, pp. 50–52.

Annex B: Statistical terms and analysis

Throughout this book we have referred to data and analysis of the data, such that we have been able to offer insights and to suggest courses for action. The statistical techniques used include the following:

Factor analysis – examination of the intercorrelation of survey items to determine which items tend to reliably 'hang' together and should be treated as one factor or 'category' of items (e.g. employee engagement, customer focus). Factor analysis also provides a sense of the core themes in the data.

General descriptive statistics – examination of means, standard deviations and response distributions to identify trends in the data, including response patterns of various demographic groups, key themes within the data that affect employee attraction, engagement and retention, as well as general strengths and opportunities for the organization.

T-tests, analysis of variance (ANOVA) – analysis of group differences to determine whether demographic differences are statistically significant.

Linkage analysis – multivariate statistical modelling technique used to analyze the causal structure of a group of variables (e.g. linkages between employee, customer, operational and financial metrics) to understand their direct and indirect relationships. Linkage analysis identifies and validates employee measures that have the greatest influence on business outcome measures.

Correlation, regression and multiple regression – 'Driver' analysis to understand the direction and magnitude of relationships among a set of items or variables to determine, for example, which survey items and survey categories predict engagement index scores, turnover intention, or other outcome variables of interest.

Impact analysis – helps to set priorities for action by looking at survey items and categories along multiple dimensions. Impact analysis prioritizes areas of focus by looking at impact (statistical relationship to employee engagement) and probability of movement (percent favourable and distance from norm).

Unit scorecard – creates unit comparisons to show key demographic differences in survey categories to illustrate strengths, potential opportunities and opportunities for improvement.

Say/Do analysis – highlights the key values that management says are important and the values (e.g. employee and customer focus) that management demonstrates are important; identifies gaps in what managers say versus what employees perceive that they do.

Conjoint and total rewards optimization analysis – analysis of the relative preferences employees have for various reward programme design levels. Conjoint analysis also models the effect various reward designs would have on employee engagement and retention. Combined with programme cost information, the analysis can be used to identify optimal cost/benefit total rewards designs. Conjoint analysis requires a different survey design from traditional surveys.

Index